THROUGH THE MOUNTAINS

JOHN E. ROSS

THROUGH THE

MOUNTAINS

The French Broad River and Time

The University of Tennessee Press | Knoxville

Library of Congress Cataloging-in-Publication Data

Names: Ross, John E., author.
Title: Through the mountains : the French Broad River and time / John E. Ross.
Description: First edition. | Knoxville : The University of Tennessee Press, [2021] | Includes
    bibliographical references and index. | Summary: "More than two generations have elapsed
    since Wilma Dykeman wrote her iconic environmental history, *The French Broad*. Building
    on fifty years of scholarship, John Ross has written an updated natural and cultural history
    of the French Broad watershed that encompasses the northern half of the Great Smoky
    Mountains, Asheville, and Gatlinburg. In her book Dykeman asked, 'What has the river been
    to those who lived within the French Broad watershed?' In *Through the Mountains: The French
    Broad River and Time*, Ross probes what we must start doing now to ensure the watershed
    sustains future generations"—Provided by publisher.
Identifiers: LCCN 2020057468 (print) | LCCN 2020057469 (ebook) | ISBN 9781621906636 (cloth) |
    ISBN 9781621908548 (paperback) | ISBN 9781621906643 (kindle edition) | ISBN 9781621906650 (pdf)
Subjects: LCSH: French Broad River (N.C. and Tenn.) | French Broad River Valley (N.C.
    and Tenn.)—History. | North Carolina—History. | Tennessee—History.
Classification: LCC F443.F8 R67 2021 (print) | LCC F443.F8 (ebook) | DDC 976.8/895—dc23
LC record available at https://lccn.loc.gov/2020057468
LC ebook record available at https://lccn.loc.gov/2020057469

TO MY GRANDCHILDREN

Amanda Jane, Lincoln, John, Claudia, Remy, and Monty

and for grandchildren everywhere

who will inherit their own watersheds.

Contents

Illustrations

MAPS

Preface

Every year some 16 million tourists visit the Great Smokies; drive the Blue Ridge Parkway; and vacation in Asheville, Gatlinburg, and Pigeon Forge. They come seeking respite and restoration as have century upon century of visitors. Perhaps the first were Indians of the Archaic era who may well have relieved their aches 5,000 years ago with a good soak in Hot Spring's steaming waters. Perhaps to direct others, they daubed orange and blue markings half way up a cliff on the French Broad River marking the border of North Carolina and Tennessee. Before crossing the bridge into Hot Springs, take the gravel road down the river to see Paint Rock.

From the hidden mound just inside the gate to Biltmore Estate, where Indians celebrated the summer solstice, to the once-secret radio telescope site above Rosman, where the Department of Defense eavesdropped on Russian satellites, and to Dollywood and the historic mill in Pigeon Forge, the French Broad watershed offers much to explore for tourists and residents alike. *Through the Mountains: The French Broad River and Time* presents the "how and why" underlying the "what and where" of one of the world's oldest and most heavily visited mountain regions.

To reach the watershed, most tourists arrive via Interstates—81, 26, 40, and 75. To a large degree, each follows routes like I-81, once the Great War Path taken by ancestors of the Cherokee bent on commerce or conflict and later, as the Great Wagon Road, carrying poor Scots-Irish and German immigrants seeking new lives on hardscrabble farms in high mountain coves. Every time I catch and release a native Southern Appalachian Brook Trout, I marvel at this descendent of the ice ages. Brook trout are genetic cousins of Lake Trout and must have migrated during the Ice Age from the Gulf of Mexico up the Mississippi, up the Ohio, up the Tennessee, up the French Broad, and up the Pigeon to take up refuge in Yellowstone Prong, just below the parking area for Graveyard Fields on the Blue Ridge Parkway.

While studying geology in college, I plotted the structure of formations underlying the Asheville basin from NASA's remote sensing data. Having later worked part time for TVA analyzing dam sites on the Upper French Broad and Pigeon rivers, I can picture the evolution of the mountains, which seem so permanent, rising and eroding again and again and again through at least three cycles of mountain building and maybe as many as seven to produce the Blue Ridge we see today. Through all the terrain's ups and downs, for several million years, the French Broad has been cutting its way through the mountains.

Moving to Asheville in 2014 was like coming home to a watershed I had never left. Upon returning, among the first regional histories I reread was *The French Broad* by Wilma Dykeman, published in 1955. Though ensuing decades of research and scholarship have added tremendous depth and specificity, *The French Broad* remains indispensable for witnessing the human evolution of the watershed through the eyes of those who lived it into the first half of the twentieth century.

For me, relationships among terrain, climate, and human history are inescapable. Growing up in Knoxville, I collected arrowheads and pot sherds with a friend while his father and other members of the Tennessee Archaeological Society documented prehistoric Indian occupation on the Little Tennessee River before it was flooded by Tellico Lake. From my first book, *A Guide to the Physical Environment of New Hampshire*, written for middle-school students coauthored with William Taffe of Plymouth State College in 1977, through almost a dozen guide books for fishing and hunting to *Rivers of Restoration*, which profiles 21 of Trout Unlimited's major watershed conservation efforts, I have worked to help readers understand a bit more about how the natural environment crafts the lands and waters they so enjoy, and maybe to encourage them that their role and mine in the grand all-encompassing ecology is to conserve them for future generations.

John E. Ross
Asheville, North Carolina
2021

Acknowledgments

Through the Mountains: The French Broad River and Time has been in gestation since 2013 when I began thinking about the relationship between the course of Little Tennessee River, the people who lived along it, and its role in the economic development of that watershed. After moving to Asheville in 2014, it dawned on me that the story of the French Broad watershed involved essentially the same geology, climate, and archaeology but much more diverse populations.

From the onset, Jefferson Chapman, former Director of the McClung Museum of Natural History and Culture at the University of Tennessee–Knoxville, has been unstinting in his encouragement and counsel. Our paths first crossed more than 50 years ago when I was a shirt-tail kid collecting arrowheads and pot sherds from fields along the Little Tennessee, and he was a graduate student documenting prehistoric Indian habitation of river terraces soon to be flooded by TVA's Tellico Dam. Without him, there would be no book.

Equally important was encouragement from Jim Stokely, Wilma Dykeman's son. Her book, *The French Broad*, will forever stand as an icon of environmental histories. Her question: Who Killed the French Broad? spawned community activism that is, still today, restoring and protecting the mainstem of the river from its headwaters downstream to Knoxville where it joins the Holston to form the Tennessee.

In similar vein, Robert D. Hatcher Jr., Professor and Distinguished Scientist Structural Geology and Techtonics, University of Tennessee, Knoxville, has been singularly important in providing his new research that shows that the Great Smoky Mountains are *not* among the oldest mountains in the world.

Uplifted around 5 million years ago, not 260–300 million years ago, they are the most recent of several mountain ranges to occupy this space on the North American continental plate.

I am deeply indebted to my editors, Thomas Wells and Jon Boggs, at the University of Tennessee Press for their encouragement and patience.

Western North Carolina and East Tennessee are very fortunate to have patrons who financially support an extensive array of public libraries, archives, and historical societies that provide easy access to extensive original materials documenting the past. Foremost among librarians who have steered me to significant sources are Katherine Cutshall and Zoe Rhine of the Pack Library's North Carolina Room, Asheville; Marcy Thompson of the Rowell Bosse North Carolina Room, Transylvania County Library; Tim Fisher of the Rel & Wilma Maples History Center, Sevier County Library, Sevierville; Kaila Clark, Anna Porter Public Library, Gatlinburg; Gene Hyde, Ramsey Library Special Collections, University of North Carolina–Asheville; Archivist Jen Bingham, Archives of Appalachia, East Tennessee State University; Elizabeth Hall, director, Stokely Memorial Library Newport; Billie Chandler, Madison County Public Library, Marshall; Karen Paar, Director of Southern Appalachian Archives, Mars Hill University; and volunteers of the Henderson County Historical Society, Hendersonville.

Scores of individuals provided extremely important information. Scott Schumate, Biltmore Estate's archaeologist and historian was a font of critical documents. David Moore, professor of anthropology at Warren Wilson College, has been unstinting with his time in guiding me through prehistoric Indian and early Spanish presence. I was fortunate enough to attend the Cherokee History and Culture Institute led by Barbara Duncan, former education director of the Museum of the Cherokee Indian. She introduced me to Russell Townsend, Tribal Historic Preservation Officer, Eastern Band of the Cherokee Indians. Bart Cattanach and Rick Wooten of the Asheville Regional Office of North Carolina's Geologic Survey provided maps and information about why the French Broad flows where it does. Donald Hughes, project director of the Cecil Sharp in Southern Appalachia Project, and Doug Orr, coauthor with Fiona Ritchie of *Wayfaring Strangers: The Musical Voyage from Scotland and Ulster to Appalachia*, were vital sources on the region's indigenous Bluegrass music.

Finally, I am indelibly indebted to Meredith Whiting, my partner and decades' long friend, for her patience in reading draft after draft and abundance of helpful suggestions that we hope make *Through the Mountains* an enjoyable read.

THROUGH THE MOUNTAINS

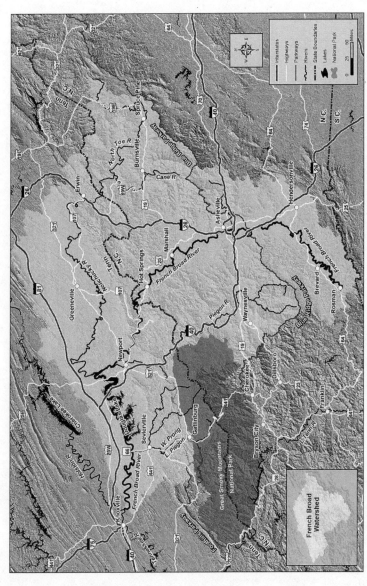

Covering 5,124 square miles, the French Broad watershed is home to more than 1,000,000 people. It includes the northeast third of Great Smoky Mountains National Park, the most heavily visited national park in the country. Fed by four major tributaries—Swannanoa, Pigeon, Nolichucky, and Little Pigeon, the French Broad River rises above Rosman, N.C., and flows 219 miles to its mouth at Knoxville, Tenn. (Cartography: Greg Dobson.)

Introduction

Cup your hands tightly together and tilt them toward the floor. Imagine the seam where they meet as a river and the lifelines on your palms as tributaries. If someone slowly poured water into your hands, it would run out over the tips of your little fingers like a tiny waterfall. You have just created your own watershed. Geographers define watersheds as basins surrounded by mountains and ridges drained by streams that coalesce in a single river. Social scientists think of watersheds differently, as turning points in one's life or in human history. *Through the Mountains: The French Broad River and Time* presents the inseparable integration of the evolution of place and people in the watershed of the French Broad River, which swings northeast around the Great Smoky Mountains, the third most heavily visited national park in America.

A watershed's terrain, its rivers, and its climate shape its flora and fauna. Though present in the French Broad watershed for about five milliseconds of the earth's history, our influence on the course of its waters and weather is far greater in the short run of millennia than its sculpting of us. The impact of our past and future deeds along the French Broad, though varying in specific details, is in aggregate no different from the effects of human habitation along any or all of America's rivers.

Every major watershed—from the Kennebec across the country to the Sacramento—has been fashioned by periods of geologic upheaval and subsidence; colonization and settlement by paleo-people arriving from Eurasia; invasion of European immigrants driven west in flight from ravages of the Little Ice Age and in pursuit of dominating wealth; eviction of native Indians;

internecine warfare; unfettered industrialized exploitation of natural resources and resulting rampant pollution; economic depression and pandemic, and, of late, environmental awareness and pockets of restoration. Thus, the story of the French Broad is the large story of all of America's great rivers, but small enough to tell.

Rising in the Blue Ridge of North Carolina and passing through Asheville, the French Broad river swings wide to the north around the Great Smokies before breaking out of the mountains near Newport, Tennessee, bound for Knoxville. There it joins the Holston to form the Tennessee River. Four smaller rivers feed the French Broad: Swannanoa, Pigeon, Nolichucky, and Little Pigeon. The Pigeon marks the northern boundary of Great Smoky Mountains National Park. Its smaller sibling, the Little Pigeon, carved the valley occupied by the tourist meccas of Sevierville, Pigeon Forge, and Gatlinburg. The Nolichucky drains North Carolina's rugged mineral district above Spruce Pine. The shortest is the Swannanoa, but in many ways it cradles some of the watershed's oldest prehistoric Indian sites. The French Broad watershed is the heart of Western North Carolina and the epicenter of tourism in East Tennessee. More than 1 million people make their homes in the French Broad watershed and nearly 16 million visit annually.

Remember the game: "Rock, Paper, Scissors"? Your parents or grandparents may have played it with you. Paper wraps rock. Scissors cut paper. Rock breaks scissors. Which of the three is most powerful? Now consider this: water or rock? Those clear drops falling from the sky that dampen our gardens feel so benign—except when delivered in deluges that flood our farms and cities, laying waste to much we have built in a river's path. Rock, on the other hand, appears totally enduring. So utterly permanent the Blue Ridge Mountains seem—but they are not.

More than 335 million years ago, the continents of North America and Africa began grinding together to form a new super continent called Pangea. Many geomorphologists believe that shortly thereafter in geologic time—300 to 260 million years ago—today's Appalachians began to rise and that the French Broad began to flow, making it one of a handful of the world's oldest rivers. However, four decades of research by Robert D. Hatcher Jr., recipient of the prestigious Penrose Medal from the Geological Society of America for his analysis of Appalachian tectonics, suggests that the mountains we see today and the river that cuts through them are probably only about 10 million years old. Further, he believes that this is at least the third, and perhaps even the seventh, mountain range to occupy this space on the North American continental plate.[1]

As the formation of Pangea and other movements of continental plates caused mountains to rise in the zone occupied by the southern Appalachians, rains fell. Peaks froze and ice pried boulders from their slopes. Continuous cycles of freeze and fracture reduced them to gravels and sands washed into ancient oceans, among them the ancient Atlantic, filling the gap as Pangea was rifting apart. As sediments piled layer atop layer, they sank deeper and deeper. Each layer increased pressure on the ones beneath solidifying them into sandstones and shales. When these were subject to intense pressure and heat deep in the earth's crust, they were welded into gneiss, schist, and other metamorphic rocks. Highly resistant to weathering, these formations underlie the Asheville basin with its abundance of low hills and steep ridges. In warm oceans—like those surrounding the Florida Keys—calcium carbonate precipitated and settled as fine grey mud that became the deeply weathered limestone and dolostone that underlie the gentle valleys of the lower French Broad watershed in East Tennessee. Taken together, the ancestors of today's Appalachian mountains and the valleys between them have moved some 2,000 miles northwest from their point of origin in the mid-Atlantic. They are moving still, but at a speed far slower than fingernails grow. The little tremblors that every few years rattle the china in our kitchen cabinets are tiny earthquakes. Each reminds us that the mountains that give us such a comforting sense of permanence are as dynamic in their own way as the seasons of flora and fauna, us among them, that inhabit them.

As the mountains and the river were driven westward, the earth wobbled back and forth on its axis. In the atmosphere, huge zones of high and low pressure battled, as they do today, for control of climate and weather. Storms in the mountains feed floods that soon drain away. Cataracts recline into riffles where I cast my flies for trout. I marvel, though, at massive rounded boulders, some the size of compact cars, which I must surmount to reach the next pool upstream. What arctic force cleaved them from the peaks? How did the seemingly gentle flows of, say, the West Prong of the Little Pigeon River above Gatlinburg tumble them, smooth their jagged edges, and deposit them in my way? What power that current must once have wielded. With such violence it must have raged.

As climate warmed and the crumbling front of the most recent glacial advance retreated northward, the first humans—Paleo Indians—entered the watershed. They and successive cultures, the ancestors of the Cherokee, sustained themselves for nearly 14,000 years.[2] First were nomad hunters who thrust their spears into mastodons. They burned forest to promote tender fresh green browse for elk, deer, and turkeys. They evolved into farmers who cleared plots and planted corn, squash, and beans. In less than a micro-second of geologic time, Indians were all but driven out, replaced roughly 300 years ago by European immigrants whose industriousness in the form of roads, farms, factories, and cities shaped the watershed of the French Broad that we live in and work in today.

Still, with its surrounding ridges, the French Broad basin remains a natural sanctuary. Plants common to boreal Canada thrive on the mountains' spine while isolated subtropical species of lichens have taken root on lower south-facing slopes.[3] Brook trout, the state freshwater fish of North Carolina, are cousins of Lake trout which sought refuge in mountain streams as lowland flows were heated by the warming climate that melted continental glaciers. Finding shelter in the mountains as well were those few hundred Cherokee who escaped infamous eviction on the Trail of Tears. Seeking freedom to raise their families as they pleased on lands they could afford, Scots-Irish put down their roots in isolated mountain coves. Legendary for their independence, they preserved ballads like Barbary Allen and their proclivity for distilling spirits of high octane. Mountain moonshine fueled hot cars that delivered booze to flat-landers who voted dry but drank wet. Thus was born NASCAR, America's leading spectator sport.

Next time you fly from Atlanta to Asheville, look out the window and marvel at the broad level valley that runs from Rosman to Hendersonville and picture occasional clusters of tiny daub and wattle huts, homes of ancestral Cherokee farmers. As you circle to land, you may well spy Biltmore House, the largest private residence in America, and once the center of George Vanderbilt's estate of 125,000 acres. Should you be driving toward Sevierville from I-40, when you cross the bridge over the French Broad imagine de Soto and his conquistadors camped five miles upriver in 1540, having just become the first Europeans to traverse the Blue Ridge. If you listen carefully on your way to Dollywood, you might hear the clang of Isaac Love's hammer pounding bars of glowing pig iron into axes and ploughs at his works known now as Pigeon Forge.

Through the Mountains: The French Broad River and Time tells the story of how the waters of the French Broad and the landscape through which they flow came to sustain us, as they have people for millennia. In her landmark environmental history, *The French Broad*, Wilma Dykeman asks the question: What has the river been to the people living in the watershed?[4] To this I add: The river and its tributaries have nurtured humans for thousands of years. What issues must we resolve today to ensure they will continue to do so? That is the question that the narrative of the watershed's geologic and climatological history, the story of the first people to inhabit it, and nearly 500 years of our varied stewardship of it leads me to address in "*The Planner's Paradox*," the final chapter of this book. And this is the conundrum faced by all who live along America's rivers, and perhaps a metaphor for the currents each of us navigates in our own personal lives.

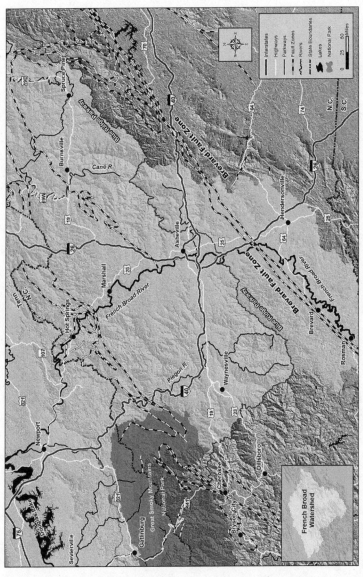

Uplifting and folding created extensive fault zones in the Blue Ridge. The French Broad follows the Brevard Fault Zone to Asheville and courses northwest over soft and fractured formations before cutting through the mountains via another fault zone at Hot Springs, epicenter of a 3.8 earthquake in 2005. Interstate 40 runs with the Pigeon River through related zone of faulting as they cross from North Carolina into Tennessee. (North Carolina Geologic Survey.)

ONE

The Headwaters

On a cold morning, pause for a moment at the Haw Creek Valley overlook on the Blue Ridge Parkway at Mile Point 380. Look south. Beyond a low ridge to your left, white steam plumes from Duke Energy's once-coal, now gas-fired power plant south of Asheville. Far to the right and wearing a transmission tower stands Mount Pisgah, called so not in native Cherokee tongue but by the ancient biblical word for "summit" or "peak." Stretching southward from where you stand is the 400 square-mile Asheville basin, carved by the French Broad River and its tributaries. The mountains you see in the distance—the backbone of the Southern Appalachians—were once thought to rank among the most ancient in the world as was the river. New research suggests that they may be only about 10 million years old. Even so, as they began to emerge, the French Broad started cutting its path through them as did its sibling, the Little Tennessee, which bookends the southern boundary of Great Smoky Mountains National Park.

Rising about 35 miles to the southwest on the eastern flanks of the Blue Ridge, the four forks of the French Broad come together in narrow floodplains near Rosman. For 55 miles before reaching Asheville, the river twists languidly through gentle bottomlands bent here and there by low hills. In its course though the basin, the river drops a scant three feet per mile. Joining the French Broad at Asheville is the Swannanoa River. Twenty-two miles long, it is the shortest of the French Broad's tributaries. But prehistoric Indians followed its route, and that of other tributaries, into the watershed, paths also taken by some of the region's earliest colonial settlers. Downstream from Asheville, the shoulders of the Southern Appalachians close in. Rapids froth over rock ledges, and the river quadruples its descent to around 12 feet per mile in a section adored by whitewater fans. It finally breaks free of the mountains above Newport, Tennessee, 60 miles downstream.

Newport itself is located on the Pigeon River, one of two principal tributaries to the French Broad. Named for the passenger pigeon that clouded the skies when migrating over its route through the mountains before being hunted to extinction in the late 1800s, the Pigeon gathers its waters on the western flank of Richland Balsam, elevation 6,382 feet and the highest point along the Blue Ridge Parkway. Fed by streams draining Waynesville and Maggie Valley, the river's 60-mile course is followed by Interstate 40, where it runs its gorge from North Carolina into Tennessee.

About 10 miles downstream from Newport, the Nolichucky River joins the French Broad impounded now by TVA's Douglas Dam. Whelped by run-off from west-facing slopes in the shadow of North Carolina's Grandfather Mountain, the Nolichucky's headwaters wind through Spruce Pine, known for historic gem and mica mining and the famed Penland School of Crafts. In 1540 de Soto, the first European to traverse the Blue Ridge, followed the Nolichucky on the route that led him to the Mississippi a year later.[1] Colonial settlers gave its nickname to Tennessee frontiersman John Sevier, hero of the Revolutionary War battle of Kings Mountain and Tennessee's first governor, known in these parts as "Chucky Jack." The Chucky provided the route for the Clinchfield & Ohio railroad to reach Spruce Pine by 1903. Completed in 1914, the final leg of its connection with the Southern Railway at Marion, N. C required blasting 17 tunnels in the 11 miles from Altapass to the other side of the Blue Ridge. Called "The Loops," to maintain an easy grade for heavy coal trains from southwest Virginia, this section traversed 16.5 miles in a long horseshoe curve, the open ends of which are separated by only 1.9 miles. A similar railroad, the East Tennessee & Western North Carolina, called fondly by some the "Tweetsie," and by others the "Eat Taters & Wear No Clothes" line, traced the Doe Rivers' path from Elizabethton, Tenn. in the 1880s to reach deposits of iron ore at Cranberry, N.C.

Though significantly smaller when it comes to water flow, the gentle valley of a third tributary—the Little Pigeon River, which enters the French Broad about four miles below Douglas Dam—carries more than 50,000 vehicles per day on the route from I-40 through Sevierville, past Pigeon Forge and Dollywood, into Gatlinburg. By comparison, only half as many cars and trucks hustle on I-40, along the "big" Pigeon as it cuts through the Blue Ridge between Tennessee and North Carolina. And fewer than 8,000 vehicles per day follow the West Prong of the Little Pigeon, where raging torrents at the end of the Ice Age tumbled car-sized boulders downstream, to Newfound Gap, as US 441 crosses Great Smoky Mountains National Park bound for Cherokee, N.C.

While pierced by the French Broad and its tributaries, the Blue Ridge themselves seem massively impervious and immobile. Their dusty blue sawtooth ridges on the horizon actually float on the earth's crust like jagged dumplings in a pot of stew simmering on the stove. Convection, that same force that roils the stew but this from the earth's core, drives continental plates on which mountains ride into collision and apart again. When plates collide, mountains are pushed up, but at a rate far slower than fingernails grow. And during the building of the mountains, huge masses of molten magma can be injected into rock strata. Cooling, they may form plutons of granite that—when surrounding less-resistant formations—weather away, appear as rounded domes such as Looking Glass Rock, which dominates the view from the Blue Ridge Parkway at Mile Post 413.

From the point in the mid-Atlantic where the North American and African plates collided, the terrain on which the French Broad and its tributaries flow has drifted northwestward for some 2,000 miles. The Southern Appalachians are still being driven westward at about half an inch per year, according to measurements taken at the Pisgah Atmospheric Research Institute, site of an impressive array of radio telescopes tucked in a Blue Ridge hollow above Rosman high in the headwaters of the French Broad watershed. They were first used to track the first NASA satellites 50 years ago.[2]

Thrust faulting created linear zones of softer and broken rock, which the French Broad follows from Rosman, past Brevard and Hendersonville, to a few miles beyond Asheville.[3] There, its course bends north, eating its way over another district of fractured formations that underlie Marshall and Hot Springs and through the spine of the Blue Ridge into Tennessee. The basin is widest and the terrain gentlest around Asheville, where these zones of faults and fractures intersect.[4] No other broad swaths of rolling land surrounded by mountains exist in the Southeast. Thus the Asheville basin is as unique to the Southern Appalachians as are the flats of Lake Bonneville to the Rockies.

For more than 2,000 years, Indians raised crops throughout the forested valleys of the basin. Their paths became roads. Where trails crossed streams, European immigrants built cabins and, where gradients were steep enough,

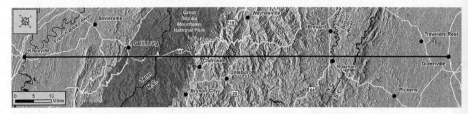

Cross-section from Knoxville, Tenn., to Greenville, S.C., crossing French Broad River
headwaters at Rosman, N.C.

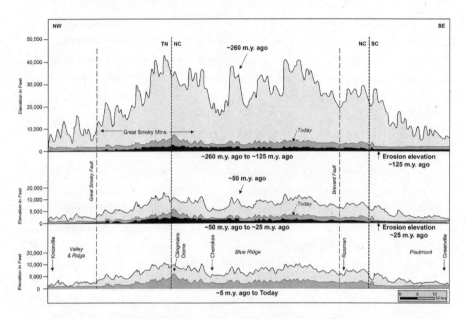

Speculative Southern Appalachian topography from ~260 million years ago (end of
African–North American plate collisions forming Pangea) to present. Lightest grey
shading in each set of cross-sections indicates maximum uplift. Black profile (two
upper cross-sections) represents ultimate erosion surface before next uplift. Dark grey
areas indicate today's elevation of the Great Smokies and adjacent mountains. Based
on research by Robert D. Hatcher Jr., PhD, Professor and Distinguished Scientist,
Structural Geology and Tectonics, University of Tennessee-Knoxville. Cross-sections'
vertical exaggeration 3:1. (Topographic interpretation: Andrew L. Wunderlich,
GIS analyst/cartographer. Artwork: Greg Dobson.)

grist and saw mills. Houses at crossroads added spare rooms, took in travelers, and became inns. A store would open nearby. Across the road, another house would be built. Thus were planted seeds for settlements that blossomed into towns—Brevard, Hendersonville, Marshall, and Asheville. Other smaller lowlands at the base of the Blue Ridge attracted additional European immigrants. One such intermountain cove, White Oak Flats, became Gatlinburg after Radford Gatlin opened a post office in his store in 1856.

GLACIAL SPRING

As continental plates were butting heads and splitting asunder, the earth's atmosphere was doing likewise. Huge zones of high pressure spun clockwise over tropical and arctic regions north of the equator. Between these massive weather-making wheels, low pressure cells rotate counterclockwise like little gears in a giant engine brewing storms that brought deluge and blizzard. The location of highs and lows was governed, then as now, by the tilt of the earth's axis toward or away from the sun. The vigor of their circulation was determined by the earth's rotation, differences in the temperatures of their air masses, and currents in the oceans below. They competed then, as they do still today, to dominate the weather, ushering in eras of intense drought and wind; of high humidity and pounding rain; of bitter cold, glaciation, and ice caps. Volcanic eruptions and impacts of asteroids elsewhere on earth, with their transglobal clouds of sun-shrouding dust, temporarily altered the world's climate and weather.

The most recent period of glaciation began to wane 22,000 years ago. Conventional wisdom holds that glaciers were found no further south than the latitudes of Ohio and northern Pennsylvania. Yet above the headwaters of Boone Fork on Grandfather Mountain at 4,500 feet elevation, a rock outcrop carries grooves, striations, and polishes first thought to be characteristic of Alpine glaciers. Though later investigation has shown that those scars were made by logging chains and cables, most geologists surmise that the highest peaks of the Southern Appalachians may well have worn year-round caps of snow during the Ice Age.[5] At the height of the last glacial advance, the floor of the Asheville basin likely resembled high Arctic desert, a barren and bitter land gnawed at by incessant wind and bereft of all vegetation save rare clusters of lichens.

As climate warmed, occasional torrential spring rains and tropical storms

Though not glaciated, the southern Blue Ridge wore thick caps of ice, which when melted by the warming climate 20,000 years ago, produced raging cataracts that rolled huge boulders down rivers like the West Prong of the Little Pigeon above Gatlinburg. (Great Smoky Mountains National Park archives.)

drenched mountain icefields and snow packs. Cataracts of meltwater charged narrow, winding stream channels to their brims with slurries of cobbles, gravels, sands, and clays. In maelstrom eddies, pebbles swirled round and round, drilling potholes in bedrock beneath currents. Tumbling along were massive blocks of rock that had been pried from cliffs by ice. And when no more snows capped the peaks, and ferocious run-offs abated, the boulders with their jagged edges, now rounded smooth, were left where they sat. You can see them in the West Prong of the Little Pigeon River in Great Smoky Mountains National Park below the Chimney Tops and in the West Fork of the Pigeon, south of Canton as NC 215 climbs toward the Blue Ridge Parkway.

Where the gradient of streams lessened, currents slowed and could no longer carry their thick loads of sediments. First to be dropped were boulders, then cobbles and gravels, and finally sand and thin layers of rich silt. With each flood, new soil—known as alluvium—was deposited. As climate warmed, a tundra of mosses, grasses, and stunted shrubs spread across valley floors. Each new generation of flora left a bed of rich humus in its wake, which was eroded by new spring floods and deposited further downstream. Streams meandered, eating away first the right bank then the left, broadening river bottoms as they aged.

Snow and ice vanished, and the ground lay barren like the emerging terrain of Antarctica. Permafrost abounded. With rising temperatures, stunted shrubbery of the tundra thickened. Tree species that had found refuge from glacial extinction on the continent's southernmost coastal plains began to migrate north. First came jack pine and spruce. As the climate continued to warm, pine and spruce climbed higher up mountain slopes. In the lowlands, they were replaced by oaks and hickories. Grasses and berry bushes began to proliferate. Diversifying flora attracted herds of musk ox and caribou found now in boreal Canada. Mammoth and mastodon browsed grasslands at forest edges.

Among fauna of glacial heritage still resident in the headwaters of the French Broad are brook trout, the official freshwater fish of North Carolina. Vermicular dabs of gold splotch their dark blue-green backs. Roundels of red, sometimes surrounded by halos of sky blue, dot their flanks. They spawn in October when the bellies of males turn orange as bright as autumn leaves. Brookies are not trout at all, but a long-isolated char that evolved in the Canadian Shield that migrated up southeastern rivers from the Atlantic and Gulf during ice ages and found refuge in the little creeks of the highlands as climate warmed. Brook trout, *Salvelinus fontinalis,* are the wildflowers of mountain streams.

INTO THE BASIN

Humans entered the French Broad watershed more than 14,000 years ago. The first were Paleo Indians. By about 8000 BC, their culture had evolved into the Archaic period, which stretched to roughly 1000 BC. They were followed by those of the Woodland era whose latest phase, the Mississippians, developed about AD 700 and extended into the 1600s, when they came into contact with European explorers and immigrants who followed.[6] The Paleo people are the first known ancestors of the Cherokee. Armed with spears, they were nomadic hunters and gatherers incessantly foraging for food. Most archeologists believe they migrated westward across North America, having arrived from eastern Eurasia via the Bering land bridge between Siberia and Alaska, by watercraft crossing the Pacific, or both. A few, however, hold that the first people in the region are descendants of the Solutrean culture, having traveled from northern Europe along the edge of the Arctic ice cap and down the Atlantic coast.[7]

Tracks of Paleo people in the watershed are extremely scant. Their presence is evidenced by tips of lances occasionally found throughout the basin. Distinguished by a long groove called a flute down each side, they resemble spear points found alongside bones of mammoth near Clovis, New Mexico. That some Paleo points were made of quartzite and chert and that concentrations of broken points and chips are occasionally found near outcrops of those rocks in the Blue Ridge suggest that the earliest people may have established semipermanent seasonal camps rather than just hunting their way through the watershed.

Radio carbon data date the presence of Paleo people in the region to about 14,500 years before the present era. Archaeologists found stone scrapers, knives, and related tools along with musk ox and mastodon bones near the marl of an ancient lake along the north fork of the Holston River at Saltville, Va., about 150 miles northeast of its junction with the French Broad at Knoxville, Tenn.[8] For nomads who have traveled clear across the country, it is reasonable to assume they passed through the lower French Broad watershed. It is also highly likely that America's first people, traveling in small family groups probably of no larger than two dozen or so, ascended the river into the Asheville basin from the Tennessee Valley. As well, they filtered into the watershed from the Piedmont.

At first they stalked mastodons and giant ground sloths that had retreated into the highlands before migrating further north into cooler climes and then into extinction as climate warming continued. Later Paleo generations hunted bison, elk, deer, and turkey for meat and hides for shelter and clothing. Essential in their diets as well were acorns, hickory nuts, and chestnuts; roots and tubers; and fresh green shoots.

Their most precious possession was fire, but for thousands of years they may have been unable to start one every time they wanted. How did they acquire it? Without a doubt, prehistoric Indians relied on lightning. According to Cherokee legend, the animals sent forth the water spider to a sycamore tree smoldering on an island from a lightning strike. In a basket spun from her web,

Following mastodons, mammoths, and other mega-fauna, nomadic Paleo Indians were the first humans to enter the watershed about 14,000 years ago. (McClung Museum of Natural History and Culture, The University of Tennessee, Knoxville. Artwork by Madeline Kneberg.)

she placed a glowing ember and brought it back to the other animals. From that time on, the Cherokee have been known as the *People of One Fire*.

Embers from wild fires were carefully husbanded, perhaps in bundles of finely shredded reeds or wood shavings wrapped like cigars. To start a new fire, a glowing coal would be flaked from the bundle into a wad of tinder. Indians would blow on the hot ash until it lit dry twigs onto which kindling had been laid. Also passed from generation to generation was the art of fiercely rotating one very dry pointed stick into a notched conical socket in another stick fast enough so friction ignited wood shavings in the little gap. Or they may have struck a sharp rock of flint or quartz against a block of pyrite, crystalline iron sulfide also known as fool's gold found throughout the mountains, to send sparks into tinder.

Use of fire separated humans from animals, but of equal importance was discovery of how to make cord. No doubt thin strips of hide or intestine were first used to bind sharp stone points to spear shafts. No longer did Indians have to rely on sharpened and fire-hardened sticks to kill game. Later evolved techniques of twisting fibers from stringy plants and braiding them into twine.

Cord allowed skins to be stitched into clothes and nets to be fashioned for catching fish. Alas, Blue Ridge climate has been too humid to preserve their ancient twine.

As climate warmed, it continued to become drier. Rivers in the watershed ceased to ravage flatlands as violently or as frequently. Deer, black bear, elk, and turkey became more common. Nut trees and fruit-bearing plants abounded. Around 8000 BC, the opening of the Archaic era, Indians slowed their nomadic wanderings. On Zimmerman's Island in the French Broad a few miles downstream from Newport, Tenn. and now submerged by Douglas Lake, Archaic Indians developed a more or less permanent village. From there, small groups would follow the river and the neighboring Pigeon upstream into the Asheville basin.[9]

Archaic people established villages where Garden Creek joins the Pigeon southeast of Canton, N.C., on the plain on Biltmore Estate where the Swannanoa flows into the French Broad, and further up the Swannanoa on the campus of Warren Wilson College. Scores of families took up residence along the French Broad near Hendersonville and Brevard. As well, evidence of Archaic encampments has been found along the Nolichucky in Tennessee below its exit from the Blue Ridge at Erwin and in Sevierville not far from Dollywood.

Drive highways along rivers in the watershed and picture clusters of Indian huts covered with sod or reed mats where now stretch acre upon acre of agricultural plastic through which tomatoes bound for packing plants now grow. Imagine an Indian lurking, arm cocked and ready to spear a bison, in a bunker by a fairway on the famed Donald Ross-designed golf course at Asheville's Grove Park Inn.

A more settled life gave Indians the time to improve tools and weapons. Creeping stealthily to get close enough, Paleo Indians had thrust spears into huge late ice-age mammals. To slay faster-moving deer and elk, Indians of the Archaic period perfected spear throwers, short wooden shafts two or three feet long with a hook on one end and a handle on the other. The hook fit into a notch in the end of the spear. A tapered stone weight was often tied to the short shaft to add leverage. An Indian would hook the spear to the shaft, lay the shaft back over his shoulder, grasp the handle and spear with his fingers, and with a mighty lunge fling the shaft forward and release the spear. Known by the Aztec word *atlatls*, the short shafts permitted Archaic Indians to hurl their spears farther and faster than their Paleo ancestors.[10]

Deer and black bear were highly prized, not just for their protein but, of course,

Archaic Indians established semi-permanent villages like the one on the Warren Wilson College campus on the Swannanoa River around 4,000 years ago. (Warren Wilson College Archaeology. Artwork by Gwen Diehn.)

for their hides. Skins roofed lean-tos or other primitive shelters and provided clothing. When hunters brought hides into camp, women scraped them clean of flesh and fat and dried them in the sun. After being soaked for several days, they were taken up again and the other side was scraped to remove hair. They were immersed again but this time with ground-up deer brains. Taken out and beaten until supple, they were dried and browned over small fires and perhaps rubbed with fat and powdered hematite, a soft, native red-orange ore of iron, to color and preserve them. Then they would be cut and sewn into garments.[11]

Also, women had learned how to weave baskets so tightly that when wet, their fibers swelled and became virtually watertight. Submerged in water along with tubers and shoots of plants newly greened in the spring, venison and other meats could be stewed when hot rocks were added to the broth. Chestnuts and hickory nuts were very important to the Indians' diet. They were gathered in the fall and stored in baskets. Boiled, the meat came loose from the shell, and its oil rose to the top, where it was skimmed off and saved. Below the oil floated a soft mush of nut meat. It too was dipped out, maybe with a curved piece of clean bark or perhaps a ladle of woven reeds or sturdy grass stems, to be dried and stored.

Toward the middle of the Archaic period, rainfall decreased, and the French Broad and other rivers became shallower. In the spring, bottom-feeding suckers ran up river and collected in shallows as they spawned. They were easy to harvest. By flaking notches in thin cobbles, bigger by half than flat round stones children skip across streams, Indians created weights to sink loosely woven nets for fish. They built fish traps, weirs of boulders pointing downstream from opposing banks. Nets were placed in the narrow gap where the two veins came together. As Indians thrashed the river above the trap, fish turned and fled downstream into the nets. They were caught, their entrails which spoil easily, were stripped away, and their flesh was dried and smoked to preserve it. Hooks fashioned from small bones of deer were also used for fishing.

As the Archaic era progressed through its late and final phase (3,000 BC–1,000 BC), tools became more sophisticated. Rounded river rocks were ground into axe heads with a groove to which the split ends of a stout handle could be tightly bound. Not only were they used to fell trees but also perhaps to hollow thick trunks into dugout canoes. Bowls of soapstone, also known as steatite, began to appear. So soft that it can be easily shaped with scrapers of chert or dried bone, the bowls were carved where the rock was quarried in the Great Smokies. Alas, they broke easily, and pieces that could not be mended were made into personal ornaments.[12]

The Archaic Indian's main thoroughfare into the French Broad basin was the Catawba Trail, which ran from South Carolina to Ohio through Tennessee and Kentucky. Originating below Greenville, S.C., it was joined at Asheville by another trail coming up from the Charlotte area, which crossed through Swannanoa Gap. Together the paths ran down the French Broad to Zimmerman's Island, now flooded by Douglas Lake. There, it connected with the main artery of the Indian trading and war path, which follows the length of the Great Appalachian Valley from Lake Champlain between Vermont and New York at the Canadian border into northern Alabama.[13]

The route of the trails into the Tennessee Valley and French Broad watershed is still today among the region's most vital transportation corridors and essential to the basin's economic vitality. On the north side of the French Broad at a point that would come to mark the Tennessee–North Carolina border, the trail passes beneath a 100-foot-tall cliff. About 5,000 years ago, Archaic Indians inscribed symbols and daubed them with intense orange and blue colors thought to tell of warm springs across the river. Known today as Paint Rock, these petroglyphs are among the most visible evidence of prehistoric Indians in the watershed.[14]

For more than 9,000 years, first the Paleo people and then those of the Archaic era, Indians led extremely unsettled lives. The quest for food drove them ever up the next draw, across the next ridge, and down into the next valley, inevitability dictating that they would encounter Indians from other cultures. Whether rooted in commerce or conflict, the exact nature of those meetings time has forever worn way, but their importance remains in artifacts discovered at places where they camped. Their exchanges revolutionized their existence.

Paleo spears had carried heavy lance-like blades. Those of the Archaic era were lighter and smaller, and stone projectile tips found at the Warren Wilson site on the Swannanoa were smaller still. Resembling points found in the Piedmont to the east beyond the mountains, some were shaped like triangles, little more than an inch long and less than an inch wide at their bases. On others, a short stem projects from the base. Radio carbon dates of organic remains at sites where the points were found give them an age of about AD 700. Commonly held among archaeologists is the belief that use of arrows and bows by Indians of the basin began about then. No longer restricted to hurling spears, they could harvest rabbits, squirrels, raccoons, opossums, turkeys, and other birds. Lighter and less cumbersome than spears, arrows could be shot with accuracy even by youngsters. Thus the number of hunters in a family group increased dramatically as did the amount and variety of protein in their diets.

But of even greater importance to their diet was the emergence of pottery at about the same time.[15] Also gleaned from contacts with other Indians residing in the Piedmont, pottery revolutionized the way food was stored. No longer were families forced to depend on baskets that, no matter how tightly woven, began to rot in ever-present dampness. Food could be preserved for increasing periods of time, but pottery was fragile and a challenge to move.

Though squash and gourds had been grown for more than 4,000 years before the current era,[16] With the onset of the Medieval Warm Period about AD 900, an increase of about 2°C, family groups discovered they could reliably plant seeds of nutritious native plants such as sumpweed. Small plots of gourd and squash were planted. Husks of gourds may have been dried to serve as cups, bowls, and dippers. Though their vegetable flesh was no doubt was consumed, it was far less important to the Indians' diet than nuts and wild grapes, which were smoked and saved as raisins. Together the abilities to grow and store food expanded the permanence of seasonal camps into year-round villages.

These, the first semipermanent settlements in the watershed, were small, consisting of half a dozen or so more or less square houses of about 20 feet on a side with a single door. Posts anchored walls made of woven reed mats daubed with mud that dried and hardened. Stout central posts supported thatched roofs shaped like rounded pyramids. Floors of packed earth were sometimes covered by thin mats of plaited split cane. Family life centered around the ever-smoldering hearth of fire-hardened clay.[17]

Advances in implements for harvesting game and the ability to grow food sped progression from a culture of hunting and gathering, in which everyone prowled in the never-ending quest for sustenance, to one of specialized tasks. The strongest and most agile members of a village hunted. Those adept at weaving baskets or making pottery or flaking rock into points or tools spent increasing amounts of time doing so. As Jared Diamond suggests in *Guns, Germs, and Steel* . . . , a more settled style of life allowed prehistoric people time to contemplate the world around them and the forces that shaped it. Use of native plants to treat disease became codified as medicine. As in other cultures throughout the world, practices of everyday life evolved into ritual. In ritual were sewn the threads of spirituality so prominent among descendants of the first humans to enter the basin.

The earliest communities in the French Broad watershed continued to attract Indians from other regions intent on commerce. Among the most prominent trading partners entering the watershed were the Hopewells. Their culture was centered in southcentral and southwestern Ohio, where their burials occasionally contained grizzly bear teeth and obsidian from the Rockies, marine shells from the Gulf Coast, and mica from the Carolinas. Blades of a type of chalcedony outcropping only in Ohio and associated with Hopewell culture have been found in burials on the lower Little Tennessee River.[18] Along with exotic trinkets, these visitors may have brought with them a new outlook on physical manifestations of spirituality. Their predecessors, the Adena, had constructed earthworks in the form of effigies such as the famous Serpent Mound near Chillicothe, Ohio. Coils of this one- to three-foot-high 1,348-foot-long earthen snake are aligned with solstices and equinoxes suggesting cosmological rituals.

The hand of the Hopewells is evident in mounds at Warren Wilson and Garden Creek on the Pigeon near Canton, but none more obviously than Biltmore Mound about a mile upstream from where the Swannanoa flows into the French Broad. Constructed about 1,500 years ago, it does not rise as a prominent landform like many major Indian mounds in the Southeast such as the Nikwasi mound at Franklin. Rather, it was expanded outward from its center and appears faintly as a low and gentle rise of only a few feet above the floodplain. Its spiritual significance is by far more important. A large post about two feet in diameter was placed in the center of the mound, precisely on a straight line between Mt. Mitchell, the highest peak east of the Rockies, and Mt. Pisgah, the second tallest peak in the Blue Ridge framing the Asheville basin.

As the sun rose over Mt. Mitchell on the morning of the summer solstice in AD 590, its rays would have passed directly over the post and illuminated Mt. Pisgah behind (see map next page). Few archaeologists doubt that Biltmore Mound was the site of astronomical observations and ritual feasts. Along with bones from whitetail deer and turkey, shells from mollusks and turtles, and scales from fish and plentiful remains of nuts and seeds—all evidence of feasting—archaeologists recovered "power parts" of animals—jaws of bear, canids, bobcats and fox, and even a bear's penis bone—thought to be used in spiritual or shamanistic ceremony. Documented as well are paraphernalia including crystals, gorgets, objects of mica and copper, and awls believed to be for scratching marks on the skin of participants who may have been part of solemn rites.[19]

Clusters of Indian houses dotted the broad 8,000 acres of floodplain of what is now Biltmore Estate. Surrounding the settlements were gardens growing squash, pumpkin, beans, corn, and sumpweed. They were likely cultivated with digging sticks. About the same time, grey wolves were domesticated into dogs selectively bred for prized traits such as aptitude for tracking and baying game and for loyalty. Their prowess as hunting companions was memorialized in small effigy pots bearing their likenesses. Occasionally, their skeletons are found in male burials, testimony that dogs had already become man's best friend.[20]

Not only did Indians living in villages surrounding the mound and those throughout the basin take part in the celebrations, but the mound's location close to the junction of two major trails suggest that others living outside the region may have journeyed there to participate as well. They may have also gathered medicinal plants from surrounding ridges. Perhaps Indians turned to the heavens to pray for bountiful hunt and harvest seasons, protection from marauding interlopers, and explanations for that which they could not fathom. Weather must have lain near the foundation of their concerns. Seasons neither too cold or hot, too wet or dry presaged a good growing season and a healthy year to come.

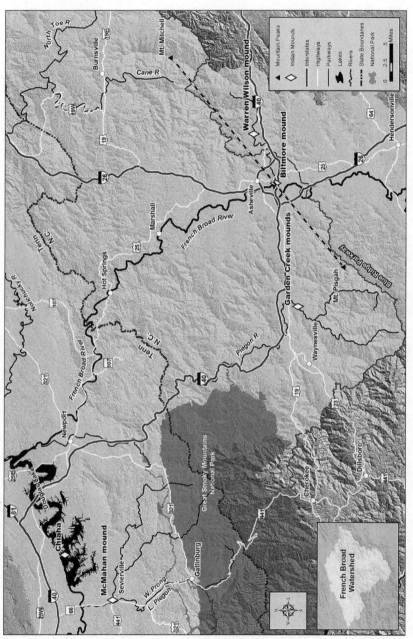

In AD 590 as the sun rose over Mt. Mitchell on the summer solstice, its rays passed over a tall pole placed in the Indian mound near the entrance to Biltmore estate where Indians of the Woodland period living nearby are thought to have been feasting in celebration of the new growing season. (Cartography: Greg Dobson.)

Though archaeologists draw lines in time dividing Indian cultures by material traits such as types of spear and arrow points, pottery, mounds, and other evidence of physical presence, they speak of them as phases implying an uninterrupted continuum of evolving civilization. The Paleo culture was gradually supplanted by the Archaic, which grew into the Woodland and its most recent prehistoric iteration, the Mississippian. It is wrong to think of these peoples as tribes, and it is just as erroneous to believe that newer Indian cultures defined by their tools and abodes supplanted older ones. Equally misguided is the notion that they were displaced by invading tribes, the Iroquois for example, in the same manner that Europeans replaced prehistoric people in the French Broad watershed. Rather, it is reasonable to assume that the original people of the watershed evolved adopting new technologies, practices, and rituals the same way we do—holding on to the old, trying bits of the new, and adapting what proves better suited to the environments in which they live.

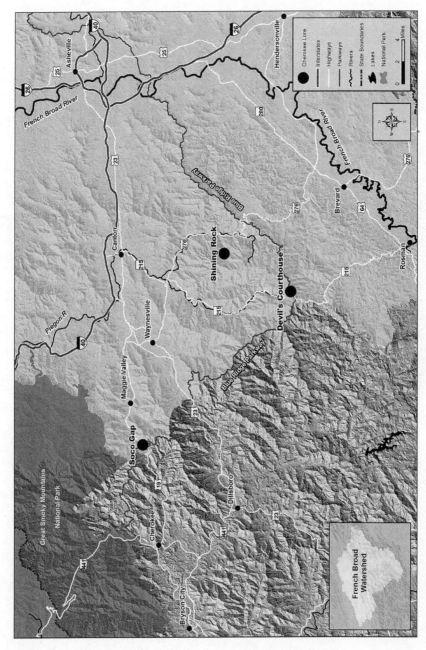

Follow the Blue Ridge Parkway to Devil's Courthouse where Judaculla, the slant-eyed giant of Cherokee lore, sat in judgment. To the northeast is Shining Rock where the Creator placed the first Cherokee couple, Selu and Kaná ti. (Cartography: Greg Dobson.)

TWO

Cherokee (ᏣᎳᎩ), the Principal People

The Cherokee are among the most prominent Indian cultures in the East. At the opening of the sixteenth century, lands dominated by Cherokee, but not all inhabited by them, spanned nearly 200,000 square miles, stretching from the central Shenandoah Valley in Virginia nearly 500 miles west to the mouth of the Tennessee River at Paducah, Kentucky, and from Cincinnati south for almost 400 miles to just north of Atlanta. The vast tracts from the Ohio River southward across Kentucky and central Tennessee were hunting grounds, shared, but not harmoniously, with neighboring Indians.[1] Though victorious in battle against the Creeks to the south and the Shawnees to the north, the Cherokee lived in a perpetual state of warfare.

According to James Mooney in his authoritative *Cherokee History, Myths, and Secret Formulas*: "The name the Cherokee call themselves is Yûñ'wiyǎ' or Ani'-Yûñ'wiyǎ', in the third person, signifying 'real people' or 'principal people.'" While the origins of the appellation are obscure, it may well be that they chose the name to distinguish themselves from invading tribes. The language spoken then and now by the Cherokee is linguistically linked to that of the Iroquois. Exploring its genesis, Mooney writes of the migration of Iroquois southward into Cherokee country after the former's defeat by the Algonquians.[2] Cherokee legend has it that the Iroquois and Cherokee were once one people then divided deep in prehistory. Because of similarities in the languages, some linguists tend to support this view.

Working for the Bureau of American Ethnology under John Wesley Powell at the Smithsonian Institution from 1885 into 1890, Mooney was a prominent

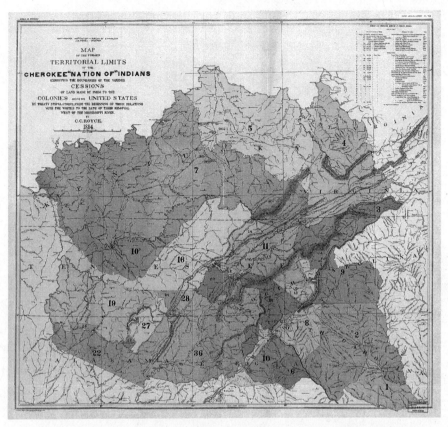

While the homeland of the Cherokee was centered where North Carolina, Tennessee, South Carolina, and Georgia meet, at its height their territory extended from the Ohio River to Atlanta and west to the Mississippi. (Royce, C. C. Map showing the territory originally assigned Cherokee Nation of Indians, 1884, Library of Congress.)

Indian ethnographer of his day. He lived among the Eastern Band of the Cherokee for several months and collected stories from a shaman named Swimmer. He paid Swimmer for his interviews, raising doubts among some of today's ethnographers about their veracity because of their intense parallels to stories from the Judeo-Christian and classical traditions. Observing that the Cherokee were eager to adapt to the ways of white settlers, Mooney suggests that the stories had been colored by contacts over the preceding 100 years with Christian missionaries whom, he reports, James Adair describes as "a nest of apostates" in his landmark *History of American Indians*, published in 1775. They were also likely influenced by African American folk tales learned from slaves with whom

Cherokee shared the auction block. Kinship between Joel Chandler Harris's "Brer Rabbit" stories in *The Complete Stories of Uncle Remus* and portrayal of the rabbit as a trickster in Cherokee lore is inescapable.[3]

Prehistoric Indians were highly mobile as the presence of grizzly bear jaws and obsidian from the Rockies and North Carolina mica in Hopewell graves of central Ohio illustrates. Indians of the French Broad may have traded language with those from other regions—including the Deep South and Great Lakes—that they met on their travels. And it is also probable, according to Mooney, that Iroquoian speaking peoples filtered in from the north and others of related lineage drifted in from coastal Virginia and North Carolina, intermarrying Indians of the mountains and valleys, establishing the linguistic culture that became Cherokee.[4] Finding the climate reasonably benign with a longer growing season and the furrows of an agrarian society already beginning to be tilled, they may have simply stayed. They occupied sites along river valleys including the French Broad, the Pigeon, the Nolichucky, the Little Tennessee, and other rivers heading up in the Southern Appalachians that had hosted Indians since end of the last glacial advance.

HOW THE CHEROKEE CAME TO BE

In the beginning all the Animals lived in Gălûñ'lătĭ, the land beyond the sky, and it was crowded. The earth below was covered with water. Down was sent the little Water Beetle. She dove to the bottom of the sea, clutched a great glob of mud with her forelegs, and swam as hard as she could for the surface. Just before she reached it, she ran out of breath. Struggling, she had to let go of the mud. Breaking free, she floated on her back and gasped fresh air. The mud bobbed up nearby and grew larger and larger. The Animals, seeing that she was safe, dispatched a wise old Buzzard to see if any of the mud was dry. He flew and flew and became very tired. Lower and lower he circled until the tips of his wings dipped into the mud making valleys. When he raised his wings, the mud flew off and landed as mountains. Thus were created the valleys and mountains of the Cherokee homeland.

MOONEY | *Cherokee History, Myths and Sacred Formulas*

At the dawn of human time, according to Cherokee legend, there lived a widow with one daughter in the ancient town of Kanuga along the headwaters of the Pigeon River above Waynesville. She instructed her daughter that she must take no other than a great hunter for her husband. One night, there came to the house where the daughter slept a stranger who lay with her. The daughter told the stranger of her mother's edict. Awakening in the morning, she found by her door a deer. Night after night, the stranger would come to be with the daughter, and in the morning a buck, a doe, or perhaps a turkey would be found by her door.

Her mother insisted that she see the stranger. This the daughter told him, but he demurred, saying that his looks would frighten her. She began to cry, and the stranger relented. In the morning, she went out and fetched her mother. They returned and beheld the stranger. He was a giant. His face was kindly but his eyes were very long and angled downward. He lay curled with his back on the floor. He was so huge that his head brushed against the rafters at one end of the hut, and his feet touched the roof on the other. He was called Judaculla, so named for his slanting eyes. And it came to pass that the girl gave birth to a daughter and left with him to live high in the Blue Ridge in a cave at the base of what is known today as Devil's Courthouse along the Blue Ridge Parkway. Judaculla administered justice from his throne above the cave. Cherokee myth holds that Indians who transgressed tribal law were bound hand and foot, taken to the cave, tried by Judaculla for their crimes, and put to death.

The promontory offers stunning views of the headwaters of the French Broad and its sibling, the Little Tennessee. To the west is the ridge where Judaculla farmed, known now as Old Fields Bald. "Old Fields" are plots where Cherokee and their ancestors are thought to have cultivated food. Beneath the bald along Caney Creek lies a soapstone boulder covered with ancient petroglyphs. It is said that Judaculla leapt from his seat on the Courthouse, landed on the boulder, and put his hand down to steady himself. The handprint is easily seen.

The boulder itself is steatite, very soft soapstone composed mainly of talc, a principal ingredient of Johnson & Johnson's now discontinued baby powder. Talc is formed from ancient sea sediments that were subject to intense heat and pressure during the process of metamorphism that fused muddy shales and sandstones into gneiss and granite that make up much of the Blue Ridge. Steatite was readily carved with tools of quartzite and antler. From it Indians fashioned bowls, atlatl weights for their spear throwers, ceremonial pipes, animal effigies, and personal ornaments.

Other etchings on Judaculla Rock may map the surrounding country, believed to be the core of the Cherokee homeland. Not far away, according to their lore, the Creator made a home for the first man and woman below Shining Rock, so named from its gleaming outcrop of white quartzite at its peak a few miles south

In a cave beneath Devil's Courthouse along the Blue Ridge Parkway, Judaculla imprisoned transgressors of Cherokee law. (Photograph: John E. Ross.)

Leaping from his seat on Devil's Courthouse, Judaculla landed on this boulder near Cullowhee and bent to steady himself. His handprint is clearly visible in this petroglyph, one of several in Western North Carolina. (Milas Parker with Judaculla Rock, North Carolina Department of Natural and Cultural Resources.)

of Waynesville. The peak is inscribed with petroglyphs showing human-like figures. The first couple, Kaná ti and Selu, his wife, lived there with their young son. Kaná ti was a lucky hunter. When he went out, he always returned with a buck, or a doe, or maybe a turkey. She provided corn and beans whenever desired. Food was always plentiful and easy to obtain.

But one day Selu butchered a deer and washed away its blood in the river. Unthinkingly, she had violated the purity of water which the Cherokee held sacred. The blood begat a wild boy who led the couple's son astray. The son had been told never to follow his father on his hunts. But the wild boy's curiosity could not be stilled. Together they tracked Kaná ti to the cave at the base of Devil's Courthouse where all animals lived. They saw him roll a boulder aside. A fine buck stepped out and fell to Kaná ti's arrow. Not long thereafter, the boys made bows and arrows for themselves, ventured to the cave, pushed aside the rock, and shot a deer as it emerged. But their aim was bad. They hit it in the rump, causing it to raise its tail like a white flag as it fled. That is why deer are called "whitetails." In the commotion, all the other animals escaped from the cave. And that is how deer, turkey, and bear, on which Indians depended for meat and hides for clothing and shelter, became so elusive, and why, ever after, Cherokee men were forced to devote most of their time to hunting for food.

CORN, MOTHER OF LIFE

Upon learning what the boys had done, Kaná ti was incensed. In the back of the cave, he found four deep clay jars He kicked them open and out swarmed a plague of biting insects—lice, bedbugs, fleas, and gnats—eager to feast on the young boys' tender skin. No matter how they swatted and howled, the insects would not be deterred. Tormented, the boys fell to the ground and curled up to protect themselves. After a time, Kaná ti felt they had been punished enough. He drove the the plague of painful pests away and sent the boys home to their mother. He then picked up his bow and crept into the forest. Now, for the very first time, he had to hunt for meat for his family to eat.

Chastened, the boys made their way home. When they reached their cabin, they were exhausted. Famished, they asked their mother to make them a meal. With sadness, she shook her head and told them there was no meat. But she asked them to sit and rest while she went to the storehouse to fetch some corn. Set atop high poles, the corncrib was made of small logs to protect the grain from animals but sparsely chinked with clay so air could dry the corn

The first Cherokee wife Selu, the Corn Mother, and her husband Kaná ti, the Lucky Hunter, were given their home by their Creator beneath Shining Rock above the headwaters of the Pigeon River. ("Kaná ti and Selu," a painting by Cherokee artist Lynn Lossiah, from *Seven Cherokee Myths: Creation, Fire, the Primordial Parents, the Nature of Evil, the Family, Universal Suffering, and Communal Obligation*, G. Keith Parker, McFarland.)

and preserve it. Every day Selu went to the storehouse and returned with her basket full of corn and beans for supper.

Their curiosity undeterred by Kaná ti's punishment, the boys waited until Selu had rounded a bend in the path to the storehouse. Once she was out of sight, they followed her. Hiding in the brush, they saw her climb the ladder to the corncrib's door, open it, and vanish inside. Like squirrels, they shinnied up the poles, perched on the bottom log, removed a piece of chinking, and looked in. They saw their mother place her basket on the storehouse floor, uncover it, straighten up, rub her belly, and lo, the basket filled half-way up with corn. Standing taller, she rubbed her armpits and miraculously beans filled the basket to its top.

The boys were frightened. They had learned that their mother was a witch. Knowing nothing of the difference between good and bad witches, silently they vowed to kill her. But Selu, ever attuned to the spirits, knew immediately of their plans. She confronted them and told them that after they had killed her, they must clear a large round field in front of their house, drag her body seven times over the ground, sit and watch the field all night long, and by morning fresh corn would be grown and they would always have plenty to eat. Seven is a magic number in Cherokee lore.

With clubs, they beat their mother to death. Then they cut off her head and placed it on a spike on top of their house facing west to watch for Kaná ti. The boys were lazy. Rather than preparing the field as Selu instructed them, they cleared only seven small plots. Instead of dragging her body seven times over the ground, they did so only twice. Where her blood fell, corn sprouted. The boys watched it overnight and by morning it was ripe, but it grew only in the little plots the boys had prepared.

By and by, strangers from other villages learned of the boys' good fortune. They came to the house where the boys lived and asked for grains of corn they could plant themselves. The boys were kind and gave them seven kernels, told them how to plant and watch them through the night, and said that in the morning, they would have plenty of corn for their people. The strangers lived seven days' travel from the boys. On the first night of their journey home, they did as they had been told, and by morning fresh corn was ready to pick. Each cut a stalk and continued their way home. When night came again, they planted kernels from their new ears, watched over it all night, and with dawn they harvested more corn. Growing weary on the long hot journey, on the next night they sowed their seeds and lay down. Instead of remaining watchful, they slept. In the morning they found that the corn had not grown at all.

Still they believed in the power of the magic grains the boys had given them. On a floodplain, they cleared away brush and with sharp hoes of split wood loosened the dirt. With sticks, they poked holes in the soft earth, pushed in seeds as they had been shown, and tamped the soil lightly around them. They retired to their houses to sleep and every morning they returned to the fields to see if the corn was fully grown. Nothing had come up. Weeks passed before the seeds had even sprouted, and when they did, weeds threatened to choke the stalks to death. With their hoes, day in and day out, they chopped at the weeds. The work was hard and wearisome. When the sun was highest in its trail across the sky and the days were as long as they would get, green ears were finally just ripe enough to eat. Instead of overnight, due to the strangers' laziness, corn now demanded months of cultivation before it was ready for harvest.

By then, summer's zenith was washing across the land. With their white tails flying, spotted fawns frolicked in freshly verdant woods. Black bear cubs peeked at their new world from crotches in trees they had just learned to climb. Freshly fledged, chubby turkey poults had fluttered up to the lowest branches of trees and teetered awkwardly where they would roost come winter. Fat suckers had begun to swim up the rivers to spawn. From isolated farms and family hamlets, Cherokee trekked to towns where council houses sat atop mounds for the Green Corn Ceremony, a joyous celebration of universal renewal. Shamans prayed for a bounteous fall. After feasting and dancing, Indians gathered glowing embers from the perpetual fire burning in the council house and carried them home to rekindle their own fires, which would sustain them for the year to come.

PEOPLE OF ONE FIRE

The world was cold so the Thunderers, Ani'-Hyûñ'tĭkwălâ'skĭ, loosed a bolt
of lightning from their home in the sky into the base of a hollow sycamore tree
rooted on an island far from shore. Seeing smoke from the smoldering trunk,
the Animals were eager to get coals to warm themselves and for cooking.
At first the raven was sent because he was big and strong. He landed on a limb.
But as he pondered what to do, heat scorched his feathers. Badly scared, he
returned. That is why all ravens are black. Owls volunteered next but fire burned
their eyes. Bright light bothers them to this day which is why they fly only at
night. After all the other animals tried and failed, the little water spider stepped
up. She was so light that she ran across the water, spun a bowl with her web,
and in it placed a glowing coal from which the first Cherokee fire, and all
others thereafter, was kindled.

MOONEY | *Cherokee History, Myths and Sacred Formulas*

Though each Cherokee town was independent and a central government did not exist, the Cherokee were united by shared tradition and belief. At the core is the hallowed fire. According to legend, the fire brought by the water spider kindled the blaze that burned in the hearth of the council house at Kituhwa, the historic mother town of all Cherokee. Surrounded by hundreds of acres of rich farmland on the floodplain of the Tuckasegee River nine miles southwest of Cherokee, Kituhwa is identified by a low mound in a field identified by a historical marker by highway US 19. In the council houses of every Cherokee town flickers a sacred fire, allegedly the progeny of the original blaze. Today, when one Cherokee asks another where they are from, they ask "What is your fire?"

Atop the mound at Kituhwa stood a council house. Council houses were large, 40 to 50 feet in diameter sheathed with wattle or rivercane, and weatherproofed with daubs of clay. Four posts supported a peaked roof of bark and, perhaps, turf. Benches may have been arranged around the walls where both men and women sat. Here, decisions for the town and surrounding villages were made. Women and men had equal voice, for Cherokee culture was matrilineal. Women were the heads of households. Kinship passed from mother to her children. When a man married, he left his own clan and became a member of his wife's clan. Their children were members of her clan, not his.

Most often Cherokee towns were assumed by Europeans to have chiefs, white and red. The white chief was beloved male elder or, occasionally, a woman and responsible for domestic affairs—raising children, planting and harvesting vegetables, preparing food, making pots and baskets for cooking and storage, and harmonious relations with neighboring villages—all essential for the survival of the town. The red chief was traditionally a man. Selected for his prowess as a hunter, he led robust young men in gathering meat, in warfare against peoples encroaching on the town's territory or in conquest of neighboring land, and in making sure that the central fire never went out. The Cherokee never identified their leaders as "chiefs"—that title was bestowed on them by Europeans who believed that every community must have a single leader who was elected or gained power through wealth, inheritance, political savvy, and physical strength and cunning.

About the time of the Green Corn Ceremony in high summer, fires in all villages and homes around council houses were extinguished. A runner from Kituhwa would bring embers to satellite mother towns from which they would be distributed to council houses such as the one on the mounds at Biltmore and the one at the junction of Garden Creek and the Pigeon River upstream from Canton. From there, a shaman would distribute hot coals to leaders of surrounding villages, and from there they would be carried to farmsteads in isolated coves. Thus was life rekindled.

PREHISTORIC CHEROKEE OF THE WATERSHED

Though Cherokee territory covered thousands of square miles west of the Blue Ridge, it was concentrated in the southern Appalachians. While they dominated a large swath of the east central United States, their population was quite small by today's standards, only about 60,000. Ethnologists in the early

1800s divided the Cherokee into five clusters. Most heavily populated were the *Middle Towns* from the headwaters of the Little Tennessee above Rabun Gap, Ga. to its confluence with the Nantahala River. Today's Cherokee Reservation, properly known as *Qualla Boundary*, is located in the midst of the *Out Towns* along the Tuckasegee and Oconaluftee. Along the Valley and Hiwassee Rivers near Murphy, N.C., villages were members of *Valley Towns*. Stretching down into South Carolina with a few in northeast Georgia were the *Lower Towns* centered on former British Fort Prince George. Across the Blue Ridge along the Little Tennessee lay the *Overhill Towns*, now flooded by Tellico Lake.

Absent from this assemblage of Cherokee communities are any prominent clusters of towns in the French Broad watershed. Drive from Asheville to Rosman. Along the route, the French Broad twists and turns through miles and miles of rich river bottomland, roughened here and there by veins of intervening hills. The same can be said for the Pigeon downstream from Lake Logan to the huge paper mill at Canton and to lesser degree for Jonathan Creek, which rises beneath Soco Gap and drains Maggie Valley. Ditto for the valleys of the Nolichucky and Little Pigeon. Walking over ploughed floodplain fields after a rain nearly always turns up shards of Indian pottery and arrowheads, broken or sometimes whole. Occasionally, one comes across cracked fire-blackened rock, sign of a prehistoric camp fire.

Aside from council houses on mounds at Biltmore and Garden Creek, tangible evidence of Cherokee presence in the watershed is limited. Yet obviously they farmed these floodplains. Why then are traces of their habitation so scant? There may be two major reasons. The upper French Broad watershed is relatively far removed from the core of Cherokee population along the border between North Carolina and Georgia. As well, the onset of the Little Ice Age, beginning about 1350, coincides with the decline of the final era of prehistoric Indian occupation in the upper watershed known to archaeologists as the Appalachian Summit region.[5]

From about 900 to 1300, the Southeast experienced a general increase in temperature that corresponds to the Medieval Warm Period. During that time, Viking settlements were established in Greenland and northern Labrador. Southern Appalachians became immensely favorable to the expansion of agriculture and the paralleling spread of the Mississippian culture, known regionally as the Pisgah phase, throughout the French Broad watershed. Crops and wild game thrived. Villages grew and strong chiefdoms were established. Warfare among residents of neighboring regions seems to have been relatively minimal. Small Pisgah communities of usually fewer than a dozen houses prospered on floodplains.[6]

Excavations of the Pisgah village on the Swannanoa's floodplain at Warren Wilson College suggest that Indians lived in small more or less rectangular houses about 20 feet square walled with wattle and daub. In the center was a hearth of fire-hardened clay. Stout posts supported roofs shaped like pyramids, probably thatched or covered with bark and having a hole at the peak for smoke to escape. Other postholes indicate that walls may have divided a few interiors, and at about half them an arch of bent over saplings may have created a tunnel-like entrance. Food was probably stored outside in cribs, such as the one where the curious boys had found Selu. At the cores of the villages may have risen low mounds such as those at Garden Creek and Biltmore. Family farmsteads spread outward from the center of the communities, and small, satellite hunting camps may have been established at the heads of coves or near outcrops of rock used to fashion arrowheads and spear points high in the mountains. This was a time of relative plenty and peace and may represent the zenith of prehistoric Indian culture in the watershed.[7]

The Three Sisters—corn, beans, and squash—had been domesticated and were farmed together on broad river bottoms and on narrow floodplains in high mountain coves. First earth was mounded into a flat-topped hill about 12 inches tall and several kernels of corn were punched in. When the corn had sprouted and stalks reached six inches or so, beans were planted alongside; the growing corn stalk would provide a pole for them to climb. Squash was planted too. As it spread across the ground, its broad leaves would help to crowd out weeds. Eaten together, the three provided the essentials of a good diet: carbohydrates, proteins, fats, and amino acids. As nutrition improved, life-span lengthened and populations increased.

Though corn had been introduced from Mexico into southern Appalachian Indian diets about AD 400, ears and kernels were tiny compared to today's hybrid versions. Cobs were less than half an inch in diameter and not much longer than an inch or two. Being good farmers, Indians saved larger seeds and planted them and new stalks produced larger ears.[8] But the importance of corn to their nutrition was not nearly as significant as bushels of chestnuts, hickory nuts, and acorns that fell in the forest every fall and could be gathered by anyone with a basket. Nuts, not corn, was the staple of Indian diets in the French Broad watershed.

The earth wobbles very slowly on its axis, tilting its northern and southern hemispheres closer toward or farther away from the sun ushering in eras of relative warmth or coolness. About AD 1350, annual temperatures across North America began to fall but only by a few hundredths of a degree Celsius per year, ushering in the beginning of the Little Ice Age. In the Arctic, Viking outposts on Greenland and Newfoundland failed while famine, food riots, and the dreaded Black Death mushroomed across Europe. Summers were plagued by extreme crop-withering drought, but winters and springs saw increased rainfall. Growing seasons throughout mid-America were disrupted and shortened. As harvests of corn, beans, and squash declined, grain stored in cribs and clay-lined pits molded and rotted. Destroyed as well were seeds essential for successive plantings and supplies of stored nut meats. Malnutrition and disease spread throughout America. The Little Ice Age profoundly affected prehistoric Indian culture as it would, in its waning years, European settlement along North America's east coast.[9]

The average lifespan of prehistoric Indians had been increasing as ways of hunting and gathering, cooking, and preserving food had been improving. In the Tennessee Valley just west of the Blue Ridge, those of the Archaic era lived to be between 25 and 30 years old and were about five feet tall. By early Woodland times about 1000 BC, with the advent of agriculture, the bow and arrow, and pottery, a typical Indian was six-inches taller and lived five years or so longer. However according to analysis of more than 500 skeletons dating from around AD 1400 from Toqua, a Mississippian age town on the Little Tennessee west of the Blue Ridge, lifespan had shortened considerably. Though men still averaged 5' 6" tall, most lived not longer than 17 years. Women were typically 5'1" tall, and many succumbed at about age 15 years. Jefferson Chapman, who directed extensive documentation of prehistoric sites along the Little Tennessee before it was inundated by Tellico Lake, writes that the people of Toqua were nutritionally stressed and probably suffered from anemia and related diseases that result from diets too dependent on corn and too weak in iron, other mineral-rich foods, and protein from the meat of wild game.[10]

Perhaps the most severely impacted Indians of the Little Ice Age were those living in the lower Ohio Valley, Kentucky, and central Tennessee, the north-western fringes of vast hunting lands claimed by the Cherokee. During the

Medieval Warm Period, accumulation of surplus crops allowed chiefs to gain power over their people who were less successful farmers. The onset of periods of intense drought spanning four to fourteen years from AD 1385 through AD 1413 placed Indian communities under extreme stress.

Intense drought, deluge, and cold resulted in declining agriculture and in reduced abundance of wild plants, nuts, and game. Shortages of food eroded the power of chiefdoms to control the people they led. Construction of ceremonial and even burial mounds as well as long distance trade abated. Periods of warfare became more frequent as opposing groups fought for increasingly scarce food supplies including farm land, herds of deer, and flocks of turkeys. Residents of villages sought new lands and began to move south seeking acreage with longer growing seasons. Soon the few became a mass migration. Before long the area from the confluence of the Mississippi and Ohio Rivers and extending up the latter's valley nearly to Cincinnati began to empty out of people. By the beginning of the fifteenth century it was largely depopulated. It is known today by archaeologists as the Vacant Quarter.[11]

Indians living in the French Broad watershed were not immune from these decades of extended drought, downpours, and cooling temperatures. Many migrated down from highland villages on the floodplains along the upper reaches of the river and its tributaries to the Tennessee Valley and Piedmont. There temperatures were a little warmer, growing seasons were longer, the soil richer, and there was more land to farm. Villages surrounded themselves with palisades for protection from invading tribes. Among them were the Shawnees, the prominent tribe of the Ohio Valley in the thirteenth and fourteenth centuries. At Soco Gap, on the Blue Ridge Parkway between Maggie Valley and the Cherokee Reservation, the Cherokee always kept watch for invading enemies coming up Jonathan Creek, a tributary of the Pigeon. According to Cherokee lore, a large party of Shawnee approached, were ambushed and all but one were killed. After his ears were cut off, he was allowed to return to his people carrying word of their defeat.[12]

In the century before Hernando de Soto entered the Blue Ridge, the Indian population in the French Broad watershed was about 20,000, much diminished from the heyday of Pisgah culture in the 1200s. But without a doubt the first Americans were very much present. They lived in small villages, clusters of a few houses near their farms on river floodplains and in coves in the mountains. Their lives must have been hard, a hand-to-mouth existence, as they scratched whatever sustenance they could raise or gather. They must have kept one eye

Cherokee were farmers and hunters, living in small villages before European explorers arrived. ("Kanasta or Connestee," a painting by Cherokee artist Lynn Lossiah, from *Seven Cherokee Myths: Creation, Fire, the Primordial Parents, the Nature of Evil, the Family, Universal Suffering, and Communal Obligation,* G. Keith Parker, McFarland, p. 143.)

cocked toward gaps in the ridgeline, ever wondering whether dawn or dusk would bring a raid by others intent on securing for themselves what little their victims had amassed.

Unlike the thorough documentation by Chapman and others of the network of large towns in the drainage of the Little Tennessee, tangible evidence of prehistoric Cherokee in the upper French Broad watershed is limited. Yet fresh archaeological research is uncovering more prehistoric Indian communities in the watershed. And stories passed down from one generation to the next confirm their presence as do journals kept by conquistadores who accompanied de Soto on his expedition through the mountains in 1540. Resilient and adaptable to natural and cultural forces that engulf them, the Cherokee and their ancestors are, indeed, the first settlers of the region.

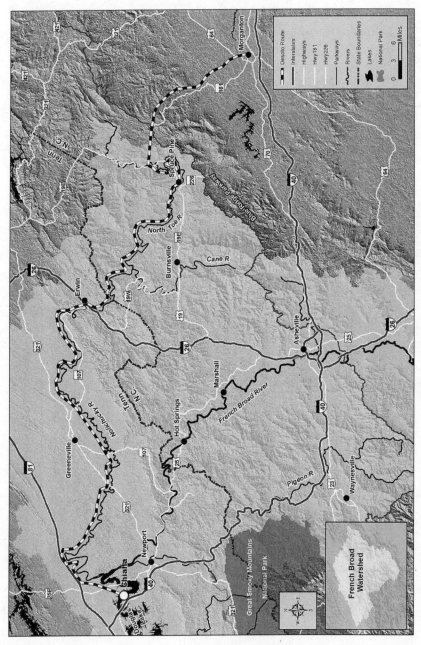

In May 1540 Hernando de Soto and his 600 conquistadors became the first Europeans to explore the Blue Ridge and the French Broad watershed. Their route can be followed today by car. (Cartographer: Greg Dobson.)

THREE

Conquistadors

Hernan de Soto led the first Europeans known to have traversed the Blue
Ridge. During the afternoon of May 21, 1540, he and his conquistadores arrived at Joara, a major Indian town located on a broad floodplain surrounded
by low foothills at the base of the Blue Ridge about a dozen miles northwest
of Morganton, N.C., and just a little southwest of the hamlet named Worry.
He was a man of his time: aggressive, arrogant, vain, and violent. Along with
Francisco Pizarro, Hernan Cortes, Ponce de Leon, and other Spaniards, he had
plundered the Incan empire, slaughtering and pillaging southward from the
Spanish foothold in Nicaragua into the mountains of Peru. Though he amassed
tons of gold and silver, wealth did not satisfy him. He longed to be a *marqués*,
the royal rank below that of a duke, with his own territory in the New World.
Returning to Spain in 1536 with riches held in partnership with de Leon but
which he refused to share, de Soto was appointed by King Charles V to be
governor of Cuba and given the right to claim for Spain all of *La Florida*, as
the North American continent in its entirety was then known.[1]

In late May 1539, de Soto had arrived off Long Boat Key below the mouth
of Tampa Bay. On a short stretch of open beach among impenetrable groves
of red mangrove, he landed 620 conquistadors, horses, pigs, and provisions.
After spending the fall forging north, fighting Indians, and capturing slaves
to serve as porters, he halted for the winter near Tallahassee amidst the
Apalachee, the Indian tribe from whom the name of the Appalachian Mountains is derived. While in camp, one of his officers told him that a young
Indian—Perico—came from a place far to the northeast "on another ocean."

Perico allegedly made his living by trading, was facile with languages, and spoke knowingly of how gold was mined and smelted. He reported that a woman chief of Cofitachequi, a province near his own, collected taxes from her subjects that were paid in gold and silver. Thus was cast the die that would bring de Soto into the Blue Ridge.

They would reach Joara at the foot of the mountains in the spring of 1540. The village lies at the confluence of Irish and Upper Creeks at the crossroads of two major Indian trails and is known today as Ft. San Juan or the Berry archaeological site. The route of one of the trails,, running nearly east-west, is shadowed more or less by Interstate 40 as it climbs toward Swannanoa Gap bound for Asheville. The other, a principal trade route between South Carolina and East Tennessee, follows Upper Creek as it stairsteps up from one bucolic vale to the next before reaching the swampy break among the peaks near Jonas Ridge not far from an exit off the Blue Ridge Parkway for Linville Falls. Deeply weary from wearing their iron armor and toting arquebuses, those heavy and clumsy matchlock hand canons, and plagued by hunger and sickness, the Spaniards rested in Joara. On the day before they reached the town, one of their horses, so crucial for the success of their journey, had died most likely from lack of feed.

LA SENORA DE COFITACHEQUI

Accompanying de Soto was the chief of Cofitachequi, a woman, whom he held hostage. Weeks earlier upon entering her village, thought to be just south of Camden, S.C., de Soto's men found tools flecked with soft yellow metal they assumed to be gold just as Perico had promised. Arriving in a sedan chair born by her warriors, she was identified by de Soto's scribes as "La Senora de Cofitachequi." In a manner of friendly hospitality, she ordered the conquistadors provisioned with grain and meat. Yet after the Spaniards looted stored provisions and pillaged bodies in the mortuary temple of their strands of freshwater pearls, she turned frigid and refused to be of further assistance. De Soto then took her hostage and forced her to guide his expedition to the alleged gold mines. Portuguese chroniclers describe the mountainous country into which she led the conquistadors as the land of the Chalaque, among the earliest phonetic references to the people we know as the Cherokee. The "Lady of Cofitachequi" was revered by people of the region. As de Soto's expedition progressed northwestward toward the Blue Ridge, at her command Indians

Upon reaching the village of Cofitachequi, thought to be near Camden, S.C., de Soto was hospitably welcomed by its chief, a woman, whom he later took hostage forcing her to lead him into the Blue Ridge on a fruitless search for gold. (Orr, John William, Engraver. *Indian Princess Presenting a Necklace of Pearls to de Soto / J. W. Orr, N.Y.* South Carolina, 1858. Library of Congress.)

along the way provided conquistadors with porters and provisions including little dogs to eat. Learning of the chief's plan to escape as soon as she saw the opportunity, de Soto had her guarded every movement.

Refreshed by the delivery of corn by Baltasar de Gallegos, whom he had sent to gather grain, de Soto left Joara on May 25 and began his journey over the backbone of the Blue Ridge. They ascended Upper Creek and paused for the night just east of the gap in the mountains. During the next day, the "Lady of Cofitachequi" pleaded to be excused to relieve herself. She took with her one of her slaves and, when out of sight, fled down the mountain with a small container of valuable pearls, which de Soto had allowed her to keep hoping to ensure her obedience. She returned to her people at Joara, where she met up with Spanish-speaking slaves who had deserted de Soto's expedition.[2]

On the morning of her escape, the conquistadors suffered from "great cold," according to Rodrigo Rangel, one of de Soto's chroniclers.[3] Bitter cold was not uncommon at that time of year, least of all in the mountains, especially in the mid-1500s as the Little Ice Age was settling in. After crossing the Eastern Continental Divide, which separates waters flowing eastward toward the Atlantic from those headed west and eventually into the Gulf of Mexico, de Soto's party entered the headwaters of the Nolichucky River, the largest tributary of the French Broad. There they picked up streams feeding the North Toe River. Unlike Upper Creek's valley, that of the North Toe is narrow and hemmed in by steep rocky slopes. Icy water often covered the trail, and the conquistadors were forced to wade, soles of their leather boots soaked and sliding with every step on slippery rocks.

Near Huntdale, N.C., Cane River joins the North Toe to form the Nolichucky. De Soto's party was certain they had come upon the river *Spiritu Sancto*, the Mississippi. They had, indeed, reached one of its innumerous mountain headwaters, but it would take them almost a year before they stood on its banks south of Memphis, Tenn.

Four days after leaving Joara, they camped close by Erwin, Tenn., and then pushed down through the river's last gorge before breaking free of the mountains at Embreeville. How relieved they must have been to march again on a nearly level land between easy hills along the now-gentle Nolichucky. They moved from Indian village to village, past the birthplace of Davy Crockett on Big Limestone Creek near Greeneville, and on June 5, entered Chiaha, a large Indian settlement on Zimmerman's Island in the midst of the French Broad. There they rested for three weeks, exhausted from having traversed the Blue Ridge.

De Soto and his conquistadores would continue on down the French Broad, passing its junction with the Holston at what would become Knoxville and following the Tennessee on south. Two years later, he would die from fever on the banks of the Mississippi. Until his final days, he no doubt believed he had claimed a vast empire for Spain, an empire of untold riches, an empire that he would never rule. A generation later, in 1566, a second Spanish explorer, Juan Pardo, would arrive in Chiaha, having crossed the mountains from Joara following the Watauga River. By then the Indians of the French Broad had begun a robust trade with Spaniards living at St. Elena, known well by US Marines as Parris Island, S.C.[4]

When de Soto arrived at Cofitachequi, he found beads of green glass, which he first thought were emeralds, and iron axes made in Castile. He noted that Indians living there seemed more civilized and that their footwear resembled the conquistadors' own. The hatchets and beads, most likely, had been traded to the Indians by members of the colony at San Miguel de Gualdape, established by Lucas Vázquez de Ayllón in 1526 on Sapelo Island, south of modern Savannah. Harsh winter wiped out Ayllón's town after a few months, but not before houses and a church had been built. Even so, he gained a toehold in coastal Georgia and the Carolinas, one that would grow, attract the English who settled at Jamestown in 1607, and initiate British conquest of the French Broad watershed.

Ayllón's immigrants brought more than trade goods to Indians of the coastal plains. They delivered disease, particularly smallpox and influenza. Many scholars suggest that resulting pandemic reduced Indian populations by 90 percent.[5] Though many villages maintained large stocks of corn, some had virtually none. Within a few leagues of Cofitachequi, scribes accompanying the conquistadors report "great townes depopulated, and overgrown with grasse, which shewed that they had been long without inhabitants. The Indians said that, two years before there was a plague in that countrie, and that they had moved to other townes."[6]

According to Grascilaso de la Vega, a sixteenth century Spanish historian who interviewed many men who had accompanied de Soto, "The Castilians found no people in Talmeco because the previous pestilence had been more rigorous in this town than in any other of the whole province, and the few Indians who had escaped had not yet reclaimed their homes; hence our men paused but a short time in these houses before proceeding to the temple." He writes of "four large houses . . . filled with the bodies of the people who had died of the pestilence."[7]

Diseases struck quickly and broadly. Those infected died in a matter of days or weeks. Traditional Indian cures such as immersion in cold water thought to be purifying or sweating to drive out evil spirits were counter-productive. So virulent were these illnesses that there were not enough healthy inhabitants to bury the dead. Their bodies were left to rot where they lay or to be preyed upon by scavenging dogs, foxes, wolves, and birds.

Definitive evidence of the scale of devastation caused by the introduction by Europeans of diseases against which Indians had no defense has yet to be presented. Yet few doubt that smallpox, measles, typhus, and other maladies were major factors in the destruction of Indian cultures in the Southeast. The relative peace and prosperity of the Medieval Warm Period was fading rapidly. Vanishing was the era that Indians had celebrated with the construction of great temple mounds such as those at Etowah near Cartersville, Ga., and Nikwasi in Franklin, N.C.

The southeast was entering the throes of the Little Ice Age. So dependent were prehistoric cultures on foods hunted, gathered, and grown on plots around their villages; on weapons no more formidable than arrows, lances, and war clubs; and on transportation no stronger than their own legs that little beyond their intimate knowledge of the terrain and its waters could defend their ways of life in the face of European invasion.

INVASION FROM THE EAST

The Spanish had come first to North America in the 1500s, establishing their colonies in South Carolina, Florida, Juan Pardo's fort at de Soto's old camp at the eastern base of the Blue Ridge, and a mission near the mouth of Chesapeake Bay. For France, Jacques Cartier was charting the Gulf of St. Lawrence. In 1534, he explored upstream to the bluffs on which Quebec City would be established in 1608, a year after the English settled in Jamestown. Though the French founded a haven for Huguenots, Fort Caroline, on Florida's St. John's River, it lasted but one year until destroyed by Spaniards in 1565. About 20 years later, la Salle reached the mouth of the Mississippi. In following decades, France planted colonies at Biloxi, Mobile, and New Orleans, effectively controlling the northern coast of the Gulf of Mexico and the full course of the Mississippi River.

Relatively speaking, the English were newcomers. Their short-lived colony on Roanoke Island just inside North Carolina's Outer Banks was found abandoned in 1590. More successful were settlements at Jamestown, Va., in 1607, in Bermuda in 1609, at Plymouth, Mass., in 1620, and on Newfoundland that same year. During the same decade, the British established themselves on Caribbean islands of St. Kitts and Barbados, holding the sea gates to the Gulf of Mexico. They established Charleston, S.C., at the mouth of the Congaree River in 1670. At present day Columbia, S.C., enters a wide and shallow tributary thus earning its name "Broad River." To the equally shallow and wide river flowing northwest toward territory claimed by Louis XIV, the English gave the name "French" Broad.

Following de Soto's path twenty-seven years later, conquistador Juan Pardo built Ft. San Juan at the Catawba tribe's village of Joara now known as the Berry Site. Tiring of Spanish occupation, twenty years later Catawbans laid siege to the fort and killed its occupants save one who escaped to tell the tale. (Warren Wilson College, Department of Archaeology. Art credit: John Klausmeyer.)

After disease, bitter climate, and war with England withered the first Spanish settlements along the middle Atlantic coast, the English dominated trade in the Carolinas. Establishment of Jamestown opened colonial Virginia's vast interior, which stretched all the way to the confluence of the Ohio and Mississippi rivers. As well, the British planned to acquire everything west of Pennsylvania and south of the Great Lakes. For them, the shortest route from Jamestown into the interior led up the tidal Appomattox River, past the little falls at present-day Petersburg, over a low height of land west of Farmville, and into valley of the Upper James. The rapids were as far upstream as ships could sail, and on a bluff above them in 1646 the British built Fort Henry. The fort was the Crown's principal post for trading with Indians of Virginia's frontier. The treaty ending the Third Anglo-Powhatan War mandated that all Indians living west of the rapids must pass through the fort to trade.[8] The same stricture applied to all merchants heading into the interior barter with them.

The fort's commander would be in a lucrative position, indeed. Securing the appointment was 26-year-old Abraham Wood, already a wealthy landowner and member of Virginia's House of Burgess. Soon after his posting, he and a few friends began to probe toward the valleys beyond Blue Ridge. In 1650, he crossed the top of the Roanoke River drainage into rivers flowing westward, among them surely the New and perhaps the headwaters of the Holston not much further south. On May, 17, 1673, Wood sent James Needham with his servant Gabriel Arthur, eight Indians, and four horses on an expedition to establish trade with the Tomahitans, considered by some to be the Cherokee. Their route is thought to have taken them into the lands of the Occaneechi living in the Piedmont, thence west over the Blue Ridge into the rich limestone valley beyond the Nolichucky's gorge through the mountains.

Along the way, Needham was killed in an argument with Indian John, one of their guides. Saved from being burned at the stake by a benevolent chief, Arthur was befriended by the Cherokee and accompanied them on travels into Spanish settlements on coastal plains and north into the Ohio valley. There, he was captured by other Indians, taken for a Cherokee, found to be English after washing away months of grime, and returned to Wood's post at Fort Henry on July 20, 1674. Needham and Arthur are likely to have been the first English traders to enter the French Broad watershed.[9]

SLAVES AND SKINS

Before the arrival of Europeans, Cherokees were not a united people. Rather, they were members of towns and surrounding villages. Their lives revolved around seasons for planting and hunting, around ritual celebrations, and, due to climatic stress, around increasing tension and warfare with neighboring and invading bands. Iron axes introduced by Ayllón in the early 1500s whetted Indian lust for European goods which never dulled.

Imagine how easy it was to fell a tree with an axe of iron compared to one of stone or to shoot a deer (or an enemy) with a gun instead of a bow and arrow. What a delight it must have been to fashion clothes with scissors, needles, and thread from bolts of cotton and woolen cloth instead of with bone awls, sinew or twine and animal skins. Add the pleasure of cooking in metal kettles, smoking tobacco in clay pipes, and wearing jewelry of brightly colored glass beads. Of utmost significance were horses, introduced by Spaniards, and rum with its debilitating effect. In less than 100 years, the Cherokee had been incorporated into the world-wide economy of the sixteenth and seventeenth centuries which transformed their culture far more profoundly than deteriorating climate and devastating disease combined.

At first, Indian slaves were as important a commodity to the British as deer-skins. English colonies in the West Indies were woefully short of laborers. To obtain slaves, the Crown fomented strife between the Cherokee and the Creeks and others whose lands abutted theirs. Cherokees swapped prisoners captured in raids against their neighbors for trade goods, a practice that only abated as the availability of enslaved laborers from Africa expanded in the seventeenth century.

For Cherokee, deerskins became their most valuable export. Plagued by the Little Ice Age, in densely populated Europe food and farm products including leather were in short supply. It was indispensable for manufacturing shoes, gloves, and coats; essential military equipment including uniforms, boots, belts, saddles, and harnesses; and industrial belting to turn machinery in mills and factories. Hides from whitetails (*Odocoileus virginianus*), native to the Southern Appalachians, could be obtained far more cheaply than from cattle raised in Europe. Ginseng, that indigenous mountain herb so valued today, was in high demand by Asians and Europeans, who sought it as an aphrodisiac and cure for venereal disease. Tons of clay were transported to Charleston and shipped to England to be used in the making of Wedgewood and similar china.[10]

To understand trade from an English perspective, listen to the report of John Lederer who made three forays from Virginia into western Carolina in 1669 and 1670:

IF you barely designe a Home-trade with neighbour-Indians, for skins of Deer, Beaver, Otter, Wild-Cat, Fox, Racoon, &c. your best Truck is a sort of course Trading Cloth, of which a yard and a half makes a Matchcoat or Mantle fit for their wear; as also Axes, Hoes, Knives, Sizars, and all sorts of edg'd tools. Guns, Powder and Shot, &c. are Commodities they will greedily barter for: but to supply the Indians with Arms and Ammunition, is prohibited in all English Governments.

In dealing with the Indians, you must be positive and at a word: for if they perswade you to fall any thing in your price, they will spend time in higgling for further abatements, and seldom conclude any Bargain. Sometimes you may with Brandy or Strong liquor dispose them to an humour of giving you ten times the value of your commodity; and at other times they are so hide-bound, that they will not offer half the Market-price, especially if they be aware that you have a designe to circumvent them with drink, or that they think you have a desire to their goods, which you must seem to slight and disparage.

To the remoter Indians you must carry other kinds of Truck, as small

To maximize their profits, British traders waylaid Cherokee
hunters and got them so drunk they were easily cheated, forcing
the once proud and self-sustaining people into virtual economic
servitude. (Cartouche from William Faden, "A map of the
Inhabited Part of Canada from the French Surveys; with
the Frontiers of New York and New England," 1777.)

Looking-glasses, Pictures, Beads and Bracelets of glass, Knives, Sizars, and all
manner of gaudy toys and knacks for children, which are light and portable. For
they are apt to admire such trinkets, and will purchase them at any rate, either with
their currant Coyn. . . .

   Could I have foreseen when I set out, the advantages to be made by a Trade with
those remote Indians, I had gone better provided; though perhaps I might have run
a great hazard of my life, had I purchased considerably amongst them, by carrying
wealth unguarded through so many different Nations of barbarous people: therefore
it is vain for any man to propose to himself, or undertake a Trade at that distance,
unless he goes with strength to defend, as well as an Adventure to purchase such
Commodities: for in such a designe many ought to joyn and go in company.[11]

To increase demand for European goods, traders relied on rum. They waited
on trails used by hunters bound for home loaded with bales of skins gathered
over several months. They plied them with drink and cheated them of their
hides, paying only a few baubles. When the defrauded hunters arrived in the
villages, they had no means to purchase cloth their families needed for clothing
except by pledging to pay in hides harvested on their next hunt. In addition,

traders deceived Indians by using shortened yardsticks to measure fabric and rigged scales to give light weight to hides. The Cherokee had no way of knowing they were being duped by unscrupulous merchants.

Ability to purchase goods in exchange for promises of future hides led Indians deeply into debt. As a result, virtually all able-bodied males were forced to engage in hunting. And when they failed to collect enough skins, they entered pernicious and inescapable economic servitude to the English. Entire villages were affected. In prior generations, males had cleared and burned fields to fertilize and prepare them for planting. But with almost all males gone to hunt or wage war, growth of corn and other crops declined. To survive, communities were forced to purchase food from traders, further accelerating indebtedness to the English. So heavily dependent on manufactured goods they became that skills of fashioning tools from stone and making pots from clay, finely honed over centuries, began to be forgotten. No longer did Indians live in sustainable harmony with their surroundings.

By the early 1700s, the governor of South Carolina and his agents had insisted that they deal with single chiefs of the Cherokee's major towns in the same manner as English nobles negotiated with European heads of state. Sir Alexander Cuming, sent by King George II to strengthen alliance with the Cherokee against the French, proclaimed an Indian named Moytoy "Emperor." Hereafter, Indian "elites," hand-picked by the Crown, would govern all Cherokee. Bowing to royal pressure, they would cede to the English lands they had claimed for hundreds of years and order warfare against peoples west of the Blue Ridge allied with the French. Gone forever was consensual community governance except, perhaps, in small villages in the upper French Broad watershed, which were not included in what the English considered to constitute the Cherokee nation. [12] The relative isolation of Cherokee in the Asheville basin may well have preserved their independence and protected them against generations of military strife to come.

FOUR

A Land Unsettled

It was known as the Great Indian Warpath, that heavily worn thoroughfare down the Appalachian valley running 1,200 miles from Quebec south through New York, Pennsylvania, Virginia, and Tennessee into Alabama. Along its route, like limbs of a mighty tree, scores of side trails branched off into Ohio and Great Lakes country, into the tidewater regions of Delaware and Chesapeake bays, and into the French Broad watershed. In the main, these corridors followed river valleys. They crossed from one watershed to another over gentle gaps separating tiny headwater streams. For centuries, Indians trod these trails bent on barter or battle. The Iroquois and the Shawnee were bound southward while the Cherokee were pushing north.

To the west of the warpath lay the Cumberland Plateau and the endless prairies of Kentucky, rich with deer, elk, and bison. To their hides, the arrival of European traders added immeasurable value, wealth on the hoof that Indians could use to barter for guns, shot, and powder; iron axes, knives, hoes, kettles; and cloth and pretty glass beads. Along with their manufactured trade goods, horses, and diseases, Europeans brought with them their wars. Conflict had permeated northwestern Europe since the era of the Franks, Gauls, Saxons, and Rome's legions. Norman conquest of England in 1066 heralded a millennium of warfare that would eventually engulf North America. Tentacles of their conflicts reached deeply into French Broad country.

The Appalachian Mountains and the great valley beyond provided a de facto boundary between the French and the British. The character of their relationships with Indians could not have been more different. Francis Parkman is best known for his landmark book *The Oregon Trail: Sketches of Prairie and Rocky-Mountain Life*. Of equal note is his seven-volume *France and England in North America*, completed in 1892 and still valued by scholars. In volume II, *The Jesuits in North America*, he writes: "Spanish civilization crushed the Indian; English civilization scorned and neglected him; French civilization embraced and cherished him."[1]

British Lt. Henry Timberlake, who mapped the Overhill Cherokee's towns along the Little Tennessee in 1762, noted in his memoir that he found Indians much more disposed to the French, "who have the prudence, by familiar politeness (which costs but little, and often does a great deal) and conforming themselves to their ways and temper, to conciliate the inclinations of almost all the Indians they are acquainted with, while the pride of our officers often disgusts them . . . as it was trade alone that induced them to make peace with us and not any preference to the French whom they loved a great deal better."[2]

Pressing ever westward from their lodgments on coastal plains, each new generation of English colonists wrested from tribes fresh concessions of real estate, opening new lands to hunting and private ownership. Many of the treaties, though, required Indians to wear a special badge or coat when crossing into country claimed by the British.[3] No one, neither Indian nor immigrant, could be certain whose land was whose. Rampant confusion over boundary lines provoked bitter conflict that prevailed through the execrable decades leading to the Trail of Tears. As the eighteenth century dawned, Indians from the Great Lakes to the Gulf of Mexico west of the Appalachians increasingly became pawns in the violent European struggle for domination of North America. Not even the Cherokee living in relative harmony with European immigrants among the ridges and isolated floodplains of the French Broad and its tributaries would be spared.

WARPATH TO WAGON ROAD

On their foray a century earlier, Needham and Arthur must have followed sections of the Great Indian Warpath and a number of its branches. The route became the primary conduit for the steady stream of Scots-Irish and German immigrants bound for western Virginia, East Tennessee, and Western North Carolina. They knew it as the Great Wagon Road. Stretching west from Philadelphia, Pa., toward Harrisburg, it then angled southwestward through the

Down the Shenandoah Valley's Great Wagon Road the first European settlers came, German Protestants too poor to afford lush farmland west of Philadelphia. After the Revolutionary War, Scots-Irish filtered into the watershed bringing their music and spirits. (https://movingnorthcarolina.net/the-great-wagon-road/.)

future towns of Gettysburg, and into Winchester, Va., and on down the valley to Roanoke. There, the route bent almost due south, following the Roanoke River's cut through the Blue Ridge into lands explored a century earlier by the Spanish and the territory where Cherokee still struggled to satisfy the voracious appetite of English traders for deer skins.

Among the 250,000 immigrants from Europe, principally from the British Isles, landed at Philadelphia from 1700 to 1775 was Squire (his given name) Boone.[4] The story of his and his family's migration down the Great Wagon Road illustrates the journey undertaken by thousands who would settle in East Tennessee and Western North Carolina. Boone had emigrated from Devon, England, in 1713, married Sarah Morgan in 1720, and settled in a Quaker community near Exeter Township outside of Reading, Pa. Son Daniel, born in 1734, was the sixth of their 11 children. Bringing upon himself what members of his meeting house called "a Godly Sorrow," Squire Boone was expelled when Daniel was 13. By then, a cavalcade of Scots-Irish and Germans was passing through

Exeter along the Great Road bound for the fertile valleys of the Shenandoah, where good land could be had for far less than it cost in southeast Pennsylvania. Most bundled their goods on pack horses, but some packed their belongings in those four-wheeled, hooped-canvas covered, sway-bedded wagons that would take the name of their principal maker on Conestoga Creek.

In early May 1750, the Boones and members of their immediate and extended families loaded their possessions into three or four wagons. Given a dry road, they may have covered the 70 miles to Harrisburg on the Susquehanna in four days. A week later, in company of Germans, Swiss, and Irish travelers, they probably forded the Potomac at Williamsport, Maryland. After another week or so, they pitched camp at Linville, a little north of Harrisonburg, Va., where they would farm for a couple of years. On the family's trek south, young Daniel carried a long-barreled, flintlock rifle with a slender stock probably of maple with the sharply dropping cheek piece but likely lacking the engraved brass patch box and other inletted ornamentation so characteristic of famed Pennsylvania rifles. Reportedly, Boone's rifle was made by Henry Gillespie of Lancaster County. His descendant, Matthew Gillespie, located his gun smithy on Mills River in Henderson County, N.C., and his progeny would make guns well into the Civil War.[5]

The Boone family's journey into the frontier was not at all unusual. However, it fired Daniel's life-long lust to follow the next creek up and across the next gap into the next valley, where furs would be more plentiful and people far fewer. From the family's camp at Linville, he and his friend Henry Miller explored southward into the upper James River valley, which Wood, Needham, and Arthur had prowled 100 years earlier. Later, he and his father bore further south through the Roanoke water gap in the Blue Ridge and down into the forks of the Yadkin near Mocksville, N.C. There, in the fall of 1753, the elder Boone filed a warrant to purchase a fertile square mile—640 acres. The following year, the Boones built their first cabin on land that would grow into the family's estate.

Though the Boones were tillers of the land, Daniel "never took any delight in farming or stock raising." From his first "long hunt" from the camp in the Shenandoah Valley, he hankered for fall and winter, when he could escape the drudgery of chopping, plowing, and hoeing for adventure in the woods. As enjoyable as his trips might have been, they were also his primary source of cash. Single deer's skin came to be currency. A "buck" was the equal of a Spanish peso which the German's called a "thaler," easily corrupted later to "dollar." To augment his summertime income, young Boone became a waggoneer, carting loads of hides and farm produce to markets in Salisbury down the Yadkin.[6]

NO MAN'S LAND

For decades, the English and the Cherokee had been trading partners and thus, allies. On the other hand, the French, from their explorations of the St. Lawrence and the Mississippi, coveted interior North America and had established alliances with the Delaware and Shawnee. Separating the two perpetually warring kingdoms was the Great Valley and its eastern wall, the Appalachians. Caught in the middle were Europeans of various nationalities who, ever lusting for cheap land beyond the western horizon, poured down the Great Wagon road and drifted up each creek into lush valleys they thought were more or less free for the taking.

Less than a year after the Boones planted roots on the Forks of the Yadkin, English merchants trading as the Ohio Company received a grant from King George II of 500,000 acres along the upper Ohio claimed by Indians friendly to the French.[7] Seeking to oust the English, Louis XV sent his army to ignite the passions of the Iroquois and their allies, the Delaware and the Shawnee, sparking raids down the Great Warpath into English settlements in Virginia and North Carolina. They reached the Yadkin in the summer of 1753 before being repelled by local militia with the assistance of neighboring Catawba Indians. Several invaders were killed, and in their possession were crucifixes and other trade goods made by the French. Daniel Boone was then a private in the militia. He may or may not have taken part in the fighting. After the outbreak of the French and Indian War later that year, he signed on as a teamster with a force of North Carolinians recruited to support Gen. Edward Braddock's campaign against Fort Duquesne, where the Allegheny and the Monongahela Rivers meet to form the Ohio. Braddock was soundly defeated in 1755, and Boone returned home.

Picking up where he had left off, Boone resumed his long hunts. He frequented the headwaters of west-flowing rivers beyond the Blue Ridge. Local lore maintains that he camped where Needham and Arthur had on the Nolichucky before moving on to Boone's Creek, where he hid beneath a waterfall to escape hostile Indians. Near there on a beech tree, he allegedly inscribed, "D. Boon CillED A BAr on tree in the YEAR 1760." John Mack Faragher, considered to have written Boone's definitive biography, asserts that the carving is a forgery. Boone was quite literate for his time. His favorite book was *Gulliver's Travels*, which he often read by the light of his camp fires, and he was fastidious in always spelling his surname with its final "*e*."[8] Even so, this is the most famous of several Boone bear trees encountered in the lands he hunted. Felled by a storm about 1917, its wood was stored, dried, and in the 1960s made into gavels for local judges and other keepsakes that the local chapter of the Daughters of the American Revolution sold to raise money to memorialize his presence along the Nolichucky.[9]

The Treaty of Paris ending the French and Indian war was signed in 1763. It ceded to England all territory beyond the Appalachians to the Mississippi claimed by France. Shortly thereafter, the British issued a proclamation establishing the Indian Reserve. Within its bounds, European settlers were prohibited from purchasing land from the Cherokee and other tribes.[10] Having hunted with Boone in the valleys of the lower Nolichucky and Holston, in 1769, William Bean became the first settler in East Tennessee. He built a cabin near the falls where Boone allegedly hid from the Indians. Two years later and 16 miles south, Jacob Brown secured land on the Nolichucky. From South Carolina, he arrived with two pack horses laden with goods and set up a small trading post. In so doing, he became the first European to establish a permanent residence in the French Broad watershed.[11] He was an intimate of other European settlers who were collecting a day's travel north on the Watauga River at Sycamore Shoals. In 1772, they formed the Watauga Association, perhaps the first colonists to create a democratic independence from the Crown.[12]

A DARK AND BLOODY GROUND

Among the Watauga Association's founding magistrates was John Sevier, who would gain fame as an Indian fighter and the first governor of Tennessee. Like Daniel Boone and Jacob Brown, Sevier was also from a family of a roving nature.[13] While living in New Market in the Shenandoah Valley, he was commissioned as a captain in Virginia's militia by George Washington. He scouted the headwaters of the Holston and French Broad in 1771. By 1773, he had migrated down the valley and settled near Long Island on the Holston close to today's Kingsport. With Richard Henderson, he was a principal in negotiating the Treaty of Sycamore Shoals with the Cherokee in 1775. Though in direct violation of edicts by the Crown and North Carolina, the treaty ceded vast tracts that would become central Kentucky and Tennessee to Henderson's Transylvania Company for trade goods worth 10,000 British pounds. The treaty was also interpreted as legitimizing Brown's settlement on the Nolichucky.

Signing for the Cherokee was Attakullakulla, also known as Little Carpenter, the tribe's elder statesman. In 1730, he had been one of six Cherokee who traveled to England to negotiate an alliance. Back in North America, he was taken prisoner by the Iroquois in 1739, transported to Canada, adopted by the family of their principal chief, and became friendly with French officers and traders. Seeing firsthand how they played the Iroquois as pawns against the English, he became adept at navigating their conflicting demands in efforts to gain security for his people. By the late 1740s, he was living among the Overhill Cherokee, and from the English colonial governor of South Carolina, he wrested the promise of building Fort Loudoun on the Little Tennessee to protect his people from French and their Indian allies' encroachment from the west.

For the Cherokee, goods received from the Treaty of Sycamore Shoals proved to be a paltry exchange compared to those earned from hunting on the lands they gave up. Attakullakulla's son, Chincanacina, aka Dragging Canoe, was enraged by the agreement and vowed to turn Middle Tennessee into "a dark and bloody ground."[14] No treaty could withstand constant expansion of colonial presence in the valleys of the Holston and Nolichucky. News of the outbreak of open warfare between colonists and the Red Coats in Massachusetts arrived in 1775 and alarmed white settlers. So, too, did rumors in the spring of 1776 that Dragging Canoe had invigorated his allegiance with the British and planned to attack. Until then, attacks by Indians had been sporadic, isolated plunder of individual white farms.

When news of Dragging Canoe's intention reached pioneer families settled along the Holston and Nolichucky, they fled their farms and retreated behind Fort Watauga's stockade at Sycamore Shoals, near today's Elizabethton, Tenn., awaiting the assault. Slipping silently through the forest, the Cherokee surprised several women milking cows beyond the walls. Among them was "Bonnie Kate" Sherrill, who was pulled over the palisades to safety by Sevier, her future husband. Unable to take the fort, the warriors retreated, and within weeks a relief column of Virginia militia under Colonel William Christian arrived. Reaching North Carolina about the same time were fresh reports of Indian

BURNING A CHEROKEE TOWN AND DESTROYING THEIR CROPS.

To cleanse British-backed Cherokee from their homelands
in southwest North Carolina, in the fall of 1776 General
Griffith Rutherford and his force of 2,400 militia burned
36 towns and destroyed crops forcing most Indians to flee
and join the Creeks in northern Georgia and Alabama.
As a nation, the Cherokee never recovered. (Savannah
Images Project.)

attacks on Moravian settlers along the Holston. One recounted that warriors
had "horribly mutilated them, scalping the entire head, and hacking the body
into many pieces."[15]

Such atrocities provoked a coordinated response by the newly united states
in the Southeast. By early July, state governments of Georgia, North Carolina,
South Carolina, and Virginia were planning attacks to eliminate the "Indian
threat." Georgia dispatched Col. Samuel Jack with 200 militiamen to destroy
the Lower Cherokee towns at the headwaters of the Chattahoochee, Savannah, and Saluda rivers. The plan was for him to rendezvous with 1,100 South
Carolinians under Major Andrew Williamson. Col. William Christian led
1,800 Virginians against the Dragging Canoe's base in the Overhill towns on
the Little Tennessee. Gen. Griffith Rutherford, commander of Salisbury, N.C.
militia, was ordered to coordinate with Williamson and Christian and attack
towns in the eastern Blue Ridge.

Rutherford gathered 2,400 volunteers at Davidson's Fort (Old Fort, N.C.) on the headwaters of the Catawba River in late August. Departing on September 1, he led his men up the rugged Indian trail over Swannanoa Gap and down the river's gentle valley. After making 11 miles that first day, he went into camp for the night. On the following evening, he put up near the junction of the Swannanoa and the French Broad on today's Biltmore Estate, near the ancient Indian settlement by then long vacant. The next morning, he and his troops waded the French Broad at War Ford just upstream from the lagoon on the estate. Bearing a bit north, he picked up the Hominy Creek drainage, where the army again overnighted near Sulphur Spring.[16]

Commanding one of his companies was Capt. William Moore. Dismounting wearily, he was struck by the beauty of the vale. As his horse drank from the wide stream, he thought: "This is Eden's Land" and vowed to return.[17] Return after war he would, becoming one of the first white settlers in the region. In the morning the troops followed Hominy Creek west and crossed into the watershed of the Pigeon, which carried him through Canton and Clyde, now essentially the route of US 23. Turning southwest, he headed for the Cherokee town of Nikwasi at Franklin on the Little Tennessee River, and to Cowee, a few miles downstream.

About a year earlier in late May 1775, a month after colonial militiamen fired on the Red Coats at Concord's Old North Bridge, American botanist William Bartram was exploring down the Little Tennessee, identifying plant species native to the Southern Appalachians. He traveled alone or in company of Indians and traders he met along the way. As recorded in *Travels and Other Writings*, his sketch of the countryside and its inhabitants is nothing if not pastoral:

> I passed through (Echoe), and continued three miles further to Nucasse (Nikawsi), and three miles more brought me to Whatoga. Riding through this large town, the road carried me winding about through their little plantations of Corn, Beans, &c. up to the council-house, which was a very large dome or rotunda, situated on the top of an ancient artificial mount, and there my road terminated. All before me and on every side, appeared little plantations of young Corn, Beans, &c. divided from each other by narrow strips or boarders of grass, which marked the bounds of each one's property, their habitation standing in the midst. Finding no common high road to lead me through the town, I was now at a stand how to proceed further, when observing an Indian man at the door of his habitation,

three or four hundred yards distance from me, beckoning me to come to him, I ventured through their lots, being careful to do no injury to the young plants, the rising hopes of their labor and industry; crossed a little grassy vale watered by a silver stream, which gently undulated through, then ascended a green hill to the house, where I was chearfully welcomed at the door and led in by the chief, giving care of my horse to two handsome youths. During my continuance there, about half an hour, I experienced the most perfect and agreeable hospitality conferred on me by these happy people, I mean happy in their dispositions of rectitude with regard to our social and moral conduct. O divine simplicity and truth, friendship without fallacy or guile, hospitality disinterested, native, undefiled, unmolested by artificial refinements!

My venerable host graciously and with an air of respect, led me into an airy, cool apartment; where being seated on cabins, his women brought in a refreshing repast, consisting of sodden venison, hot corn cakes, &c. with a pleasant cooling liquor made of hommony well boiled, mixed afterward with milk; that is served up either before or after eating in a large bowl, with a very large spoon or ladle to sup it with."

His host asked Bartram if he had come from Charleston and whether he knew John Stuart, Britain's Indian agent. After answering in the affirmative, the two smoked pipes of tobacco as Bartram recounted his travels and requested direction to Cowee, a principal town of the Cherokee farther down the Little Tennessee. Together, they walked, Bartram leading his horse, for two miles before shaking hands and parting company. "This prince is the chief of the Whatoga, a man universally beloved, and particularly esteemed by the whites for his pacific and equitable disposition, and revered by all for his exemplary virtues, just, moderate, magnanimous and intrepid."[18]

A year after Bartram's bucolic visit, Rutherford and his troops descended the Little Tennessee a few miles beyond Cowee, which he found abandoned. Rutherford returned to Nikwasi and continued his march toward Cherokee living in the Valley towns along the Hiwassee River. Barring his way was the sharp spine of the Nantahala Mountains. In that day, the "common crossing place" was Wayah Gap. Either by plan or happenstance, he led his men through a gap further to the south. Trailing Rutherford and hurrying to catch up, Williamson's army were ascending the narrow trail up Wayah Creek and entered the steep gorge known as the Black Hole. There, Cherokee warriors encircled the advancing army in ambush. For two hours, both sides held their ground until Williamson mounted a bayonet charge scattering the Indians. In the firefight, 14 Indians and 12 militiamen were killed.[19]

Rutherford, meanwhile, had continued down the Hiwassee, burning villages, trampling crops, confiscating deerskins and ammunition, and destroying anything else of value before Williamson reached him on September 26. All told, the expedition destroyed 36 towns, forcing most of the Cherokee to flee south, where they joined the Creeks.[20] A few sought refuge in the mountains, facing the prospect of winter with scant food or shelter. From Rutherford's scorched earth campaign, the Cherokee would never recover.

KING ON THE MOUNTAIN

In the wake of Rutherford's campaign, Cherokee attacks on Europeans living in the French Broad watershed continued sporadically, but white settlements remained relatively peaceful. When the commander of British armies in North America captured Charles Town (Charleston) in May 1780, he ordered General Charles Cornwallis to march inland to protect loyal settlers,[21] sweep rebelling colonials from North Carolina, and carry the war to the mouth of Chesapeake Bay. There he was to rendezvous with the British fleet and defeat the rebels once and for all. Major Patrick Ferguson, a superb marksman and designer of a breech-loading flintlock rifle, served under Cornwallis and led the vanguard of British forces up country. Along the way, he recruited scores of loyalists who would comprise the bulk of his force. He dispatched a stark warning to patriots living across the Blue Ridge, vowing that he would "march his army over the mountains, hang their leaders, and lay waste to their country with fire and sword."[22] As he moved northward, he was continually harassed by North Carolina militia. Because they refused to come out and fight in classic continental fashion—preferring to fire from behind trees and boulders—he despised them as uncouth ruffians and "the dregs of mankind"[23]

When Col. Isaac Shelby, who commanded the North Carolina militia with Charles McDowell, learned of Ferguson's intent, he saddled his horse, raced across the mountains, and alerted Sevier to the impending attack. Choosing to confront Ferguson on ground of their choosing, the pair sent out word to muster militias and assemble as soon as possible at Sycamore Shoals. More than 1,000 men, most on horseback but a few afoot, assembled from as far away as Wolf Town (now Abingdon, Va.), the Patriots were a homespun lot, woodsmen turned farmers by necessity and eager to return home to harvest their crops.

They were defined by the fact that each carried a rifle, far more accurate but slower to load than the smooth-bore Brown Bess muskets with which most of Ferguson's men were armed.

The Patriots departed Sycamore Shoals on September 27, beginning their journey over the mountains, a trek that earned them the nickname for which they would be forever known. At Quaker Meadows, Charles McDowell's plantation outside of Morganton, N.C., the Overmountain Men rendezvoused with militiamen from the Yadkin watershed. Suspecting that Ferguson remained at Gilbert Town, a now-abandoned settlement near Rutherfordton, they set forth in that direction on October 4. Shortly after beginning the march, two men suspected of loyalist leanings vanished, hurrying forward, it was later learned, to warn the British commander of the size and intention of the force that would confront him. Alarmed, Ferguson began withdrawing toward Cornwallis's main force near Charlotte.

After making 21 miles on October 6, the column halted for the night. They learned from local farmers that Ferguson had camped on Kings Mountain—in reality a rocky knoll a couple hundred feet higher than the surrounding countryside. To attack before Ferguson could be reinforced or withdraw further, Sevier and Shelby dispatched 900 of their best riflemen astride the campaign's finest horses. With their flintlocks covered to protect them from the cold drizzle, these make-shift dragoons rode some 35 miles. Closing in on Ferguson's sleeping troops, the patriots dismounted. Rain had softened leaves flooring the forest allowing them to creep quietly forward without alerting loyalist pickets.

Surrounding the hilltop, the Patriots advanced, firing from behind trees and boulders. Brown Bess muskets were designed to deliver deadly volleys of fire from troops standing erect in straight ranks. Even in the hands of the most skilled marksman, these smoothbores were notoriously inaccurate. But unlike the patriot's rifles, British muskets could be fitted with bayonets. Ferguson ordered his men to fix bayonets and launched a charge down the hill. Frightening as it must have been, the Overmountain Men refused to bolt. They advanced slowly, steadily, aiming and shooting so as not to waste a single precious bullet. Ferguson was shot out of his saddle. With their commander dead, the battle sputtered to a close. The Battle of Kings Mountain forced Cornwallis to delay his planned campaign through North Carolina. And he learned that citizen farmers loyal to the Crown were no match for patriots fighting for independence.

Returning from Kings Mountain, Sevier was informed that a large party of

Indians was preparing to attack settlements in on the Nolichucky, Watauga, and Holston rivers. He reorganized his patriots, moved down the French Broad, crossed the river at Big Island, and encountered the Indian camp. In the ensuing battle, 28 of them were killed while Sevier suffered no casualties. The Battle of Boyd's Creek effectively ended any hope that the Crown's Indian allies could reverse the course of the American War of Independence in the Southeast.[24]

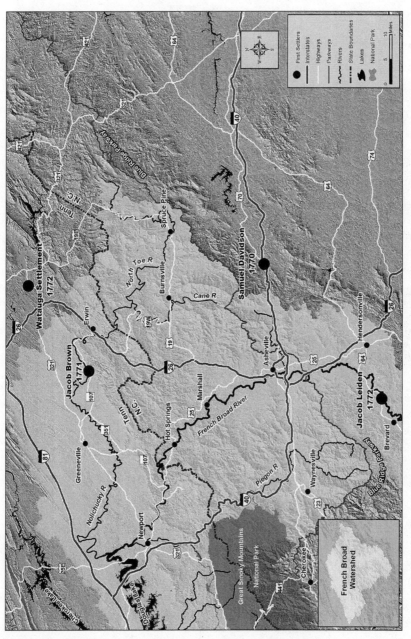

The first settler in the French Broad watershed was Jacob Brown from South Carolina who built a trading post in 1771 near the confluence of Cherokee Creek and the Nolichucky River in what would become Washington County, Tenn. A year later Jacob Leiden established a farm on today's "Lyday" Creek near Penrose. (Cartography: Greg Dobson.)

FIVE

Eden of the Mountains

With this command: *Get thee up into the top of Pisgah, and lift up thine eyes westward, and northward, and southward, and eastward, and behold. . . .* Thus the Lord showed Moses the promised land. That passage from Deuteronomy surely was in Vanderbilt's mind as he viewed the tallest peak on his immense estate. Walk the short and strenuous trail from the Blue Ridge Parkway to the top of Mt. Pisgah. No matter which direction you look, you see ridge after succeeding ridge separated by valleys. When the first wave of Europeans arrived, slopes were thickly forested with oaks, hickories, chestnuts, and poplar. Growing straight and tall, poplar was the easiest to fell and fashion into cabin walls and furniture.

Between ridges ran streams cold and pure and teeming with native brook trout. Where their gradients lessened, torrents of spring and summer carved floodplains, the only more or less level land in the mountains. Smaller ones were flat enough for a cabin, maybe a shed with a garden and an apple tree or two for the kitchen. Progressively down the mountain, floodplains widened and were increasingly topped by rich mantles of fertile sandy loam. Some carried overgrown plots known as "old fields," where Cherokees had grown corn, beans, and squash. On those that had not been farmed grew thick but easily cleared stands of river cane. At the foot of ridges rising above them, gently sloping hillsides offered sites for houses, barns, and paddocks.

Drive up any of the myriad state and county roads that climb mountain valleys in the watershed. Follow the progression of floodplains from broad river bottoms where streams join the rivers: the French Broad, the Nolichucky, the Pigeon, and the Little Pigeon. Let your mind wander back to the mid-1780s.

America had won its war for independence from Great Britain. Spirits of self-reliance and self-sufficiency swept the country. If one were determined enough and not indentured or enslaved, one could escape poverty in sea coast cities by loading up scant possessions and heading west into new lands wrested from England's Indian allies. For American veterans of the Revolutionary War, the Blue Ridge and the Great Valley beyond were, indeed, the fabled Garden of Eden.

TO THE VICTORS . . .

Rutherford's campaign in 1776, incessant reciprocal raids between colonists and Cherokees, the Battle for Kings Mountain, and Sevier's subsequent forays against Indians at Boyd's Creek and Newport on the French Broad forced the Cherokee out of their settlements and down into far southwestern North Carolina, southeastern Tennessee, and northern Georgia and Alabama. Under the Treaty of Long Island, signed in 1777, the Cherokee ceded to North Carolina all but the lower end of the Nolichucky watershed. Nine years later, the Hopewell Treaty turned over a thin strip containing the Swannanoa and many of the French Broad tributaries rising in Madison County. In 1791, the Treaty of the Holston removed the balance of the lower French Broad and most of the Pigeon from Cherokee ownership. The remaining land drained by the Pigeon containing Waynesville, the upper French Broad, and Mt. Pisgah was signed away by the Treaty of Tellico in 1798. The 1819 Treaty of Washington all but purged Indians from the headwaters of the French Broad. It concentrated Cherokees in what was supposed to be their new and sovereign homeland within the United States of America. The election of Andrew Jackson nine years later would prove just how much that treaty was worth.

Signing of the treaties did not cleanse the Cherokee from the watershed. Instead, they retreated up streams, seeking refuge in highland valleys, a migration not dissimilar to the way climate warming drives native species to higher and cooler habitats. The first US Census taken in 1790 records few Cherokee in the Blue Ridge drained by the French Broad. Some historians have taken these data to mean that Indians no longer lived here. But others offer a more realistic explanation. For fear of being deported from their farms, many Cherokee no doubt decided not to identify themselves as such. According to Stephen J. Yerka, historic preservation specialist with the Eastern Band of the Cherokee, "If you didn't participate in the census, nobody knows you're here."[1] And because of intermarriage with Europeans and adoption of their lifestyle, many may have felt that they were no longer members of the tribe.[2]

For victors in the Revolutionary War, land seemed almost free for the taking. Until 1796 and the creation of the State of Tennessee, North Carolina extended westward all the way to the Mississippi. Deeply impoverished by the war, the state had no funds to pay militiamen who had fought for independence. Instead, it issued warrants for unclaimed western lands. Privates received 7.6 acres for each month of service. If they had served for the full seven years of the war, they were entitled to 640 acres—one square mile. The higher the rank, the greater the size of the warrant. A captain could receive up to 3,840 acres; a colonel, 7,200 acres; and a brigadier general, 12,000 acres. Heirs of deceased veterans received warrants issued to their fallen kin. They could be sold, and often were.[3] To convert the parcel into a grant of land, it had to be surveyed, fees paid, and the plat accepted by North Carolina's secretary of state.

Until 1785, the boundary between lands available to colonists and those reserved for the Cherokee excluded the French Broad watershed from the Swannanoa northwest to the present North Carolina–Tennessee line. That strip would not be open for settlement until the signing of the Hopewell Treaty in 1786 and constituted something of a no man's land wracked by outbursts of conflict. To avenge raids by Patriots returning from service in Virginia, in 1783 Indians stole horses from nascent settlements near today's Newport. A band of colonists led by Peter Fine pursued them up a tributary to the Pigeon and attacked their village. It was winter. Peter's brother Vinette was killed. Having no time to bury his body, Peter and his men chopped a hole in the ice and lowered the corpse into the stream. Its name, "Fines Creek," denotes Exit 15 on I-40, through the Pigeon River gorge.[4]

FIRST TO PUT DOWN STAKES

Though he had no grant or warrant, the first Patriot to build a cabin in the upper French Broad watershed, according to most historians, was Samuel Davidson. Infected like Daniel Boone, by the notion that fields were more fertile and game more plentiful beyond the western horizon, Davidson had arrived at the base of the Blue Ridge in 1770 to take up residence on 640 acres in today's Old Fort. To accommodate Gen. Rutherford's troops, a stockade was erected on Davidson's land in 1776; known then as Davidson's Fort, it was considered the "westernmost outpost of Colonial civilization."

Come spring eight years later, in 1784, Davidson, his wife, their infant daughter, and a female enslaved servant crossed Swannanoa Gap, put up a cabin where Christians Creek enters the Swannanoa, cleared a few acres, and began farming. Having no paddock for his horse, he attached a cow bell to its halter so he could find it when it wandered off. Early one morning, he heard the bell ringing. Going in search of it, he headed into the forest toward the sound. Not long thereafter, his wife heard gun shots. Samuel failed to return. Terrorized and fearing the worst, she and her young family fled up the river, over the gap, and down into the safety of his brother's, Major William Davidson's, house in Old Fort. Recruiting some of his neighbors to join him, he promptly set off across the mountains, scoured the area around Samuel's cabin, and discovered his scalped remains on Jonas Mountain. After tracking down a band of Cherokee, they attacked, killed two, and withdrew back over the mountains.[5] That same year, Capt. William Moore filed for a grant of 450 acres of the land he had called "Eden" on Hominy Creek near Sulphur Springs, later the site of a hotel by that name. He made his way back and erected a wooden blockhouse for protection from the Indians. Three years later, after the Cherokee had ceded the land where his brother had been killed to North Carolina, Maj. Davidson's and his sister Rebecca Alexander's families and several friends settled where Bee Tree Creek enters the Swannanoa, just east of Warren Wilson College.

The Davidsons and Moore were not the first Europeans to settle in the upper French Broad watershed. That distinction may belong to Jacob Leiden, who immigrated up the Estatoe Path, an ancient Indian trail leading from Cherokee towns in northwestern South Carolina into the Toe River valley in Mitchell County, N.C. Leiden, whose name was later anglicized to "Lyday," established a farm near Penrose, not far east of Brevard most likely in 1772. Lyday Creek flows through his land and into the French Broad. Leiden fought the British at Kings Mountain and is reported to have neighbors who had come up from South Carolina by the late 1770s.[6]

Across the Great Smokies, Samuel Wear built a blockhouse in 1782 at the junction of Walden Creek and the Little Pigeon River, now subsumed by Pigeon Forge's amusement and shopping mecca. On the Little Pigeon's East Fork in 1785, another veteran, Frederick Emert, became the first European to settle near Gatlinburg, Tenn. He put down roots in the cove named for him near Pittman Center. Emert had served with Gen. Anthony Wayne, who earned the soubriquet "Mad Anthony" for his outlandish tactics, which resulted in the capture of the British fort at Stony Point on the Hudson River, netting 550 Redcoat prisoners in all of 25 minutes.

The Leidens, Moores, Davidsons, Wears, and Emerts were the vanguard of the flow of veterans and their families who would immigrate into highland valleys of the French Broad watershed. They were followed by merchants bent on serving new customers. And along with them came a trickle of "summer people" in search of healing waters and seeking refuge from fetid and miasmic swamp airs of South Carolina's low country.

THOROUGHFARE ALONG THE RIVER

Running from the rolling Piedmont below the eastern front of the Blue Ridge near Greenville, S.C., into the Tennessee Valley, the Catawba Trail and its tributaries constituted the first thoroughfares through the upper French Broad watershed. Routes were arduous and perilous. Coming up from the Southeast, they followed tortuous paths squeezed along boulder-laden streams that twisted up tight gorges often bound by sheer cliffs and frequently cut by cataracts gushing down clefts in the mountains. Would-be settlers, merchants, and the forerunners of today's summer tourists on which the economy of the region now depends were preyed upon by bands of Cherokee angry and unwilling to accept removal from lands they considered by all rights to be their own. Perhaps marginally less difficult—though at times as fraught with danger—was the "road" along the river from the valleys of the lower French Broad, Nolichucky, and Holston in what would become the state of Tennessee in 1796.

By the census of 1790, southwestern North Carolina had a population of about 1,000, not counting Cherokee. Colonists from the Piedmont and the area around the Watauga Settlement were drifting into the Upper French Broad watershed. So rapidly were new settlers arriving that, in 1791, North Carolina's legislature created Buncombe County from portions of Burke and Rutherford Counties. Known then as the State of Buncombe, the new county contained Clay, Graham, Haywood, Henderson, Jackson, Macon, Madison, Swain, Transylvania, and parts of Polk and Yancey counties.

Transforming trails into roads was among the new settlers' highest priorities. Buffalo and Indian footfalls had worn narrow grooves, three or four feet wide, through forests and canebrakes along waterways. Buffalo, or more correctly American bison (*Bison bison*) still wandered through river bottoms. Among the

Into upper French Broad country early settlers followed the Drovers' Road so named because herds of cattle and pigs and flocks of turkeys and ducks were driven along it from Tennessee to markets in South Carolina. It came to be known as the Buncombe Turnpike. (Ora Blackmun, *Western North Carolina Its Mountains and Its People to 1880*, Appalachian Consortium Press, Boone, NC.)

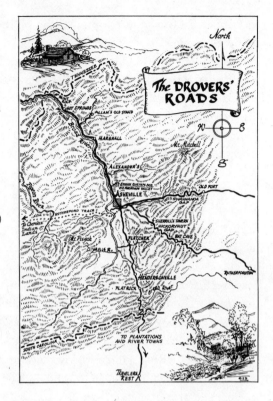

last of the bulls harvested was felled in 1799 by Joseph Rice near his homestead on what has come to be known as Bull Creek near the community of Riceville a few miles east of Asheville.[7]

With axes, picks, and shovels, settlers widened these trails. A first-class road was to be wide enough—about 12 feet—to accommodate a wagon or carriage.[8] Road building was high on the agenda when the court (governing body) of newly formed Buncombe County met on April 6, 1792, at Gum Spring, the residence of Col. William Davidson (not to be confused with his cousin, Maj. William Davidson of Bee Creek) near the entrance to Biltmore Estate. Earlier in the meeting, James Patton had been appointed surveyor. In later sessions, the court appointed an overseer of roads. Every able-bodied male was ordered to devote a set number of days to road construction and repair.

Where they could, roads went around outcrops of granitic rock. Where they could not, sledge-wielding road builders pounded steel star drills, boring holes that were then filled with black powder. Around a fuse made from a powder-filled reed, earth was tamped down tight. Leading to the fuse was a line of dried leaves, which, when lit from a safe distance with flint and steel, burned to the wick, which set off the small blast.[9] The explosion was only powerful enough to fracture the rock into rubble that had to be removed by pick, iron pry bar, and hand. At the bases of cliffs that rose from the river, a pavement of submerged boulders was laid, forming what came to be called "side fords."

In 1793, Buncombe's official courthouse was established at Morristown (renamed Asheville in 1797), located on a highland a mile north of the confluence of the French Broad and Swannanoa. Seeking to open a store there, Zebulon and Bednet Baird half-carried a wagon loaded with supplies up the trail from South Carolina through Saluda Gap.[10] Two years later, the first wagon exited North Carolina, passing Paint Rock into future Tennessee loaded with produce.[11] Thus began the flow of freight, tourists, and later, livestock, on one of today's main routes through the southern Blue Ridge. Travelers were lured up these roads by stories of graceful valleys lush with easily cleared cane, an excellent fodder for livestock. But also, they sought the region's healthful clime. Lowland South Carolinians—loyalists and patriots alike—who fought in Revolutionary War campaigns in the mountains had come to appreciate, first hand, the watershed's healthful climate.

SOOTHING WATERS

When word arrived that two militiamen, Henry Reynolds and Thomas Morgan, chasing stolen horses along the French Broad near Paint Rock had waded into the warm flows of a little stream entering the river along the southwest bank in 1778, residents of Watauga Settlement and other nearby communities were delighted. Having traveled down the great valley from Virginia, many were aware of the therapeutic qualities of comforting mineral springs. They perhaps knew of those at Warm Springs, Va., where the affluent had gone to take the waters since the 1760s. Indians were aware of them. Archaeologists believe that the orange and blue petroglyphs on Paint Rock by the Archaic people 5,000 years ago perhaps alerted Indians traveling along the river to pools of 100°F water a few miles upstream.[12] Not a year after Reynolds and Morgan returned with their story, according to Ramsey's *Annals of Tennessee*, "the warm springs were resorted to by invalids."[13]

In 1791, William Neilson bought land along the river holding the springs and erected a large house, built to accommodate dozens of travelers. Among them was Methodist Bishop Francis Asbury who logged some 6,000 miles

Circuit-riding reverend Francis Asbury preached Methodism throughout the western mountains stopping frequently at Neilson's Inn in Warm Springs. (*The Heart of Asbury's Journal*, Ed. Ezra Squire Tipple, Eaton & Mains, NY.)

by horseback and wagon every year between 1800 and 1814 crisscrossing the mountains shared by Tennessee, North Carolina, and Virginia, delivering sermons wherever he found an audience. On Thursday, Nov. 6, 1800, he arrived at Neilson's and reported the visit in his meticulous journal:

> Crossed Nolachucky at Querton's Ferry, and came to Major Craggs, 18 miles. I next day pursued my journey and arrived at the Warm Springs, not however without an ugly accident. After we had crossed the Small and Great Paint mountain, and had passed about thirty yards beyond the Paint Rock, my roan horse, lead by Mr. O'Haven, reeled and fell over, taking the chaise with him; I was called back, when I beheld the poor beast and the carriage bottom up, lodged and wedged against a sapling, which alone prevented them both being precipitated into the river. After a pretty heavy lift all was righted again, and we were pleased to find there was little damage done. Our feelings were excited more for others than ourselves. Not far off we saw clothing spread out, part of the loading of household furniture of a wagon which had overset and was thrown into the stream, and bed clothes, bedding, &c., were so wet that the poor people found it necessary to dry them on the spot. We passed the side fords of French-Broad, and came to Mr. Neilson's; our mountain march of twelve miles calmed us down for this day. My company was not agreeable here—there were too many subjects of the two great potentates of this western world—whisky, brandy. My mind was greatly distressed.[14]

SEEDS OF THE INTERSTATE

Standing in Pack Square in the center of Asheville are bronze castings of hogs and turkeys. They are replicas of millions driven down the more than 200-mile route from farms in East Tennessee, Kentucky, and Southwest Virginia to buyers in South Carolina and Georgia. At first a seasonal trickle beginning in late summer, reaching full throttle in autumn, and tapering off in the midst of winter, the cavalcade grew steadily until railroads arrived in the 1880s. How else, other than as feed grown into muscle and fat on the hoof, could farmers transport prodigious crops of grain and hay to market? Easy it is to picture a herd of 400 cattle or mules strung out along the primitive riverside road, but imagine driving a flock of as many ducks even though their wings' pinion joints had been clipped so they could not fly. Such drives were fortunate to average eight to ten miles per day.

Drovers labored mightily to avoid spending the night in the open. They much preferred to reach a "stand." Stands were well-known places of rest, typically a long, low, two-story log or frame house fronted with a deep porch and stone chimneys at both ends. Rising from the center was a large chimney, leading from a wide kitchen fireplace where massive kettles of mush and stew swung from iron cranes. For about 25¢, roughly $6 today, drovers bought hearty suppers and breakfasts, washed down with buttermilk, coffee, or more likely whiskey, brandy, or cider. Their meal tab afforded them a place to sleep on the floor of the great room, but for a few cents more they could share a bed upstairs. Stands also provided lodging for increasing numbers of tourists.

Adjacent were ramshackle sheds and barns and pens and paddocks for live-stock. Turkeys roosted in large oaks and maples nearby. To feed 100 hogs, eight bushels of corn were required, thus providing a market where neighboring farmers could sell their grain or barter it for merchandise. Stand owners were also storekeepers. Occasionally, drovers would settle their bills in exchange for a lame hog destined for dinners or with the promise of filling a shopping list of goods that could only be obtained from merchants down in Greenville or Charleston. Trust was seldom an issue, for herdsmen had to pass by the same stands on return trips to their farms in Tennessee and Kentucky and again as they herded their livestock to market in years to come.

David Vance Jr., who kept a stand at Marshall, recorded feeding 90,000 hogs in a single month. Some nights, more than 50 drovers would put up at an inn.[15] To operate his stand, he depended on enslaved African Americans, as did his neighbor James Alexander.[16] So great was the traffic on the road along the French Broad that the North Carolina legislature in 1824 authorized the formation of the Buncombe Turnpike Company, to be capitalized with 1,000 shares of stock valued at $50 each. Beginning at the base of the Blue Ridge in South Carolina, the turnpike climbed through Saluda Gap and followed the

The path along the
French Broad brought
the first tourists
into North Carolina
as early as 1779.
(*Picturesque America or
The Land We Live In*,
Ed. William Cullen
Bryant, D. Appleton &
Company, 1872.)

river valley past Buncombe County's courthouse in the center of Asheville,
by Alexander's stand about midway to Marshall, through the gorge to Warm
Springs and the Tennessee line at Paint Rock.[17]

  Breaking free of the mountains southeast of Newport, the turnpike was
recognized as the finest road in North Carolina and the primary route through
the Southern Appalachians, due to the course carved by the French Broad. It,
and feeder roads crossing Swannanoa Gap from the Moravian settlements near
Salem and Hickory Nut Gap from Charlotte, would carry increasing numbers
of lowlanders seeking relief from summer's stifling heat and humidity. By 1827,
the Buncombe Turnpike was completed from Paint Rock to join the Poinsett
Highway in upper South Carolina. That year, Charles and Susan Baring, he
of the family who established Baring Bank in England, the second oldest
merchant bank in the world, arrived in Flat Rock from Charleston. They built

Mountain Lodge, with its adjacent spring and billiard houses, on 2,300 acres. Their mansion became renowned by Southern plantation society country and painted the community with the first shades of the summer resort patina that defines it still today. Among others traveling the turnpike were hundreds seeking their fortunes in gold, as had de Soto nearly 300 years earlier.

ALL THAT GLITTERS

Rumors of Spaniards mining gold in the headwaters of the French Broad since the eras of de Soto and Juan Pardo persist still today, though hard evidence is as elusive as the precious metal's traces in the sands of Appalachian mountain streams. However, until the California gold rush began in 1849, North Carolina yielded more of the precious metal than in any other state. So rich were deposits, that the US Mint opened a branch in Charlotte in 1835 to produce gold coins.[18] Though little was found in the French Broad watershed, the prospect that it might be lured hundreds of new settlers.

It all began in 1799, when 12-year-old Conrad Reed went fishing in Little Meadow Creek on his family's farm in Cabarrus County on the eastern edge of Piedmont. He stumbled upon a shiny rock of unusual yellow color and took it home. His mom and dad, John, must have thought it was pretty too for they used the 17-pound boulder as a doorstop for the next three years. Finally, curiosity got the best of John, and he took it to a local silversmith in nearby Concord. The silversmith was not sure, but thinking it might be gold delivered it to a jeweler in Fayetteville, who confirmed that it was. Smelted, it produced a bar about six inches long, which John, not knowing its value, sold to the jeweler for $3.05 or about $70 in today's currency.

John soon realized his mistake. With friends and their enslaved workers, they prospected his and surrounding farms. As Little Meadows Creek withered in summer drought in 1803, they discovered a 28-pound nugget and enough other deposit in its sands and gravels to open the first documented gold mine in the United States. When the news spread, thousands left cities along the coast and headed to counties in the Piedmont, stretching from Charlotte to south of Greensboro. Scattered deposits were also found at the foot of the eastern flank of the Blue Ridge along a band running from Columbus to Morganton. While not as rich as those found by the Reeds, they were ample enough for Christian Bechtler to open a private mint in Rutherfordton in 1832 and produce the first US $1 gold coin. In the headwaters of the French Broad, traces of gold

Though little was found in the French Broad watershed, nuggets discovered in streams at the base of the mountains triggered America's first gold rush and led to the eviction of the Cherokee on the Trail of Tears. (*The First Book of History for Children and Youth*, Carter, Hendee, and Co. 1833, p. 75.)

were also discovered but never ample enough for sustained mining. Yet it was the lure of gold, rather than its actual discovery, that accelerated settlement in the watershed.

Regional impact of gold mining in North Carolina was soon eclipsed by massive strikes in North Georgia. Like tossing gasoline on a fire, these new discoveries ignited the lust for Cherokee land that ultimately drove all but a few hundred of them into exile. No one is sure who found gold first in these, the southernmost foothills of the Blue Ridge. It may have been Benjamin Parks, returning from spreading salt on a "lick log" for his cattle on the Chestatee River; John Witheroods, hunting along Dukes Creek near Cleveland; or John Ward, prospecting not far from Parks' lick log. Whatever the case, the *Georgia Journal* of August 1, 1829, carried the following article:

Gold.—A gentleman of the first respectability in Habersham county, writes us thus, under the date of July 22d:

Two gold mines have just been discovered in this county, and preparations are making to bring these hidden treasures of the earth to use.

So it appears that what we long anticipated has come to pass at last, namely, that the gold regions of North and South Carolina would be found to extend into Georgia . . .

Hoards bent on striking it rich were teeming into area by 1830. The name of the first boom town was Auraria, derived from gold in Latin: *aurum*. About four miles northeast, the hamlet of Licklog became Dahlonega after the Cherokee word Da-lo-ni-ge meaning "yellow." At first miners panned for gold, but soon began driving hard rock mines into ridges following veins of quartz. Blasted into rubble, ore was carted from tunnels and crushed by water-powered hammers into powdery sands, which were washed down sluice boxes. Particles of gold, being heavier than quartz, settled behind baffles. In 1835, a federal mint was opened in Dahlonega. It stamped out more than $6 million in gold coins before being shuttered at the opening of the Civil War in 1861.[19]

But gold dust and nuggets were not the only riches in the soils beneath the Blue Ridge in North Georgia. Where steep and stony mountain slopes succumbed into often swampy floodplains, soil was black with humus, the accumulation of eons of decayed plants felled by winter. Though the climate was too cool for cotton, it continued to prove ideal for crops long grown by Indians, principally corn, beans, and squash. Revolutionary War vets eagerly sought land grants in these rich alluvial valleys. Today, many are carpeted in row after row of white or black agricultural plastic growing vegetables to be trucked fresh to cities in the mountains, Piedmont, and coastal plains. In the 1800s, plantation owners in the lowlands were striving mightily to increase acreage devoted to cash crops of cotton, rice, and indigo. To augment income, many acquired farms for other crops and livestock in the headwaters of the French Broad's sibling river, the Little Tennessee near Clayton and elsewhere in country set aside for the Cherokee. Pressure to drive out Indians exploded with the election of Andrew Jackson in 1828.

TARNISHED TERRAIN

Though a regiment of Cherokee is credited with salvaging Jackson's attack on the Creek village at Horseshoe Bend in 1814, and he secured pensions for widows of Cherokee felled in the battle, he was an avowed "Indian hater." His campaigns in Alabama turned out to be for no purpose other than grabbing their land for speculation.[20] The Panic of 1819 ignited financial fear throughout of the country. Roads were desperately needed in western North Carolina and East Tennessee so new settlers could get their produce to market and stock their stores with needed goods. Jackson's pledge to support internal improvements, along with his stature as the hero of the Battle of New Orleans, earned him much of the vote in the 1824 presidential race and ensured his election four years later.[21]

By then, the Cherokee were well on their way to becoming a literate people, thanks to the syllabary devised by Sequoyah with the help of his six-year old daughter, Ayokeyh, in 1821. That led to the creation of the *Cherokee Phoenix*, the first newspaper in the tribe's native language. The first edition was published on February 21, 1828, in New Echota, Ga., capital of the Cherokee Nation, now recognized as sovereign by the US government. Ability to spread news by written word further galvanized their resistance to efforts by Georgians to strip them not only of lands guaranteed by treaty but even of their rights to testify in courts on their own behalf. Discovery of gold exacerbated popular pressure to remove them to reservations in Oklahoma.

For the first months of his presidency, Cherokee leaders believed that, as president, Jackson would live up to his words and protect his one-time allies. Those hopes were dampened when he signed the Indian Removal Act of 1830 and dashed in 1835 when Major Ridge, a mixed-race member of the tribes' governing triumvirate, put his name in behalf of his people to the Treaty of New Echota agreeing to exchange all Cherokee land in Georgia, North Carolina, and Tennessee for $5 million and a reservation in Oklahoma. Ridge had further promised that his people would make the journey voluntarily, but only about 2,000 did so. With most Cherokee refusing to leave, to 60 assembled chiefs on May 10, 1838 Gen. Winfield Scott issued the following edict which reads in part:

> Chiefs, head-men, and warriors! Will you then, by resistance, compel us to resort to arms? God forbid! Or will you, by flight, seek to hide yourselves in mountains and forests, and this oblige us to hunt you down? Remember that, in pursuit, it may be impossible to avoid conflicts. The blood of the white man or the red man may be spilt, however, accidentally, it may be impossible for the discreet and humane among you, or among us, to prevent a general war and carnage. Think of this, my Cherokee brethren! I am an old warrior, and have been present at many a scene of slaughter, but spare me, I beseech you, the horror of witnessing the destruction of the Cherokees.[22]

Of 15,000 exiled Cherokee, about 4,000 died during the horrendous, 1,000-mile, mid-winter march to the barren Oklahoma reservation. A few hundred sought refuge beneath the peaks of Great Smokies and nearby mountains. They would form the nucleus of the Eastern Band of Cherokee Indians and build the vibrant community of Cherokee on their reservation—formally the Qualla Boundary—which adjoins the French Broad watershed at Soco Gap. While many historians claim that no Cherokee were living Haywood, Buncombe, or Madison counties at the time of Removal, a number of family histories from Cataloochee Cove drained by a tributary to the Pigeon River, Bent Creek near Asheville on the French Broad, and Walnut down river from Marshall tell of Cherokee neighbors.

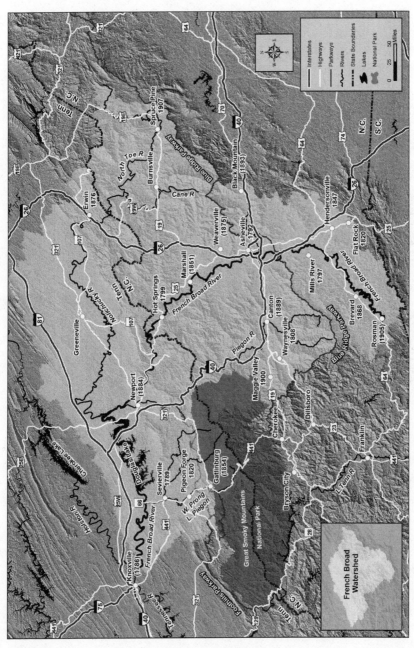

Most towns were located where Indian trails, which would become pioneer roads, crossed streams and rivers crucial sources of water for everyday use and power for grist and sawmills. (Cartography: Greg Dobson.)

SIX

Where There's Water

At times, usually in late summer or autumn, the competition of two climatic systems that dominate North America, the Polar and Bermuda Highs, stalls over the Appalachian Mountains. Occasionally trapped between them are intense low-pressure systems, frequently the remnants of hurricanes. They pump moisture north from the Gulf of Mexico and the Sargasso Sea that falls as rain all along the Blue Ridge. Intense lows have dropped nearly two feet of rain in a single day, and during 1964, more than 10 feet fell on Rosman.[1] On average, the upper French Broad watershed receives between three and seven inches of rain each month, an amount similar to the Pacific Northwest. Unlike the Cascade Mountains, however, the southern Appalachians do not create significant rain shadows that are wet and verdant on one side and arid on the other. Instead, generally speaking, precipitation varies in our watershed by elevation, with peaks receiving the heaviest amounts.

In the main, lands between the mountains are well drained. Swamps or bogs are few. Floods, devastating as they can be, pass quickly. Ample freshwater and fertile arable acreage between steep ridges, some topped by natural grassy balds ideal for grazing, lured settlers almost as powerfully as gold. Most immigrants were relatively poor and bent on finding that ideal homestead on a few dozen acres level enough for a cabin and barn with a stream close at hand. The creek, a "branch" or "prong" in local parlance, needed not be large, just sufficient for cooking, washing, and watering livestock and flowing year round. Finding such was seldom a problem.

Spring-fed runs were most highly sought. These are the purest and coolest streams in the watershed. With temperatures averaging about 56°F, they provided natural refrigeration for food. They seldom turn muddy in any other than the heaviest spates, and unlike rivers they are not prone to devastating flooding. In the upper reaches of the watershed, springs issue forth as seeps in high mountain draws. Pioneers dug basins to collect those waters in pools. Sometimes they walled them with stone and over them erected little log houses to protect milk and butter from marauding animals. Lower on the Tennessee side of the watershed, springs bubble from the bases of limestone outcrops. These were highly coveted by new settlers.

HEADED FOR THE HIGHLANDS

Most newcomers were yeoman farmers bound for plots purchased from land speculators who had bought land grants from Revolutionary War veterans or their heirs. By no means wealthy, these hard-working families set off from the lowlands with wagons loaded with essentials for wresting a homestead from the wilderness. Their tools were simple: axe, adz, rip and crosscut saws, froe for splitting shingles, shovels, plow, hoes, maul, iron wedges, whetstone, augers, hammer, and draw knives. Brought along were as many elemental household goods as they could carry: a frame for a rope bed, a table and a chair or two, cast iron kettles, bundles of bedding and clothing tightly wrapped protecting crockery and the family bible. They followed roads as far as they went toward the acreage where they planned to build their cabins.

Roads were rarely wide enough for two wagons to pass. The further into the mountains they went, the narrower and the more rutted and rocky they became. Often roads like the Buncombe Turnpike did not come anywhere close to the streamside acreage for which these families were bound. Upon reaching the limit of travel by wagon, goods were off-loaded and repacked on heavy sleds, their runners hewn from stout upturned limbs of hickory and oak. These so called land ferries were pulled by mules. Often they were hauled up creek beds jostling precariously over boulders and ledges through difficult gorges to the narrow floodplains where the valleys widened once more. Arduous is far too mild a word to describe these journeys.

And once settlers made it to their land, the first order was to throw up a shelter, often a lean-to roofed with brush and covered with canvas with a firepit out front. Here they would live by day clearing the plot for their tiny 12-foot by 12-foot dirt-floored cabin, girdling trees to kill them so a thin crop of corn could be planted beneath their dead and leafless branches come spring, and hunting for meat. By night, they slept fitfully listening for the scream of a "painter" (mountain vernacular for an eastern cougar), the grunt of a bear rummaging their provisions, or the dreaded footfall of a raiding Indian.

Corn was the staple crop, but grinding it into meal with mortar and pestle was laborious and time consuming in the extreme. Instead, more than a few entrepreneurial settlers set up small tub mills where a horizontal water wheel slowly turned the lower fluted, slightly convex millstone about 24 inches in diameter against the upper matching concave but stationary stone. Fed from above, the action of the lower against the upper sloughed freshly ground meal out a chute into a bin. Usually a tub mill served several families. They would leave a burlap sack of dried corn at the mill in the morning and return a day or two later to pick up their newly ground meal, less a quart or two the miller kept for his trouble. Presence of a grist mill, even a small tub mill, attracted additional settlers. And as more arrived, the miller might perhaps open a store and put an addition on his cabin, transforming it into a rude inn, sowing the seed, perhaps, for a new town.

Along with yeoman farmers seeking land they and their families could work for themselves were a handful of gentry from lowland plantation society. With the first decades of the 1800s came growing awareness that the fertile lands of North and South Carolina's coastal plains were wearing out. Decade after decade of planting crop after crop of cotton and tobacco was exhausting the soil. Among this batch of affluent newcomers to the highlands were veterans like Capt. David Vance, whose grandson Zebulon would become North Carolina's Civil War governor. Vance settled on Reems Creek with three enslaved laborers. He, and his neighbor Col. William Davidson, who owned eight slaves, would become principal founders of Buncombe County and Asheville.[2]

BEYOND THE RIVER'S REACH

Throughout the East, cities developed along rivers mainly because they offered the most efficient mode of transporting goods and produce to market and importing essential supplies. Yet rivers in the Blue Ridge were far too shallow and cut every few hundred yards by fields of boulders and ledges of outcropping rock. They provided little by way of navigable water, and that only by poled and oared flat boats riding crests of spring and fall freshets. A suitable location for a town might have been where Indian trails crossed rivers at shoals like War

Ford at Biltmore, where Rutherford and his men had waded the French Broad on his 1776 campaign to remove the Cherokee.

Shortly before 1790, Col. William Davidson, the late Samuel Davidson's cousin,[3] had crossed Swannanoa Gap and established his residence on a low knoll at Gum Spring a few hundred yards inside today's entrance to Biltmore Estate. Past his farm ran the Indian trail from Old Fort.[4] Nearby, this heavily trod path crossed the Catawba Trail from South Carolina to Tennessee. Less than a mile downstream, the Swannanoa joined the French Broad. The floodplain at the confluence was the site of an ancient Indian village and its low ceremonial mound. The intersection of the trails with the river could be an ideal location for a new town, a cross-roads city that could grow into the center of Western North Carolina's economy in the years to come. By then, the population of the watershed was about 1,000 according to that year's census. In his barn, Davidson and his neighbors were meeting frequently to lay the groundwork to create a new county from portions of Burke and Rutherford. It would be named Buncombe in honor of Col. Edward Buncombe, a very wealthy plantation and slave owner and patriot.[5]

> Colonel Buncombe was wounded on October 4, 1777, at the Battle of German-town, left for dead, identified by a former classmate in the British army, paroled, but unable to obtain proper medical treatment. A year later while sleepwalking, he fell down a flight of stairs, reopened his wounds, and bled to death. His name is also the root of "bunkum," that derogatory term for political hogwash, thanks to an ill-conceived, ill-timed, and extremely lengthy discourse in Congress by Buncombe's representative, Felix Walker. In 1820, on the eve of the long-debated vote to determine whether Missouri would be admitted as a slave or free state, Walker took the floor and delivered an impassioned and pointless speech, not about the issue at hand but about how well he was representing Western North Carolina, as his colleagues shouted in vain to shut him down. The newspaper reported his speech as "pure bunkum."

As they met in April 1792 to consider the site for Buncombe County's first courthouse, they were no doubt mindful of the Swannanoa's propensity to flood every few years. Twelve months earlier, an intense storm in the southern Blue Ridge dumped heavy rains on what may have been remnants of winter snow in the mountains as North America was still in the grasp of the Little Ice Age.[6] Rising rapidly, runoff rampaged down the Swannanoa,[7] French Broad, and the Nolichucky Rivers and crested five feet higher than the disastrous flood of

1916. Davy Crockett, born in 1786 on the Nolichucky just downstream from its confluence with Big Limestone Creek, remembered the flood of 1791 as the "second epistle to Noah's fresh."[8] Three years later, another flood would sweep away his father's mill and house.

Perhaps to protect the nascent town that would become Asheville (renamed from Morristown for Gov. Samuel Ashe in 1796 or 1797)[9] from flooding, Col. Davidson and other members of the county court selected a lot on a tract about a mile north on a height of land between an Indian burial ground and a stream later named Nasty Branch. With few exceptions, most towns in the watershed were first platted on ground no river could reach. As they grew with passing decades, towns expanded down onto floodplains and were ravaged by heavy flooding.

Memories of the horrific French Broad and Swannanoa flood in 1791, five feet higher than the historic crest in 1916, may have led Buncombe County's first commissioners to build their new courthouse up on a small plateau in the hills overlooking the rivers. African American Robert S. Duncanson, considered by many to be "the best landscape painter in the West," produced at least two views of Asheville while the guest of James W. Patton. (*A View of Asheville*, North Carolina, Robert S. Duncanson, 1850, Greenville County Museum of Art.)

Why Here? Travel down the watershed from Rosman and Flat Rock to Knoxville, from Maggie Valley and Waynesville to Newport, from Spruce Pine to Douglas Lake, from Gatlinburg to Sevierville. Every town has a quaint center worthy of a visit and raising the question: Why is this town here? Water, either the proximity to the French Broad or a major stream or soil deep enough and porous enough to support for numerous wells dug by hand, was a salient consideration. Most towns in the watershed trace their founding to the nineteenth century.

Upper French Broad River The French Broad in North Carolina can be divided into two sections. The upper mileage contains the headwaters originating on the flanks of the Blue Ridge. From Rosman to Asheville, the river ambles for about 55 miles and drops about 2.6 feet per mile through a gentle floodplain compressed here and there by forested ridges. Just upstream from Asheville, slopes close in on the river and for about the next 63 miles, it speeds over ledges and around low islands and falls about 11.6 feet per mile before reaching the Tennessee line at Paint Rock. The top section contains river bottoms excellent for row crops and vegetables. Along the lower mileage, flat land along the river is scarce and farms spread over neighboring rounded hills that carried native grasses ideal for grazing livestock.

Rosman Rising beneath Judaculla's perch on the Blue Ridge Parkway, Courthouse and Chestnut Creeks join their waters above Courthouse Falls. The falls drop 45 feet into a deep green plunge pool, an easy walk of less than a mile along a level trail from Forest Road 140 off Route 215, which leads from Rosman to the Blue Ridge Parkway. The creeks form the North Fork of the French Broad River. Coming in at the head of a great valley that follows the Brevard Fault Zone and winds all the way to Asheville are the river's West, Middle, and East Forks.

Among the earliest Euro-American residents of headwaters of the French Broad near the town that came to be known as Rosman was Alexander John Galloway. After herding cattle to feed the Continental Army at the Battle of Kings Mountain, he settled not long thereafter on land on the East Fork because it reminded him of his native Scotland. Nearby, over the next century a smattering of communities evolved—Tiptop, Reba, Toxaway, and Jeptha—all stops on the postal route. At Jeptha, Joseph Silversteen established a tannery in 1902, taking advantage of ample bark from mountain oak and hemlock, copious freshwater, and abundant hides from the valley's hogs and cattle. In honor of his partners, Joseph Rosenthan and Morris Omansky, he changed the name of the post office at Jeptha to Rosman, which was affirmed by North Carolina's legislature in 1905.

Brevard About 20 miles downstream from Rosman, hills pinch in on the French Broad valley, narrowing it to less than a few hundred yards. Immediately downstream it widens again and takes on the waters of the Davidson River coming in from the north, and a few miles further on, the Little River from the south. Eons of flooding deposited soils rich, deep, and first tilled, no doubt, by Cherokee and their ancestors. In the wake of the Revolutionary War, Benjamin Davidson and his family settled on both sides, where the river that bears his name leaves the mountains. Others filtered into the broad floodplain. Many like Jacob Leiden emigrated northward from South Carolina along the ancient Estatoe Path. Another favored route led up the French Broad from settlements along the Swannanoa.

The region continued to fill with pioneers. From Buncombe County, Henderson County had been cleaved in 1838 and Jackson, in 1851. By the late 1850s, residents of the broad bottom lands and up its many feeder streams were petitioning the state government to form yet another new county. They were led by Hendersonville attorney Jacob Jordan, and when approved in early 1861, he named it Transylvania—*across the forest*. Its courthouse was to be located at a place convenient to most of the county residents. Chosen was a lot on fifty acres donated for a new town to be named in honor of Dr. Ephraim Brevard, who signed the Mecklenburg Declaration of Independence, considered at the time to be the first such document produced by any of the 13 colonies.[10]

Mills River Iron was so essential to pioneering communities that in 1788, North Carolina passed an act granting 3,000 acres to anyone who would open a forge. Among those who took up the offer was Phillip Sitton. He established an iron works on South Mills River in 1790. Low grade ore was mined at the head Boylston Creek, route of today's Rt. 280 from Mills River to Brevard. Because the creek lacks flows strong enough to power a forge, Sitton had to haul the ore across Forge Mountain. There it was smelted into bars that could be heated and hammered into axes, knives, hinges, and a multitude of other tools and supplies needed by early settlers.

About 1810, Sitton's daughter married Matthew Gillespie, son of gunsmith

John Gillespie. Gillespie, whose shop was up on the East Fork of the French Broad near Rosman was famed throughout the region for his fine Pennsylvania-style long rifles. Until the Civil War at his shop near Mills River Matthew carried on the tradition forging bars of iron into tubes around a mandrel, which he then rifled by drawing a sharp cutting tool through the bore one grove at a time.

As was the case with all bottom lands well-watered by tributaries to the French Broad, population grew steadily. In 1797, James Brittain gave 10 acres to establish a Presbyterian church and a school that became Mills River Academy around which developed the town of Mills River.[11]

Flat Rock South Carolinian plantation owners eagerly suffered the rugged journey up the eastern escarpment of the Blue Ridge, knowing that the climb of two thousand feet above the elevation of their vast holdings on the coastal plain would bring them into summer temperatures averaging 6°F cooler. At the crest of the mountains, the land began to slope gently to the northwest, drained by thin tributaries that would reach the French Broad about 20 miles downstream. Charles and Susan Baring were among the first residents of the community that came to be known in the 1820s as "Little Charleston in the Mountains." On their estate, the Barings built a chapel that, in 1836, was consecrated as St. John in the Wilderness. It is the first Episcopal church in Western North Carolina. Around it grew the town of Flat Rock, so named for outcrops of exfoliating granite.[12]

Hendersonville When Henderson County was peeled off from Buncombe in 1837, debate raged regarding the location of the county seat. The River Party insisted that it be set in Horse Shoe, on a massive bend in the French Broad 20 miles downstream from Brevard. On the other hand, the Road Party demanded that it be built on a low rolling tableland 6 miles to the west along the new Buncombe Turnpike about 4 miles north of Flat Rock. So firm in its conviction was the River Party, that it began selling lots. Incensed, the Road Party petitioned the courts to block sales. The state legislature intervened and ordered a popular vote to decide the issue. By 453 to 364, the Road Party prevailed. They named the town after Leonard Henderson, former chief justice of the state's Supreme Court. He had no role in the decision, having died in 1833 well before the controversy erupted.[13] In the late 1800s, the Hendersonville and Brevard Railroad—now a spur-line of the Blue Ridge Southern—crossed the main road between the two county seats near the site favored by the River Party, spawning the unincorporated town of Horse Shoe on today's US 276.[14]

Lower French Broad River Near Asheville Regional Airport, ridges begin to constrict the river's floodplain. As its gradient increases, the river veers to the northwest and begins to tumble over rapids on its course through the Blue Ridge. Biltmore Estate and Carrier Park, at the confluence of the Swannanoa, share the last major floodplain before the river exits the mountains 90 miles downstream above Newport. In between, three low run-of-river dams impede float trips: Craggy at Woodfin, Capitola at Marshall, and Redmon two miles farther downstream. At Newport, the Pigeon adds its waters as does the No-lichucky a dozen miles below. The run from Redmon to Hot Springs with Class 4 Bell Rapids and many of Class 2 is thoroughly enjoyed by those who love floating wild rivers.

Marshall Along the dovers' road about 40 miles downstream from Asheville, a post office was established where a trail crossed the river and a large island at a shallow ford. In the early 1800s, the economy along the French Broad was rapidly shifting from agriculture to commerce. Stock stands on the route were among the most lucrative businesses in the region. With funds from his inheritance from his father, who had settled on Reems Creek, David Vance Jr. opened a stand at Lapland. Reportedly 150 feet long, it was one of the largest

An offer of turnip seeds swayed the vote that located Marshall down by the French Broad along the Buncombe Turnpike, the region's prime thoroughfare in the 1870s. (Taylor & Engle, Beauties of WNC & Florida, stereoview, ca. 1878, North Carolina History Room, Pack Library, Asheville, North Carolina.)

on the turnpike and became the hamlet's post office in 1836. He operated his stand with his enslaved workers as did other innkeepers on the turnpike.

In 1851, when Madison County was cleaved off from Buncombe, a grand debate erupted over whether the courthouse should be built in the community of Jewell Hill, now called Walnut, or on a 50-acre lot in Lapland contributed by Vance next to his stand. A vote was taken resulting in a tie. But one member of the community, Larkin Johnson as the story goes, had not voted. A delegation sought him out and found him preparing his garden. When promised he would receive free turnip seed if he voted, he did so and cast his ballot for the courthouse to be built at Vance's. The surrounding town was named after John Marshall, chief justice of the US Supreme Court.[15]

Hot Springs Since 1779, a year after warm springs had been discovered on the French Broad about eight miles upstream from Paint Rock, tourists had made their way to bathe in their soothing mineral waters. William Neilson acquired the springs in 1791 and erected the first of a succession of resorts that brought national acclaim to this little flat land hard by the Tennessee border. So popular was the destination and its location on the main route to markets in South Carolina that the court of Greene County, which in 1786 was part of the State of Franklin, ordered that a road be built to Warm Springs.[16] In 1824, the venerable James Patton, one of the founders of Buncombe County, was directed to superintend the construction of the section of turnpike from Asheville along the river to Paint Rock.[17] In 1831, Patton and his son John bought the property and erected the grand Warm Springs Hotel with its 13 massive white columns, one for each of the original states in the union.[18] Of the hotel in 1848, Charles Lanman wrote: "Of the springs there are one-half dozen, but the largest is covered with a house which is divided into two equal compartments. The temperature of the water is 105 degrees. As a beverage, it is quite palatable. The Warm Springs are annually visited by a large number of fashionable and sickly people from all the Southern States. The principal building is of brick and the ballroom is two hundred feet long. The hotel has accommodations for two hundred and fifty people. There is music and dancing, bowling, bathing, riding, and fishing."[19]

The Warm Springs Hotel burned in 1884. As a new and grander resort, the Mountain Park Hotel, was being constructed, an even warmer spring—this one with 110°F waters—was discovered in 1886, and the town's name was changed to

Hot Springs, a bit of one-upmanship over other towns named Warm Springs in Virginia and Georgia.

Pigeon River The East and West Forks of the Pigeon River rise on opposite flanks of Shining Rock, the ancestral home of the Cherokee, and Cold Mountain, site of Charles Frazier's Civil War novel. They come together southeast of Canton, a few miles upstream from the Indian mounds built 1,200 years ago at the confluence of Garden Creek. Two miles downstream from Clyde, it picks up the waters of Richland Creek up which Gen. Rutherford led his 2,400 troops on their mission to drive the Cherokee from the mountains in 1776. Another five miles downriver, Jonathan Creek joins the Pigeon.

About 30 miles downstream from Canton, the Pigeon enters its gorge traversed by Interstate 40. At the top of the narrows, just below where Cataloochee Creek comes in, Phoenix Electricity Co. completed Walters Dam in 1930. This stunning 180-foot tall, 800-foot long arch dam bows upstream and relies on the pressure of the lake to press its abutments against the walls of the gorge, a technology pioneered by Romans in the first century BC. A 6-mile long tunnel delivers water to the powerhouse at Waterville. Below the dam, the Pigeon flows another 25 miles before reaching Newport and then joining the French Broad five miles farther downstream.

Maggie Valley Who was Maggie? Her story begins with Johannes Plott, who emigrated from Germany to Pennsylvania in about 1750 with his beloved boar hunting hounds famed for their indefatigable stamina and courage. By the 1780s, the Plotts had settled near Charlotte, and a decade later his son, Henry, with his dogs had moved into the Blue Ridge on land beneath a high peak now known as Plott Balsam. Others settled nearby, and for a century that was where mail was delivered.

Around 1900, Jack Setzer, who lived down the mountain on Jonathan Creek, a principal tributary of the Pigeon River, got tired of trudging five miles up hill to collect mail for himself and his neighbors. He petitioned to have letters and newspapers delivered to his home and offered the names of his daughters Cora, Mettie, and Maggie Mae and Jonathan Valley as names for a new post office. To her enduring embarrassment, the US Post Office chose Maggie.[20] Plotts' settlement has faded with time, but in 1989 the breed of his dog—Plott Hound—was named North Carolina's state dog.[21] In the 1960s, Maggie Valley lay astride the main highway, US 19, from Asheville through Waynesville, across Soco Gap, and through Cherokee to the Great Smokies.

Waynesville On their way to banish Cherokee from western North Carolina in 1776, Gen. Rutherford's brigade camped along Richland Creek, about six miles upstream from its junction with the French Broad. At the time, the locale carried the name Mt. Prospect. Soon after the war much of the acreage in the region was acquired by Col. Robert Love, known for his blue swallow-tailed coat, knee britches with silver buckles, and silk stockings. He had served under Gen. "Mad" Anthony Wayne. In 1808, Love was instrumental in separating what would become Haywood County from Buncombe, donating lots on a ridge overlooking the creek for a new courthouse, and naming the new county seat Waynesville.[22]

Despite the presence of "21 distilleries producing 4300 of gallons alcoholic drink . . . one and a half gallons for every man, woman, and child including slaves and free blacks," according to the census of 1810, prosperity eluded Waynesville until the railroad made its way up Richland Creek in 1884. Tracks were laid atop a berm through wetlands known by locals as "frog level," which became the core of Waynesville's commercial and industrial district. Today Frog Level is known for charming bistros and antique shops.

Canton Indians had long lived in the broad pastoral Pigeon Valley, spreading northwestward from where the east and west forks of the river came down out of the mountains. Canton's First Baptist Church is the oldest in Haywood County, having been founded in 1803 as Locust Old Field Baptist Church. "Old fields" was the name newcomers gave to land that had been tilled by the Cherokee. An abundance of pure water and wood gave birth in 1908 to Champion Fibre Company, which was the world's largest pulp mill. The town draws its name from the Canton, Ohio company that built a bridge over the Pigeon. Odoriferous and carcinogenic pollution from the mill once turned the Pigeon as dark and foamy as a heady craft-brewed stout. The mill's closing in 2023 cast 1,200 Canton area residents out of work. Yet few doubt that the town will prove as resilient as the Pigeon River and the mountain forests that surround it.

Newport Before the close of the Revolutionary War, Peter Fine began to operate a ferry across the French Broad at War Ford, where militia under the command of John Sevier had routed Cherokee. Others settled nearby, and a community known as Fine's Ferry began to develop. A year after Tennessee achieved statehood in 1796, Cocke County was established. A log court house and jail were erected at Fine's. Nearly 70 years later, the Cincinnati, Cumberland Gap, and Charleston Railroad reached a broad plain along the Pigeon about five miles upstream from its confluence with the French Broad. Many prominent leaders held the opinion that the county seat should be moved a mile south and closer to industry and commerce developing where the road from the ferry crossed the railroad. There, in 1884, after exhausting debate, the town of Newport was created. Relocation protected the growing town from the French Broad's destructive floods.[23]

Nolichucky River Rising among Mount Mitchell to the south, Linville Falls to the east, and Roan Mountain to the north, the Nolichucky River flows for 115 miles through some of the most picturesque and little-developed countryside along the Tennessee-North Carolina border. Before emerging from the Blue Ridge at the old iron mining town of Embreeville, the river and its headwaters—North Toe, South Toe, and Cane rivers—tumble down tightly twisting valleys before uniting at Huntdale. Downstream from Embreeville, the river winds gently through undulating terrain underlain by carbonate rocks that weather into deep, nutritious soils. De Soto crossed the Blue Ridge in 1540 and followed the Nolichucky through the land later explored by Daniel Boone and that gave birth to Davy Crockett. Below Newport, the 'Chucky, as locals call it, meets the French Broad impounded by Douglas Dam.

Spruce Pine Gems and minerals abound in the rocks underlying this small town bisected by the North Toe River. They developed in pegmatite, a rock type formed from hot geothermal fluid intruded into metamorphic rock. As the semiliquid pegmatite cooled ever so slowly, the atomic structure of minerals like quartz, feldspar, and mica bonded together forming huge crystals. Traded by prehistoric people from the Blue Ridge, sheet mica was mined and marketed in the late-eighteenth and early-nineteenth centuries as isinglass, used in those curtains on the surrey in the musical *Oklahoma* that could "be rolled right down in case there's a change in the weather." Feldspar and kaolin, important components of scores of household and industrial products, are mined in the region, which also hosts the renowned Penland School of Crafts.

Mighty "Murderous" Mary, a circus elephant, was hanged by a railroad crane in Erwin, Tennessee, in 1916 for killing her keeper in a fit of rage after being provoked by his prod. (https://rarehistoricalphotos .com/murderous-mary-1916/.)

Erwin Erwin was the watershed's railroad town. The Charleston, Cincinnati, and Chicago Railroad laid tracks into Erwin in 1890, which became its major maintenance yard on the route from coalfields in southeast Kentucky and West Virginia to Charleston, S.C. By 1903, the railroad had followed the North Toe through Spruce Pine. Ultimately, it would climb the Blue Ridge, tunnel under Altapass, erect a station in 1910 to serve tourists staying at Switzerland Inn, switchback down the east slope connecting with the Southern at Marion, and head on toward Charleston via Rutherfordton and Spartanburg.[24]

Hauling freight over mountains on the route from Kentucky to South Carolina was hard on engines and rolling stock. Steep terrain and flash flooding were equally tough on tracks. To repair equipment and right of way, the railroad—now operating as the Clinchfield—located its major maintenance yards in Erwin. The town achieved infamy in 1916 for hanging a circus elephant, Mighty Mary. On September 11, Red Eldridge, an itinerant hotel clerk, joined Sparks World Famous Shows in Kingsport as an assistant elephant trainer. He had no experience at all. And the next day, riding atop Mary, he provoked her with his prod. Enraged she threw him against a drink stand and tromped on his head. Immediately the crowd began chanting "Kill the elephant!" To mollify the crowd, the show's owner had Mary transported to the Clinchfield yards in Erwin, where she was hanged to death from a crane used to recover wrecked railroad cars. Among the 2,500 witnesses to her execution were many of the town's children.[25]

Little Pigeon River Like its cousin tributary that joins the French Broad at Newport and referred to by Tennesseans as the "Big" Pigeon, the Little Pigeon was named for the passenger pigeon, extinct since the early 1900s. Draining the northwest slopes of Great Smoky Mountains National Park, the Little Pigeon flows through the most heavily visited section of the watershed on its way to join the French Broad, about five miles downstream from Douglas Dam. Construction began on February 2, 1942, and was completed on February 19, 1943, record time for a 200-foot high, 1700-foot long concrete dam. Built to provide electricity for war industries at Alcoa and Oak Ridge where the atomic bomb was developed, the dam impounds the French Broad in 1.5 million-acre Douglas Lake.

Gatlinburg A photo taken in 1913 shows a single farm house along the West Prong of the Little Pigeon at Gatlinburg. Today, this little town in the shadow of Mt. LeConte's three peaks and bustling with 12 million tourists annually is the primary gateway to the Great Smokies. Among the earliest settlers was South Carolinian William Ogle, whose historic cabin built in 1807 has been preserved in the town's visitor center. When Ogle arrived, the area was known as White Oak Flats, which stretched north toward Cosby along today's US 321. Radford Gatlin moved into the flats in 1854, opened a store and petitioned for a post office to be named Gatlinburg. A slaveholder sympathetic to the South, he feuded bitterly with the Ogles, his pro-Union neighbors, and was forced to move away in 1859.[26]

In his landmark book *Our Southern Highlanders,* Horace Kephart tells of the hardships faced by pioneers in the Smokies. By the early 1900s, life for mountain families had improved little and was particularly difficult for women. Not only were they expected to cook, clean, wash, weave, rear children, and care for aged parents, but they also tended livestock and guided the plow through fields often so steep and stony it's a wonder any crop grew. To teach children and help mountain women, Pi Beta Phi, a secret society for college women,

Before Pi Beta Phi sorority established their school in 1912, Gatlinburg had but few houses, a tiny inn for timber scouts, and a small store. (Great Smoky Mountains National Park Archives.)

founded Arrowmont in 1912. It was one of a number of settlement schools established in the Southern Appalachians in early decades of the twentieth century. Today, it continues as Arrowmont School of Arts and Crafts, offering an extensive curriculum of residencies and courses in pottery, weaving, caning, glass blowing, and sculpture.

Logging and tourists began to dominate Gatlinburg's economy in the early 1900s. Thanks to narrow-gauge railroads and steam-powered band saws, only three decades were required to strip hardwoods from all but the steepest and most isolated mountain sides. By the 1930s, logging was by and large done. Great Smoky Mountains National Park was established in 1934 and has become the third most heavily visited of America's national parks.

Pigeon Forge Uniting Cherokee villages on the lower French Broad with their mother town, Kituhwa, with those across the Smokies, an ancient Indian trail followed the West Prong of the Little Pigeon. On the first bit of broad floodplain beneath the mountains, Isaac Love erected an iron forge in 1820. The forge wrought hardware and implements for a growing number of immigrants, many of them Revolutionary War veterans. A decade later, his son diverted the river to power a grist mill. Operating still today, the Old Mill became the center of a sleepy community on the fringe of Gatlinburg. In the early 1960s, that began to change with the opening of the Rebel Railroad, which became Goldrush Junction, thence Silver Dollar City. In 1986, country music superstar, actress, philanthropist, and Sevier County native Dolly Parton, partnered with the theme park's owners, giving rise to Dollywood and associated hotels and amusements.

Sevierville Less than a mile downstream from Sevier County's courthouse, with its statue of Dolly Parton playing her guitar on its lawn, the West Prong of the Little Pigeon joins its namesake for the five-mile course to the French Broad. The town is named in honor of John Sevier, prominent militia colonel, first governor of the failed State of Franklin and, then, the State of Tennessee when it was admitted to the Union in 1796. Until the establishment of Great Smoky Mountains National Park, Sevierville was a local trading center served by the short line Smoky Mountain Railroad. A spur track down the Little Pigeon supplied construction of Douglas Dam in 1942. Only profitable during the war years, the rail route from Knoxville was abandoned in 1966. But four-laning Route 66 from Interstate 40 and US 441 to Pigeon Forge ignited Sevierville's tourist economy and established it as the largest shopping district in the Smokies.

French Broad Mouth, Knoxville Thirty-two miles downstream from Douglas Dam at Knoxville, the French Broad joins the Holston River, which originates in Southwest Virginia to form the Tennessee River. The third largest city in Tennessee, Knoxville was established in 1786 by Revolutionary War veteran James White on a land grant of 1,000 acres on a hill about four miles downstream, where First Creek enters the Tennessee. White surrounded his home with stockade—White's Fort—which in 1790 became the capital of the Southwest Territories. Named for George Washington's secretary of war, Henry Knox, six years later it was selected as the first capital of the new state of Tennessee.

SEVEN

Uncivil War in the Mountains

Picture pioneers who sought to grub with axe and hoe a life for themselves and their families from the meager bottom lands and challenging slopes of the Blue Ridge. The husband is worn and wiry from felling trees, building the cabin and shed, pulling stumps, splitting fence rails and shingles, tilling fields, rounding up strayed hogs, herding sheep, and tending a still. Protecting livestock and family from marauding predators—be they wolves, panthers, bears, or Indians— demanded perpetual vigilance, hour upon hour, day after day. His young old wife has grown gaunt from incessant rigor of child birth and rearing; keeping house and food on the table; doctoring the ill; minding chickens and the milk cow; and lending a hand at plowing, chopping weeds choking corn, and harvesting vegetables, apples, and peaches. Night after night, they slept with ears ever open for the slightest sound that did not belong. Amusement was scant, borne by fiddled tune, song remembered from gramma's lap, and verse from the tattered family bible. Of the future, they can think only of tomorrow and the Lord's salvation. By and large, mountain farms were small. Nearly seven out of ten contained fewer than 50 acres, much of which was too steep to be cultivated.[1]

Popular folklorists through the mid-1900s presented mountaineers as poor, ignorant, proud, and stubbornly independent—an image that endures today. In fact, the population of the watershed was far more diverse and nuanced. Well known are the landed gentry: the Barings, Davidsons, Pattons, Vances, Ogles, Regans, Seviers, and their peers with their fine houses, large spreads of rich farmland, stores, staffs of enslaved servants and laborers, and employees who owned no land. Add to population mix in the watershed, a smattering of freed African Americans, Cherokees and their descendants who found refuge in isolated coves, and the growing trove of tourists who summered, attended by their entourages of enslaved and free servants in resorts along the Buncombe Turnpike from Flat Rock to Warm Springs.

Though the soothing summer climate was a blessing for all, in the ruggedness of densely forested ridges falling into deep valleys lay the foundation of the watershed's economic isolation. Affluent and influential landowners had their roots, generally speaking, in slave-owning plantation society. Wealth of summer tourists further linked the watershed's landed gentry to the politics and society of the Piedmont and coastal plain. Those living along railroads in East Tennessee and along the Buncombe Turnpike were more likely to support the Confederate States of America (CSA) because these routes led to southern markets for their produce and products.

Politicians east of the Blue Ridge were reluctant to support new turnpikes and railroads in the mountains. Although North Carolina's legislature chartered the Western North Carolina Railroad to link the highlands with the lowlands in 1855, it neglected to appropriate adequate funding. Track made it no farther than Morganton before the onset of the Civil War.[2] Usually members of one class: owners of the growing number of tanneries, iron foundries, and lumber mills, which counted on improved transportation, were deeply resentful of lowlanders' efforts to restrict their economic opportunities.

Secession in the watershed pitted Southern-leaning wealthy merchants and residents of valley towns and their politicians against highland farmers who sought little more than time to plant their corn and feed their families. Many yeoman farmers were descendants of Revolutionary War soldiers who had fought for independence from Great Britain and believed deeply that "united we stand, divided we fall."

ARM! ARM!

So blared the page-one headline in the *Asheville News* of December 29, 1859: "From all parts of the state we perceive the most commendable zeal in organizing volunteer companies. Almost every town has one, and some two or three. We would like for our country friends in this County to take steps to organize several volunteer companies. Four or five in addition to the one we have here in the village might easily be gotten up. What say our friends

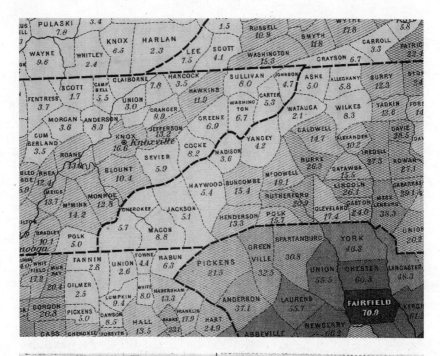

HAVE YOU SEEN IT?

IF not call and see *The Wonderful Pump* now on exhibition at the Grand Emporium of Health and Beauty, commonly known as ASTON'S. August 26. 1858.

NEGRO FOR SALE.

A likely NEGRO GIRL, 18 years old, a first rate cook washer and ironer, with a child 18 months old. In all particulars a No 1 servant — Persons wishing such a servant would do well to enquire soon, as such an opportunity for buying so good a servant is rarely offered.

Inquire at   THIS OFFICE.
August 26 1858.

CURES GUARANTEED.

SALE OF NEGROES.

THIRTEEN valuable NEGROES, belonging to the Estate of John P. Smith, deceased, will be sold at the Court House in Asheville, on Friday the 27th day of August next, on a credit of 12 months, the purchaser giving note with approved security, with interest from date.

A. T. SUMMEY,
Att'o. for Administrator.

July 22, 1858.   6t

W. H. Jackson & Co.

HAVE just received and offer for sale, a few pieces of black and colored Cloth black and fancy Cassimers, linen Lawn, Irish linen, damask

According to the 1860 Federal census, slavery was rife in Knox and Buncombe Counties; two to three times greater percentage-wise than their African American populations in 2010. (TOP: E. Hergesheimer, *Map Showing the Distribution of the Slave Population of the Southern States of the United States Compiled from the Census of . . .*, Washington Henry S. Graham, 1861. https://www.loc.gov/item/99447026/. BOTTOM: *The Asheville News*, Asheville, NC, August 26, 1858.)

on Swannanoa, Hominy, Turkey Creek, Ivy and Reems Creek? You have the material we know. Let us prepare against the evil day." Above ran this short piece on the Buncombe Rifles:

> We understand that there are nearly one hundred men enrolled in this patriotic corps. At a meeting held by the company last week a uniform was adopted to be made of steel mixed Rock Island Cassimere, manufactured in Mecklenburg of this State.
> That's right. A mountain Rifle company clad in the fabrics of the Hornet's Nest County will, we think be invincible.

President Abraham Lincoln set in formal and final motion the great American carnage of the Civil War, the ultimate resolution to the long-fermenting sectional differences over tariffs, slavery, and states' right to nullification that had been building since the 1830s, with these words issued on April 15, 1861:

> WHEREAS the laws of the United States have been, for some time past, and now are opposed, and the execution thereof obstructed, in the States of South Carolina, Georgia, Alabama, Florida, Mississippi, Louisiana, and Texas, by combinations too powerful to be suppressed by the ordinary course of judicial proceedings, or by the powers vested in the marshals by law.
> Now, therefore, I, ABRAHAM LINCOLN, President of the United States, in virtue of the power in me vested by the Constitution and the laws, have thought fit to call forth, and hereby do call forth, the militia of the several States of the Union, to the aggregate number of seventy-five thousand, in order to suppress said combinations, and to cause the laws to be duly executed.

Just nine days shy of four years later, on April 6, 1865, General Robert E. Lee, commander of the Confederate Army of Virginia, surrendered to General Ulysses S. Grant. Gen. Joseph Johnston's surrender of remaining Confederate forces to Gen. William T. Sherman at Bennett Place near Durham, N.C., on April 26, 1865, marked all but the official end of rebellion against the Union. More than 620,000 Americans of both sides had been killed, captured, or wounded. Among them, President Lincoln, felled by John Wilkes Booth's bullet on April 15, 1865. For every three killed in battle, five died of disease. In addition, at least 50,000 noncombatants—citizens and enslaved alike—were killed. Muster rolls and censuses of the era being imprecise at best, the total number of casualties must be far larger. Impossible to include would be victims of bitter recrimination that plagued isolated valleys in the watershed for years after peace was officially proclaimed.

STORM OVER THE LAND

Perhaps the region's most rabid secessionist was Senator Thomas Lanier Clingman, for whom Clingman's Dome, the highest peak in the Great Smokies, is named. Representing Buncombe County as a Whig, Clingman was first elected to Congress in 1843, lost the seat in 1845, regained it two years later and, the following year, was appointed to fill the vacant seat of Asa Briggs in the US Senate. His support of slavery intensified, and he joined the Democrats in 1858; however, he faced a staunch challenge from Zebulon Baird Vance, who would become North Carolina's war-time governor. The grandson of one of the founders of Buncombe County, "Zeb," had grown up in the watershed. While assistant editor of the *Asheville Spectator*, he scathingly attacked Clingman as a "liar and a scoundrel" for his staunch anti-Union views. Vance was elected to the House of Representatives in 1858.[3] On the eve of the Civil War, he was avowedly pro-Southern and pro-slavery though more moderate than the vitriolic Clingman.

Less than a year later, on October 16, 1859, John Brown and his followers attacked the federal arsenal at Harper's Ferry, igniting fears of a slave rebellion throughout the South. The raid was characterized thusly in *The Asheville News*:

> We publish in another column full accounts of the affair at Harper's Ferry. From this, as *The daily South Carolinian* (a newspaper published in Columbia, S.C.) pertinently remarks, everyone will perceive that there is a studied and determined intention on the part of some of the insane elements of the North to make war directly on the South. If Black Republicans would be true to its proclaimed mission, this it must do or fail and dissolve. The conservative position of the South forces it to this; and now, when we see what the "irrepressible conflict" of Seward means—when we see the feast of blood to which it will invite the South—we have but to be ready with measures firm, quiet and decided, when the popular majority of the North shall evince their approbation of it. Such atrocities designs and bloody perpetrations in the streets of a southern town, cannot be without their effect upon the southern mind; and if they are to begin, we of the present generation are as well prepared for then as any that might succeed us.[4]

The election on November 6, 1860, of President Lincoln, vilified through-out the South as a "Black Republican" for his opposition to the expansion of slavery; South Carolina's secession from the Union six weeks later; and the fall of Fort Sumter on April 13, 1861, tripped a hammer that loosed four years of unbearable personal hardship throughout the French Broad watershed. No armies confronted each other as they did at Manassas or Shiloh or Gettysburg. No armies swept through East Tennessee or Western North Carolina like Sherman's across Georgia or Hunter's down the Shenandoah Valley. The wake of those grand battles and campaigns of pillage and plunder was filled with a wretched calm. When the fighting ended, all that remained were the corpses, the maimed, the smoking ruins, and that most powerful of human wills, the unconquerable urge to somehow survive tomorrow. For the most part, the war in the watershed was fought one family at a time. People living in coves and people of river towns battled fiercely, one violent spasmodic raid followed by another.

BROWNLOW AND THE BRIDGE BURNERS

Across the mountains at the mouth of the watershed in Knoxville railed "Parson" Brownlow, as vitriolic an opponent of secession as Clingman was in its favor. Editor of the *Knoxville Whig,* Tennessee's first post–Civil War governor, and then holding a seat in the US Senate during the administration of President Grant, William G. Brownlow earned his reputation for vituperation as a Meth-odist circuit rider. Preaching to pioneers in the headwaters of the Nolichucky beneath the Black Mountains, he pilloried Baptists for insisting on "dirty" rituals such as foot washing and immersion as the only route to salvation. Similarly, he gave no quarter to Presbyterians, castigating them for their belief that one had to be "elected" or predestined in order to get to heaven.[5]

Though he supported slavery, Brownlow was so ardently a Union man that after Tennessee seceded on June 8, 1861, he raised an American flag over his house. As Confederate troops rode by on their way to defend Virginia, he would stand in the street, shake his fist and taunt them. On one occasion, troopers who sought to snatch his flag were forced to quit by his daughter, Susan, who threatened them with a pistol.[6] That October, a parcel with half a yard of brown cloth was delivered to him at his printing office. Convinced it was infected with smallpox, he grasped it with tongs, took it outside, and burned it. In his paper, he inveighed against CSA soldiers as vagabonds, wharf-rats, and riff-raff

HARPER'S WEEKLY.

A JOURNAL OF CIVILIZATION

Vol. VI.—No. 274.]   NEW YORK, SATURDAY, MARCH 29, 1862.

A THRILLING SCENE IN EAST TENNESSEE—COLONEL FRY AND THE UNION MEN SWEARING BY THE FLAG.—[See Page 195.]

Competing sentiments flamed in East Tennessee with rallies around the Federal flag and shootings of Union sympathizers by Rebels. (TOP: *Harpers Weekly*, March 29, 1862, cover. Caption reads, "A Thrilling Scene in East Tennesse—Colonel Fry and the Union Men Swearing by the Flag.")

Charles B. Douglas shot by the Rebels while sitting at his window in Gay Street, Knoxville. (Page 273.)

(BOTTOM: *Sketches of the Rise and Decline of Secession*, W. G. Brownlow, George W. Childs, Philadelphia, 1862, p. 193 [page number Google Books]. Caption reads, "Charles B. Douglas shot by the Rebels while sitting at his window in Gay Street, Knoxville.")

who'd joined the army "to get rid of their wives and children." Frequently he fulminated that they'd tank up in taverns and "swarm around my printing office and dwelling house, howl like wolves, swear oaths that would blister the lips of a sailor, blackguard my family, and threaten to demolish my house, and even to hang me."

Union partisans hit upon the plan to burn railroad bridges over the Holston and other rivers in East Tennessee up which rebel supplies traveled from Georgia to Confederates campaigning Virginia. Brownlow espoused that cause, editorializing, "Let the railroad on which Union citizens of East Tennessee are conveyed to Montgomery in irons be eternally and hopelessly destroyed!"

Learning that his arrest by Confederate authorities was imminent, he lit out for refuge in the Smokies. "I had debts owing me in the adjoining counties of Blount, Sevier, Cocke, and Granger for advertising, I accordingly left home the first week of November, on horseback." Bridges were burned shortly after he departed and "this vile man (the Rev. Col. W. B Wood who preached in the Methodist Church on Sunday and the next day encouraged his men to do acts of violence.) had sent out scouts of cavalry after me in different directions with instructions, given them on the street, not to take me prisoner, but to shoot me down upon sight."[7] Brownlow and his Unionist companions hid beneath the high ridges of the Smokies and subsisted on a bear they killed along with food provided by friends in Wear's Cove. For a month, Brownlow negotiated his surrender and in December he was granted free passage through Union lines in Kentucky.[8]

WAR IN THE WATERSHED

The war in the mountains was intensely personal. In May 1861 after Ft. Sumter had been was surrendered to the Confederacy in April, citizens of Madison County gathered to vote on whether to elect delegates for the state's convention on joining South Carolina in seceding from the Union. Well lubricated with liquor, Sheriff Ransom P. Merrill led "husawing for Jeff Davis and the Confederacy." Near the polls, a voice boomed: "Hurrah for Washington and the Union." None too steady afoot, Sheriff Merrill pulled his heavy cap and ball pistol and waved it at the crowd. Spotting Superior Court Clerk Neely Tweed, a known Unionist with whom he'd argued vehemently, he leveled his gun. Tweed dodged out of the line of fire as Merrill pulled the trigger. The ball hit Tweed's son Elisha. Enraged, Tweed drew his own pistol and tracked Merrill to the rooming house where he'd sought refuge from the furious crowed. As Merrill bellowed from a second floor window: "Come up here all you Black Republicans and take a shot about me." Tweed burst through the front door, ran up the stairs, busted into the sheriff's room, raised his pistol, took aim, pulled the trigger, and shot Merrill dead.[9] So opened the Civil War in the North Carolina county that came to be known as "Bloody Madison."

On April 17, North Carolina's governor John W. Ellis called for raising 30,000 to serve the Confederacy. A month later in Haywood County, 19-year-old Milas A. Kirkpatrick enlisted in Company L, 16th North Carolina. Two years earlier Milas had received rudimentary training as a teacher. When the call came for volunteers, he and his two brothers, Lawson and Leander, answered it promptly as did so many young men of the mountains.[10] Kirkpatrick and other members of the company formed up and marched over the mountains to Morganton, the closest railhead.[11] They took the "cars" to Raleigh, there to drill until boarding the train to Richmond, Va., on the Fourth of July. Arriving on the fifth, they joined the rest of the regiment and were ordered to Staunton, Va., two days later. Writes Captain George H. Miles in *History of the 16th North Carolina Regiment in the Civil War:* "And it will never be forgotten-the first Rebel yell ever given by the Sixteenth-was when we became suddenly in full view of the Blue Ridge, the counterpart to the homes of twelve hundred patriotic men who had scarce ever been out of sight of the mountains, there rose an impromptu shout and yell that (often after repeated on bloody fields) seemed to rend the very heavens." "Marching out from Staunton on the Parkersburg Pike," Miles continues, "with a brass band in front, the streets lined with citizens, soldiers, and ladies, and our colors gaily floating in the breeze, we began to think we were soldiers."[12]

After skirmishing with Union troops in West Virginia and taking a circuitous route through Northern Virginia along the Potomac and down to Yorktown, the 16th returned to Richmond. On May 31, 1862, it was confronting Union forces at Seven Pines. Vastly outnumbered, Confederate forces were fleeing in retreat when Kirkpatrick was felled, shot through the thigh. As a boyhood friend, Lt. Tom Ferguson, struggled to carry him from the field, his left leg bled profusely and dangled uselessly. Deposited by the side of the road, he lay through the night without water, food, or any medical attention. Evacuated to a hospital the next morning, he was attended by a team of surgeons all set to amputate. But one of them objected, saying, "That boy doesn't want to lose his leg if it can possibly be saved, and I believe it can." He was right. The wound began healing, and after six weeks Kirkpatrick was returned to Fines Creek. There, as he recovered, he taught school for a year before returning to the 16th, now assigned to Thomas' Legion in western North Carolina. Hobbled by his wound and unable to serve in the line, he was made a commissary sergeant in charge of the wagon train scouring the countryside for provisions. After the war, he taught school for a while, farmed, raised a large family, and eschewed public office preferring to 'obtain personal pleasure out of reading good books.'"[13]

DODGING THE DRAFT

For many able bodied Southern men, the romantic rose of the Confederacy began to fade in early 1862. Alarmed by the fall-off in recruitment, CSA President Jefferson Davis submitted to his congress the Conscription Act requiring all white males between the ages of 18 and 35 to serve for three years or until released. Passage of the act on April 16, triggered the flight of hundreds of mountain men through Confederate lines to Union camps in Kentucky. A subsequent bill required the terms of service for 12-month enlistees—the first to volunteer a year earlier—to be lengthened by two years. Owners of 20 or more enslaved workers were exempted. Within enlisted ranks, consternation raged over this "rich man's war, poor man's fight."

The draft was the first in American history. Among those conspiring to dodge it was 19-year-old Will A. McTeer of Ellejoy, Tenn., a hamlet at the base of the rugged knobs on the Sevier County line. In his memoir *Among Loyal Mountaineers: Reminiscences of an East Tennessee Unionists,* he reports that after a CSA soldier had been ambushed, shot, and wounded and another killed, his father was arrested and hauled off to prison. Confederates seized every squirrel rifle and shotgun they could find. McTeer had secreted away a brass-barreled, smooth bore horse pistol his grandad had carried in the War of 1812. Armed with it and a huge knife sharpened on both edges more suitable for butchering hogs than self-defense, he and three of his friends departed on July 23 for Union lines beyond Cumberland Gap.

Two harrowing weeks later, having crossed ridge after ridge as they worked their way northward and avoided rebel patrols, they came upon a group of Federal soldiers and what appeared to be a Confederate officer sitting by a spring. The officer was actually a lieutenant in the 6th Tennessee US Infantry who'd been spying on enemy movements.[14] Rising from private to major, McTeer was discharged from the 3rd Tennessee Cavalry on August 3, 1865, practiced law, and served in Tennessee's General Assembly from 1881 to 1882.

In many families kinship and patriotism went hand in hand. In others the opposite was true. Among Dolly Parton's forbearers who escaped the Conscription Act to fight for the Union were Albert Hurston Parton, 2nd Tennessee Cavalry; Benjamin Crissenberry Parton, 9th Tennessee Cavalry; Elisha Wilburn Parton, 11th Tennessee Cavalry, captured and died in the infamous Confederate prison at Andersonville, Ga.; Martin Franklin Parton, 11th Tennessee Cavalry, and Moses F. Parton, 2nd Tennessee Cavalry, captured January 26, 1863. Other of her kin joined Confederate forces including Alexander R. Parton, 39th Tennessee Mounted Infantry, killed in action, Loudon, Tenn., 1862, and John Benjamin Parton, "The Lookout Battery," demobilized, Meriden, Miss. May, 1865.[15] The Partons were one of thousands of families divided by war.

MAKE DO, DO WITHOUT

Hardscrabble farms in mountain coves never produced as bountifully as rich bottom lands along the main stems of rivers in the watershed. Even so, the Confederacy levied a ten percent in-kind tax per year on crops of corn, oats, wheat, and other grains; fodder for livestock, sugar and molasses rendered from sorghum or cane; wool; meat from hogs and beeves; and the estimated value of horses and mules. Exempt were heads of households worth less than $500 (about $13,000 today), wounded veterans and others. All businesses paid annual taxes as well including circuses, $10 per performance; jugglers, $50; and pool halls, $40 per table. Farmers were responsible for delivering their in-kind payments to the nearest railhead, which in the upper watershed meant a rugged wagon journey of several days over the Blue Ridge and down into Morganton. As well, farmers who paid taxes were required to keep detailed records of how much they paid for seed and grain. Not taxed for their own use were 200 bushels of corn, 50 bushels of Irish potatoes, and 250 pounds of pork.[16]

Mountaineers were desperate for salt, so essential in preserving meat and pickling vegetables. The Confederacy's primary source was Saltville, a hamlet at the head of the North Fork of the Holston River in southwest Virginia more than 125 miles away. Roughly 325 million years ago, about the time that the French Broad River may have begun to be formed, shallow seas were depositing their salts in thin shales and siltstones. Folding that produced the ridges and valleys of East Tennessee brought them close to the surface. Miners dug wells that collected briny ground water that was boiled down into salt. So scarce did salt become, that it was considered "white gold." The Confederacy also commandeered iron ore. Replacements for broken plows and other farm implements, tools, and such essentials as nails were almost impossible to secure.

But the greatest shortage in the mountains was labor. The wealthy who owned 20 enslaved workers or who could hire a substitute or pay $300, were exempt from Confederate conscription. To till their fields and tend their live-stock, many highland farmers had relied on laborers who owned no land. They were mostly swept up in the draft or fled north to fight for the Union. Left at home were women who, to survive, had to do all that their male kinfolk had done to provide sustenance and shelter plus their traditional roles of mother and housekeeper. Further they were victims of roving bands of deserters and bushwhackers. And all the more intensely felt were the vagaries of a hard winter or summer drought. Still more than a few women, left alone to manage farm, home, and family, grew more crops and livestock than when their menfolk had been in charge.[17]

Hardships for women depended greatly on their social station. In the be-ginning many in towns championed sending off their gallant men in defense of their country. They provided picnics for drilling militias, sewed banners and flags to wave them onward to "victory or death," and spread malicious gossip indicting others whose menfolk chose not to don Confederate grey or far worse, had snuck off bound for Union lines. And scores of women with their children and personal enslaved nannies fled family plantations in South Carolina's lowlands and North Carolina east of the Blue Ridge, seeking refuge from the war with friends in Asheville, Hendersonville, and Flat Rock with whom they'd spent peaceful summers long passed.[18]

OH, FREEDOM

In 1860, enslaved workers and free Blacks constituted about 16 percent of the population of Buncombe County, nearly three times more than the percentage of African-Americans residing in the county today. Henderson County then had about 14 percent and Madison, 4 percent. Downstream in the watershed, Tennessee counties averaged around 7 percent.[19] The reason for Bumcombe's and Henderson's high population of Black enslaved men and women and freemen is tied to the fact that their hills and valleys carried more large tracts of arable land which attracted affluent families from plantation country south and east of the Blue Ridge. Yet farmland was not suitable for row crops like cotton and tobacco which demanded intense hand-labor. While some slaves were employed as field hands, many more worked as carpenters, blacksmiths, wheelwrights, masons, and the like. Scores served as personal servants and staffed inns along the turnpike. And at the height of the summer's social season, hotels in Asheville, Hendersonville, and Flat Rock hosted enslaved men and women accompanying their masters.[20]

Life for enslaved people in the watershed varied dramatically. Those working in the house and those laboring in trades may have been somewhat better treated than field hands on large lowland plantations. But enslaved persons on small Appalachian plantations were more likely to suffer physical abuse for the tiniest infractions.[21]

Passage of the Emancipation Proclamation on January 1, 1863, freed slaves in states then in rebellion. By that time, however, much of Tennessee was under Federal control and no longer considered by Washington to be in active rebellion. By later that year, the Union had become increasingly pressed for recruits. In the winter of 1863, Gen. Grant visited Knoxville to inspect its defenses, and his chief artilleryman, Gen. Davis Tillson, asked permission to raise a regiment of "colored" soldiers. His request was granted giving birth to the 1st Regiment US Colored Heavy Artillery which was mustered into service on February 20, 1864. Four days later, Congress passed an act promising that enslaved persons who enlisted would earn their freedom and their owners would receive $100 each for those who signed up.[22] Like a fresh breeze from the north word spread through the watershed. By October, more than 1,700 were serving in Union blue, but not manning canons.[23] Instead they constructed fortifications and and hauled supplies.

Because possession of terrain in East Tennessee seesawed back and forth between Union and Confederate forces, enslaved persons could cross into US territory with much more ease than those in western North Carolina. Not only did these African Americans have the mountains to contend with but bands of Confederate Home Guard roamed the countryside ever on the look-out for fugitive slaves. So too were troops of Thomas' Legion, assigned to guard high gaps in the Blue Ridge against Union raiders. Yet enslaved men and women in the area were more than likely to help Union soldiers escaping from Confederate prisons and CSA deserters. Many escaped POWs like Albert Richardson and his colleague Junius Henri Browne, who were captured while reporting for Horace Greely's *New-York Tribune,* expressed enduring gratitude to "Black

Little Will, a White leader of the Cherokee, organized Thomas' Legion of 400 tribesmen and 800 highlanders to defend the mountains from Union invaders. (Thomaslegion.net.)

highlanders." Of them he wrote, "Every black face was a friendly face and so far as fidelity was concerned we felt just as safe among the negroes as if in our Northern homes. Male and female, old or young, intelligent or simple we were fully assured that they would never betray us."[24]

CHEROKEE CONFEDERATES

Born in 1805 after his father had died, William Holland Thomas grew up in Cherokee country and went on to become their only White chief. Ever precocious, at 13, he took on the job of managing a store on Soco Creek owned by Felix Walker who in 1820 achieved infamy in Congress for his speech of pure "bunkum." Thomas was mentored by Walker, and from his customers learned to speak Cherokee fluently. Little Will, as he was known, impressed Chief Yonaguska, who adopted him. Thomas opened his own store in Quallatown in 1822, and over the next decade, matured as a business man, politician, and one well versed in the law. In 1831, the Cherokee sent him to Washington to represent the tribe. Through the years of the Trail of Tears, he was successful in securing funds with which to purchase the lands at the foothills of the Smokies that ultimately became home of the Eastern Band of the Cherokee Indians. And he was successful in obtaining from North Carolina and the United States commitments that they would never be removed from this, their homeland, all the while growing his business interests to include sawmills, grist mills, and tanneries.[25]

By 1860 he owned more than 100,000 acres and about 50 slaves.[26] Serving as an influential member of North Carolina's Senate from 1848 to 1861, he championed building highways and railroads to serve mountain communities. Always with an eye to the future, Thomas believed that southwestern North Carolina being essentially the geographic center of the Confederacy, would become its capital when planned railroad lines were completed. In 1862, he was commissioned a colonel in the CSA and raised a regiment numbering about 1,200 highlanders including about 400 Cherokee. Thomas' Legion was active on both sides of the Smokies, building defenses from the gaps in the Great Smokies to Paint Rock and interdicting Union forays. As the war waned, the condition of Cherokee families became increasingly desperate. Some were reduced to eating roots and leaves. Thomas, from his own dwindling funds, bought meal and flour which fed hundreds.

THE PRICE OF SALT

Five miles east of Hot Springs, the highway to Weaverville crosses the Laurel River. Turn north on Route 208 and follow it to Route 212. Turn right and follow the creek up into one Madison County's loveliest and most bucolic coves. Hard it is to imagine the utter terror that permeated this tranquil valley—Shelton Laurel—in January 1863. So isolated it was from the mainstream of pro-Confederacy sentiment flooding along the Buncombe Turnpike, that it became a haven for Union sympathizers. By then, the war in Tennessee had turned against the Confederacy. Deserters were slipping over gaps into the Blue Ridge into the valley.

Well aware of the cove's politics, Confederate quartermasters conspired to starve its residents into submission. Salt, the most precious of commodities, was withheld and stocked piled in the county seat of Marshall. Left with no option but to starve or submit, menfolk from Shelton Laurel raided Confederate stores and made off with bushels of salt along with shoes, clothes, and any other goods they could carry. So incensed were they at the CSA that they raided the fine house of Confederate Colonel Lawrence Allen and stripped the blankets from the beds where his three young children lay sick with fever. Two soon died.

Allen commanded the 64th North Carolina Regiment, comprised mainly of highlanders from Madison and nearby North Carolina and Tennessee counties who had enlisted to avoid conscription. Their mission was to eradicate rogue bands of brigands, just like the ones who had ransacked his home. Their duty was odious, often pitting soldiers against relatives and former friends. His deputy was Lt. Col. James Keith, also his cousin. At the time, the regiment was split; Keith led 200 and Allen, 300. Infuriated by the raid on Marshall, they sought and received orders from the Confederate commander in East Tennessee to bring perpetrators to justice.

Arriving in Shelton Laurel, Keith rounded up women of the valley and ordered them to reveal the raiders' names and whereabouts. The women refused and were brutally tortured. Ultimately, his soldiers captured 15 men and boys, whom they assumed had taken part in the raid. Informing them that they were being taken to Knoxville for trial, Keith marched them out of the valley. Once beyond sight of their neighbors, he ordered them to kneel by the side of the road and shot them. Among those killed was 12-year-old David Shelton, who was first forced to watch his father and brother die. Though Governor Vance was outraged and ordered a full investigation of this "horror disgraceful to civilization," Keith was court-martialed, allowed to resign his commission, and faced no further punishment.[27]

LAST BASTION IN THE MOUNTAINS

So remote from major battlefields, the upper French Broad watershed was deemed of little importance to Union armies. It yielded scant exports of grain, livestock, or iron or copper smelted from local ores. At first, the establishment of an armory in Asheville to produce rifles of the English Enfield pattern favored by Southern armies seemed promising for Confederates. But poor management, a shortage of skilled gunsmiths and machinery, inconsistent supplies of raw materials, and threat of Union seizure when Gen. Ambrose Burnside captured Knoxville in late 1863 doomed the enterprise.[28] Yet Asheville's very isolation and its geographic centrality held promise that it would serve as the last bastion of the Confederacy should its armies be swept from the Piedmont.

By early 1865, that very fear was becoming reality. Gen. William T. Sherman was sweeping northward from coastal Georgia into South Carolina and little

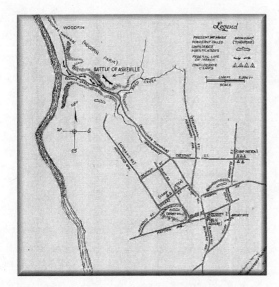

Once aspiring to be the capital of the Confederacy because of its central location, Asheville was spared from Federal raids until April 6, 1865, when a small Union force attacked and withdrew fearing it was outnumbered by CSA forces. (*Asheville Citizen-Times,* July 17, 1960.)

would prevent him from continuing through North Carolina to link up with Grant in Virginia. East Tennessee was firmly in Federal hands, and Union forces under Gen. George W. Stoneman were certain to advance eastward via gaps in the Blue Ridge. At that time, Asheville little resembled the town it would become within a decade after the end of the conflict. According to Sondley, "Its few streets were narrow, ungraded wagon roads . . . without sidewalks." Not only had the railroad failed to reach the town, but it lacked the telegraph as well.[29]

Made up of Union volunteers from East Tennessee and Western North Carolina, and commanded by Lt. Col. George W. Kirk, the 3rd North Carolina Mounted Infantry's attack on Waynesville in February 1865, was the precursor of Union plans to occupy Asheville and the upper French Broad. Kirk was born in Greeneville and served briefly in the Confederate Army. He knew the mountains, and in 1862 switched sides. Earlier in the summer of 1864, he had led a series of devastating raids from Morristown to Morganton, where he captured Camp Vance and destroyed the railroad. Departing Newport with 600 troopers, he crossed Mt. Sterling Gap, rode through Cataloochee Cove, and on February 4 attacked Waynesville. There he freed Unionist prisoners, burned the jail, and seized every horse he could. When returning to Tennessee via Soco Gap, he survived a brief but fierce firefight with members of Thomas' Legion.[30]

Long protected by the mountains from the full thrust of a Union offensive, the upper watershed's relative sanctuary withered with the onslaught of Gen. George Stoneman's cavalry from East Tennessee. His orders were to subdue that part of the remaining Confederacy not reached by Sherman's drive northward through North Carolina. He was to destroy supplies and equipment but not fight battles. Reinforced by Kirk in March, Stoneman reached Boone on the 28th and continued down the eastern flank of the Blue Ridge, attacking Lenoir, Wilkesboro, Elkin, Salem, Salisbury, and Statesville before turning west and hitting Morganton and Marion. From Marion, he bent south to Rutherfordton and then headed westward again through Howard's Gap before passing through Hendersonville on April 23 and following the turnpike to Asheville.

By then the Civil War was all but over. Lee had surrendered to Grant at Appomattox Courthouse on April 6. Sherman captured Raleigh a week later and was pushing the Gen. Joseph Johnston's remaining Confederate forces northwest toward Durham. Aware of the armistice in Virginia, Johnston and Sherman met under white flags on April 17 at Bennett Place outside of Durham and began to negotiate terms. Those proposed by Sherman and accepted by Johnston re-established state governments and certain civil rights and rearmed state arsenals. The terms were offered in accord with Lincoln's urge to "let 'em up easy." But Lincoln had been assassinated three days earlier, and the cabinet under President Andrew Johnson refused to accept them and insisted on military, not political, surrender. Johnston signed the new terms on April 26.

As Grant and Lee were meeting, 900 Ohioans under Isaac Kirby were marching up the French Broad. They spent the night of April 3 at Warm Springs. On April 5, they stole all the horses on Mrs. H. E. Sondley's farm, including a little Shetland pony belonging to her son, Foster. The pony could not keep pace and was shot. Foster went on to become a prominent Asheville attorney best known for his history *Asheville and Buncombe County*, published in 1922.

Once a tailor in Greeneville, president Andrew Johnson characterized Asheville as a "damned secessionist hole in the mountains."[31] It was the most heavily fortified town in western North Carolina. Heavy artillery was located on Battery Hill, now the site the Grove Arcade, the Basilica of St. Lawrence, and the Harrah's Cherokee Center. Later on the 5th, Kirby's force met the few remaining Confederates and members of the Home Guard occupying earthworks on the edge of what would become the campus of University of North Carolina–Asheville. The fight was brief and "as close to bloodless as a five-hour firefight can get."[32] Yet Kirby, thinking he had encountered a reinforced CSA unit, withdrew in the night.

Three weeks later and after Johnston had surrendered Confederate armies in North Carolina, Union troops were granted safe passage and allowed to free scores of Union sympathizers held in Asheville's prison. However, their commander, Gen. Alvan Gillem, left them, early departing for Tennessee to attend the state's first postwar legislative session. Absent leadership, Union soldiers returned to the town, pillaged it, and left a bitter taste of resentment that would fester for decades.[33] Eighty years later, Carl Sandburg, who won the Pulitzer prize for his four-volume biography *Abraham Lincoln: The War Years* and whom some scholars view as a pacifist, would move into Connemara, Confederal Treasury Secretary Christopher Menninger's summer retreat at Flat Rock, which survived the war unscathed. Sandburg's home is now a National Historic Site.

EIGHT

The Weed, the Doctor, and the Iron Horse

The war left the watershed much as it found: a rugged land of forests and mountains and streams, of coves and floodplains, of Indians and immigrants, of hamlets and towns, of futures bounded only by imagination and force of will. The landscape was spared grand and devastating military campaigns to be sure. But in their stead stood the blackened shell of a farm house here, a barn there, and down the road, a store. Horses, too old or lame to be requisitioned, and scrawny milk cows strayed aimlessly from their pastures bound now only by broken fences. Missing were menfolk, gone to soldier South and North, felled by battle or disease. Those who came back, often hiking hundreds of miles home, were oh so weary.

When they returned, they learned what womenfolk had come to know far too well. Salt was all but impossible to find. So was fuel for coal oil lamps. Stores carried no cloth, thread, or even sewing needles. Coffee was a distant memory. For worn cooking knives, forks, and spoons, there were no replacements let alone metal for mending pots, hoes, shovels, or plows. Hard to come by does not begin to describe the dearth of seed available for spring planting. Nowhere was the old adage *make do, do without* more apt. Had stores been stocked to bulging, goods could not have been purchased, for there was no hard cash. Confederate money was useless, and federal paper dollars, fondly known as shinplasters, were nearly so. About the only coins that retained any value were those few Bechtler gold dollars from his Rutherfordton mint remaining in circulation.

Commerce, such as it was, occurred the old fashioned way—through barter, trading a dozen eggs for a pound of butter, a gallon of brandy for a few bushels of feed.

WAR'S BITTER AFTERTASTE

If this were all women had to contend with, life would have been more than hard enough. While always keeping a hopeful eye on the road for returning husbands, fathers, and sons, their watch was fearful as well. The mountains were rife with renegade bands of brigands bent on plundering any bit of prosperity they came across and doing worse, much, much worse. On high simmer just below the surface of many coves was a cauldron of molten hatred and festering resentment over wrongs, real or perceived; examples are legion, but none so compelling as the case of Elisha Tweed.

Back in 1861 in Marshall, his father, Neely, killed Sheriff Ransom Merrill after the sheriff, well-fortified by countless swigs from a jug, took a pot shot at him, missed, but severely wounded his son, Elisha. The elder Tweed fled, joined the Union army, and died of fever while campaigning at Cumberland Gap a year later. When well enough, Elisha went north as well. Not long after the end of the war, he and a number of other Union soldiers, newly returned to Madison County, were arrested by disgruntled secessionist authorities and charged with Merrill's murder. Their plight was by no means unusual. Neighbor W. W. Rollins had served as a major in the Third US North Carolina Mounted Infantry. He led a troop during Stoneman's raid and, upon returning to his family, was charged with stealing horses. Had not Federal authorities interceded, he likely would have been found guilty. The same happened to some of his men when they came back to pick up their lives in Yancey County. Charges against Elisha were finally dropped in February 1868.[1]

ROCKY ROAD TO FREEDOM

Though Reconstruction was the law of the reunited country, pro-slavery passions remained very high, with tragic consequences for African Americans and not all at the hands of white residents of the watershed. At the tail end of the Union campaign to secure western North Carolina in April, 1865, the First U.S. Colored Heavy Artillery brought up the rear of the Federal column approaching Asheville. Their commander, Gen. Davis Tillson, had recruited the regiment in Knoxville in early 1864. Ten miles north of town, at Flat Creek, four soldiers—Alfred Catlett, Alexander Caldwell, Charles Turner, and Jackson Washington—left the column for reasons only they knew. They were apprehended by the Garrisons on their farm and, were charged with raping a white girl and assaulting her elderly aunt and uncle. On whether they were court martialed, the record is unclear. A West Pointer and a stickler for discipline, Gen. Tillson's opinion on the matter is not: "The negroes," he reported on May 8, "committed a brutal rape on the person of a young white woman, after nearly killing her uncle and aunt, two very old people, who tried to prevent the outrage. I am much gratified that they have been found guilty and shot (by a Union squad)."[2] Though he had raised a regiment of freedmen, Gen. Tillson was not their friend. Later that year in Memphis, he let it be known that freedmen who came into the city were "worthless vagrants" and allowed his agents to intercept black children carrying school books and tell them they should be picking cotton.[3]

Just as the Buncombe Turnpike had been the principal conduit for prosperity before the war, it became a main road to freedom for former slaves. George Robertson, still a youngster when the war ended, recalled seeing "hundreds and hundreds" pass "in an almost interminable procession" through Asheville, heading north down the French Broad to East Tennessee. They knew that the land across the mountains had been in Union hands far longer than the Carolinas, and they prayed that there they would finally be free. Among those joining the procession toward Greeneville was the Robertson's beloved cook, Aunt Becky. So powerful seemed her affection for the family and they for her that George was always convinced that she had to have been fooled into believing she could never be free as long as she kept working for her former masters.[4]

Though spasmed by occasional violence, life for African Americans in the lower French Broad watershed in East Tennessee was far improved over that of their brothers and sisters upstream. An acute shortage of labor opened opportunities for entrepreneurial craftsmen. One such was Isaac Dockery. Born in Jones Cove in 1832, at the start of the war he moved to Sevierville to clerk at a business in the home of Henry M. Thomas, who opposed secession. One day, Dockery was seized by Confederate raiders. Refusing to reveal where Thomas's son, a Union colonel was hiding, he was dragged through the streets. After the war, he opened a brick kiln near Middle Creek. His bricks were prized for their quality and used in the construction of many of Sevierville's historic buildings, including its iconic courthouse. He mentored his sons and grandsons, who also became highly sought after masons. Among his peers were a number of outstanding carpenters and a maker of fine furniture.[5]

'SHINE AND T'BACCY

Those who weathered the postwar years, no matter what race or politics or station in life, came to rely on the only enduring elements that defined their world, the precipitation, streams, and rivers that gave their land its life. The terrain was ideally suited for making whiskey and growing tobacco, both of which would become dominant sources of revenue for cash-strapped mountaineers. Though the federal government had levied taxes on distilled spirits periodically since 1791, highlanders paid it little heed, believing whiskey making was their God-given right. In 1862, whiskey and brandy were taxed at 20¢ per gallon, but by 1865, the levy had risen to $1.50 and reached $2.00 in 1866. Though reduced to 50¢ by Congress in 1868, by then the damage was done.

With emancipation and reconstruction came the despised Bureau of Refugees, Freedmen, and Abandoned Lands, known simply as the Freedmen's Bureau. Established by Congress in March 1865, with the war all but over, this agency of the War Department operated only in the South. It was charged with responsibility to ensure that freed slaves received full pay for their work and had access to education and health care. Most of its agents were former Union army officers. Almost without exception, they ran headlong into bitter resistance from affluent conservatives committed to reestablishing the old prewar social order.

Vastly complicating the task of Freedmen's Bureau was its perceived role in enforcing federal taxes on distilled spirits. Mountaineers associated them with hated Internal Revenue Service agents.[6] Mountaineers throughout the watershed were infuriated at this most egregious intrusion of Federal government. To destroy stills, revenuers relied on Union soldiers. They were considered to be enforcing the yoke of Yankee occupation and compliance, at gunpoint, with civil and labor rights for African Americans. Their raids on moonshiners stoked fires that distilled the sour mash of Rebel resentment into a potent liquor of violent resistance the aftertaste of which festers still today.

Along with whiskey, tobacco was a mainstay of daily life. First grown by Cherokee and other Indians, tobacco had served as an indigenous currency and

Within a decade of the Civil War, mountain farmers turned from corn to t'baccy and moonshine as their cash crops. (Great Smoky Mountains National Park Archives.)

export since Europeans came ashore at Chesapeake Bay. Early growers saved and planted the best seeds from previous years' crops, resulting in the development of robust breeds well suited to soils and climate of the watershed. Most American tobacco had been flue-cured, hung to dry in a small, tightly chinked log building over a fire, producing a dark, savory leaf, idea for chewing. Tobacco had been grown in the French Broad watershed since the 1780s.[7] About 1839, in one Caswell County, N.C., curing shed, the fire died and was rekindled with blazing hot charcoal. The temperature soared, producing leaves of lighter color and milder taste known as "bright leaf." But it was not until the development of light and flavorful burley in southwest Ohio in 1864 that farming for America's most popular weed caught fire. Combining "bright" tobacco with an equal portion of burley produced the famed *Half and Half* pipe tobacco.

Prior to the Civil War, corn was the region's cash crop. Yeoman farmers knew they could sell their grain to owners of stock stands who needed it to feed drove after drove of cattle that coursed down the turnpike. As railroads pushed through the Tennessee Valley into Georgia, they siphoned the stream of livestock reared west of the Blue Ridge away from the Buncombe Turnpike. Demand for corn, even distilled into whiskey, began to decline. In 1867, the East Tennessee, Virginia, and Georgia's tracks reached the hamlet of Wolf Creek,

Tenn., just 5 miles downriver from Paint Rock. Two years later, the Western North Carolina Railroad reached Old Fort. By then, the Buncombe Turnpike was much improved. Little more than two or three days' travel was needed to haul wagonloads of tobacco from most locales in the French Broad's upper watershed to one railhead or the other.

Planting burley seed when new leaves on willow trees were the size of squirrels' ears, moving tender new plants from bed to field, cutting suckers, topping flowers, chopping mature stalks, skewering them on stakes, hanging in the barn, stripping leaves and laying them carefully in baskets woven of wooden lattice demanded hand labor by entire families—from kids to grandparents. By the first half of the 1900s, tobacco dominated agriculture in the watershed. Filled baskets were hauled to low grey warehouses of corrugated metal that lined the French Broad at Asheville and Newport. Come November, buyers roamed aisles of tobacco warehouses, fingering leaves to an auctioneer's iconically indecipherable singsong chant made famous by a Lucky Strike cigarette ad of the 1950s ending "*soooldddd* American!" Whether Christmas was merry or bleak depended on his call, which often determined well more than half of a yeoman farm family's income for the year.

SALUBRIOUS SWITZERLAND OF AMERICA

Opulence of the Gilded Age—that period of unparalleled economic growth that followed the Civil War—rode into the watershed on carriages carrying wealthy tourists from southern plantations and industry emerging along railroads in North Carolina's Piedmont and East Tennessee. The term was coined by Mark Twain and Charles Dudley Warner in the title of their little-known novel *The Gilded Age: A Tale of Today*, which probed the irony of deep social problems veneered with glossy gold leaf.[8] Throughout the watershed, resorts began to proliferate. Most featured long verandas and manicured grounds, where guests could stroll, take in the lush scenery, and breathe pure mountain air. Like famed spas in the foothills of the Alps, others capitalized on mineral springs redolent with fetid, allegedly palliative sulfurous vapors.

As tobacco was becoming the watershed's dominant cash crop—only to be found a century later to be a primary cause of fatal respiratory illnesses—the mountains of North Carolina and Tennessee were being touted as the most healthful climate for curing pulmonary disease. About the region in 1871, H. P. Gatchell, MD, authored an extensive and laudatory treatise *Western North*

Carolina: Its Agricultural Resources, Mineral Wealth, Climate, Salubrity and Scenery. He was a respected professor of physiology and principles of medicine at Chicago's Hanneman College and "Late editor of the Department of Climatology and Hygiene in the U.S. Medical and Surgical Journal."

That year, he and his son, E. A., also a doctor, opened one of America's first sanitariums for tuberculosis patients in Asheville's Kenilworth section. It folded after two years. A dozen years later in 1885, his son opened a new sanitarium, the "Villa," a posh resort on the flanks of Battery Park in Asheville. To promote it, he produced a heavily bowdlerized version of his father's title, exclaiming:

> The mountain air is pure and bracing, there is a large proportion of sun-shiny days when out-door exercise—so important for those who suffer from lung disease—can be indulged in.
>
> It is rare to find those who come here in search of health fail of prompt and decided benefit. And those cases especially which come in the earlier stages can be assured of complete and permanent recovery.

Of those who should take their cures in Asheville, he continued:

> All of those who are victims of any sort of pulmonary disease, and particularly incipient phthisis. And in addition, those suffering from chronic bronchitis, catarrh, and asthma will find relief.
>
> Another class of invalids who will receive great benefit from a residence in this climate consists of those who are suffering from nervous debility, brain fag, or exhaustion from too close application to business. The business man of New York, Cincinnati, or elsewhere who desires to recuperate and gain needed rest will find all the conditions necessary for complete recovery.

Promoting his sanitarium, the younger Gatchell claimed that "the dryness of the climate by day and the cool nights"—the same promoting recovery from disease—destined the region "to become the chief section of the United States for the finer and fancier qualities" of tobacco. Further, he lauded a Mr. Shelton, who won a silver medal at the Vienna Exposition for his *Speckled Trout* brand. And before waxing eloquent about Asheville's healthful clime, the booklet opened with a full page ad advising: "Lovers of the Weed, who enjoy a really good smoke, should always ask for Holmes' *Pisgah*, Holmes' *Golden Leaf*, Holmes' *Land of the Sky*.[9]

Writers on both sides of the mountains vied in proclaiming that theirs was the "Switzerland of America."[10] Perhaps the sobriquet was rooted as much in the watershed's isolated independence as it was in the growing number of inns catering to tourists availing themselves of its purportedly salubrious environment. The warm springs at the North Carolina–Tennessee border had been attracting folks seeking therapeutic baths since 1779. It was the first of scores of health resorts proliferating throughout the watershed where tourists came to "take the waters."

Water pumped from thousands of wells throughout the region tastes—sometimes not so faintly—of rotten eggs. Hydrogen sulfide is the culprit, formed when rainwater percolates down as far as a mile through folded and faulted rocks and wells up again in springs. Mineral springs are fairly common throughout the Blue Ridge and their foothills. Indians and European settlers valued them for properties they deemed healthful. This was the era when mothers believed in the restorative promise of spring tonics, that scarcely palatable concoction of sulphur and molasses. So popular was drinking and bathing in mineral waters in the early 1800s that farmers whose land contained such springs often took in lodgers.

Among the first inns in the lower watershed in East Tennessee to offer its guests restorative waters was Henderson Springs in today's Pigeon Forge. By 1830, its waters were attracting folks who "brought buckets and filled them with this 'special' water that poured from an old gun barrel spout. It was said to be better than 'doctorin' medicine." The Henderson Springs Resort would continue under the ownership of successive generations as a popular health resort until 1930 when the Depression forced its closure.[11]

Completion of the Buncombe Turnpike in 1827 coincided with the discovery of a similar sulphur spring by Reuben Deaver and Sam, an enslaved worker, just west of the river at Asheville. Seven years later, tourist travel up the turnpike from South Carolina burgeoned, and Deaver opened the fledgling city's first health resort. Gallery porches offered relaxing views of Mt. Pisgah and surrounding mountains. Guests enjoyed dances in a grand ballroom as well as billiards, shuffle board, and bowling. Four hundred yards down the hill, they could comfort themselves with a soak in the spring. Under mysterious circumstances, perhaps sparked by animosity between Deaver and his son, the hotel burned on the eve of the Civil War. Rebuilt in 1887, it burned again in 1892. The site was next occupied for a time by the Malvern Hills Country Club, with its nine-hole course, one of the first in the mountains. All that remains today is a remnant of the club's concrete pavilion that shelters the now-dry spring.[12]

At the dawn of the Gilded Age, nothing seemed impossible to owners of the Mountain Lily who planned a steamboat line down the French Broad from Horse Shoe to Asheville with Knoxville as their ultimate goal. (Baker-Barber Collection, Community Foundation of Henderson County, Henderson County Library.)

THIS OL' RIVERBOAT

Owners of health resorts, farmers of tobacco and livestock, tanners, millers, loggers, and just about everybody else waited impatiently for the arrival of the railroad. By 1867, the East Tennessee, Virginia, and Georgia line had reached Buffalo Rock about five miles upstream from Newport. A year later, the Western North Carolina Railroad chuffed into Old Fort at the base of Swannanoa Gap. The Asheville and Spartanburg was stalled about 50 miles southeast of Flat Rock as surveying engineers contemplated the route which needed to climb 1,000 feet before reaching Saluda and become the steepest standard gauge railroad grade in America.

No one was more eager for the coming of the iron horse than Sidney Vance Pickens. To him and other affluent businessmen, nothing seemed impossible with the dawn of the Gilded Age. In that era, sternwheelers carried the bulk of the nation's freight on America's rivers. Packet boats, like the ones at the root of Vanderbilt wealth, plied coastal sounds and tidal rivers. Early in the

1870s, Pickens resurrected a prewar scheme to establish steamboat service on the French Broad from Brevard to his native Asheville.

The idea was not as preposterous as it seems today. Over the proposed 35-mile route, the river twists gently through a broad flat floodplain. Pickens's relative and the former governor's brother, Representative Robert B. Vance, shepherded a bill through Congress in 1874 that provided $10,000 to survey that section of the river for navigation by small steamboats drawing no more than 30 inches of water. Completing his initial report a year later, the Corps of Engineers's R. C. McCalla, estimated the cost would be $29,687.50 (about $670,000 in 2018). He wondered, though, why the route was to stop at the Henderson County/ Buncombe County line 16 miles upstream from Asheville.

Congressman Vance evidently concurred with McCalla's conjecture and authorized him to complete his survey all the way to the mouth of the river at Knoxville. In 1876, the engineer reported that the middle section of the river through the gorge from Asheville to where the Nolichucky enters below Newport would require several dams and 150 locks, each with lifts of six feet. In total, 900 feet in elevation needed to be negotiated. Deemed far too expensive, Congress funded work only on the Brevard-Asheville section. In 1877, the Corps began removing snags and building wing dams to constrict and raise the water level in the channel. The work was completed in 1881 at a cost of $37,780.22 (about $950,000 today) with only $9.08 remaining in the appropriation.

That year, Pickens, evidently enthused by this progress, obtained a new corporate charter from the state legislature for the French Broad Steamboat Company to operate on the upper section. Authorizing the sale of $25,000 of stock, the act made it illegal for anyone to fell trees into or otherwise obstruct the flow of the river. Pickens recruited John L. Porter, the Confederacy's primary architect of ironclads including the *Merrimack*, to design the *Mountain Lily*. A twin side wheeler 90 feet long and 20 feet wide, fully loaded it was to draw no more than 18 inches, quite suitable for the planned 30-inch depth of the channel at low water.

Near Horse Shoe, the location where the River Party wanted to locate the town of Hendersonville in 1837, the *Mountain Lily* was launched in August 1881. Its initial voyage up stream was a trial. Due to low water, the *Lily* had to be hauled up shoals and rapids with double pulleys and rope. Though funds had been appropriated by counties, bridges along the route had not been raised. Even with its stack lowered, the boat could not clear several. Thus, aside from

African American convicts, many arrested for petty crimes in eastern
North Carolina, carved the route with pick, shovel, and blasting powder
through Swannanoa Gap bringing the WNCR to Asheville in 1880.
(North Carolina Room, Pack Memorial Library, Asheville.)

a few short excursions, the *Lily* carried no passengers or freight, earned no
money, and was washed aground at Kings Bridge in the flood of 1885.[13]

GETTING UP STEAM

Pickens no doubt never envisioned the *Mountain Lily* making it all the way
down the river to Knoxville. His intention was to connect Brevard and Hendersonville to the railhead at Asheville. He was certain that before long railroads
would follow the route of the Buncombe Turnpike. Hadn't a steam engine—
appropriately named *Old Buncombe*—pulled a string of flat cars with crossties for
passenger seats into Wolf Creek at the Tennessee end of the turnpike in 1867?[14]
Engineers of the Asheville-Spartanburg Railroad had completed the route up
Saluda Mountain, and the first train rolled into Paces Gap, now Saluda, on
the 4th of July, 1878. A year later, it reached Hendersonville, but there it paused

due to money woes necessitating corporate reorganization. And less than 25 miles east of Asheville at Old Fort, the Western North Carolina Railroad had been halted since 1869, its finances washed out by the scandalous theft of $4 million in bonds.

The WNCR would win the race to Asheville, but not without an effort still regarded as cruelly superhuman by railroaders today. The line had to surmount Swannanoa Gap, elevation 2582′. from Old Fort, elevation 1437′, in about 5 miles as the crow flies. Steam engines of the day were just converting from wood to coal, and even the most powerful had difficulty climbing a grade steeper than 2.5%, meaning about 132 feet per mile. Surveyors laid out a route that was about 11 miles long, requiring 17 switchbacks and seven tunnels, including the 1,832-foot long Swannanoa Tunnel under the summit at Ridgecrest.

While WNCR's route was celebrated as an engineering marvel, summiting the gap was a callously inhumane enterprise, the nadir of abusive convict labor. Leased from jails in the eastern part of the state, all but a very few of the 537 prisoners were African Americans. Most had been incarcerated for minor crimes like vagrancy and petty theft. Prosecutors were under orders to find, charge, and convict more to ensure a steady supply of cheap labor. Fatalities were common from cave-ins and other horrific accidents like an exploding keg of powder. Estimates of how many died range from 75 to more than 300. Disease was common.[15] Arriving at Old Fort, convicts first had to clear the forest and build their own stockades. The tools of the day were simple: shovels, picks, sledge hammers, and star drills.

One of the seven tunnels, now known as Mud Cut, collapsed into a stew of jagged rock and mud. Debris took weeks to clear, one shovel full at a time. Completion of Swannanoa Tunnel required digging from both ends. To stay on schedule, prisoners manhandled a 17-ton steam engine—little in comparison to those in use hauling freight and passengers on the main line—up and over the mountain. They first laid planks. Then they spiked down rails one length at a time on top of the planks. With the tracks in place, they put their shoulders to ropes and pulled the engine up the new track. Next, they took up the rails the engine had just traversed, carried them ahead, and laid them on newly set planks.[16]

As they worked, they sang "Swannanoa Tunnel," recorded in *Ballads, Banjo Tunes, and Sacred Songs of Western North Carolina in the 1920s* by Bascom Lamar Lunsford, the upper watershed's premier bluegrass minstrel. As a fruit tree salesman, he traveled the country collecting songs, was hired by folksinger Pete Seeger's father to promote mountain music around the country, and was invited by President Franklin Roosevelt to the White House to sing for King George VI in 1939.

I'm going back to the Swannanoa Tunnel
That's my home, baby, that's my home

Asheville Junction, Swannanoa Tunnel
All caved in, baby, all caved in

Last December I remember
The wind blowed cold, baby, the wind blowed cold

When you hear my watchdog howling
Somebody around, baby, somebody around

When you hear that hoot owl squalling
Somebody dying, baby, somebody dying

Hammer falling from my shoulder
All day long, baby, all day long

Ain't no hammer in this mountain
Out rings mine, baby, out rings mine

This old hammer it killed John Henry
It didn't kill me, baby, couldn't kill me

Riley Gardner, he killed my partner
He couldn't kill me, baby, he couldn't kill me

This old hammer it rings like silver
It shines like gold, baby, it shines like gold

Take this hammer, throw it in the river
It rings right on, baby, it shines right on

Some of these days I'll see that woman
Well that's no dream, baby, that's no dream[17]

It is hard to imagine such labor as we speed over Swannanoa Gap on I-40 in five minutes or so. Driving Mill Creek Road from Ridgecrest to Old Fort provides a better inkling of the terrain the convicts conquered.

"What a day for Asheville, and for Western North Carolina?" chortled *The Asheville Citizen* of October 7, 1880, after the first train rolled into the depot at Best, named for the railroad's owner and now Biltmore Village, on Sunday Oct. 3. "What a splendid future is in store for our magnificent section and glorious, faithful people!" Eighteen months later, tracks were laid to the Tennessee line at Paint Rock. Completion of the line from Hendersonville in 1886 opened rail service from all points north and south through Asheville. Among passengers who arrived by train the following year to explore the town's palliative climate were two who would profoundly affect the future of the region: George Washington Vanderbilt III and his ailing mother, Maria Louisa.

NINE

Morning Greets
the Watershed

Railroads brought dawn to the watershed. Golden shafts of promise radiated through the departing night of conquest and conflict. Though a few clouds hovered on the horizon, the forecast for the coming 1900s could not have been brighter. Opportunity gleamed, so rich were the resources spread throughout the mountains. So abundant were its sweet waters, a seemingly inexhaustible supply nourishing everything from the smallest family's farm to acre after acre of industry. How could anyone who had weathered the dark past look forward to the 1880s with anything but eager anticipation?

For the next four decades, the economies in the Blue Ridge's watersheds would thrive. Mills would grind grain into flour, meal, and feed to be shipped throughout the country. Hardwoods would be felled and sawn into lumber, the finest of which would pattern parquet floors in Manhattan and London.[1] Softwood would be pulped into paper. Bark would be ground and fermented into acid to tan hides into leather. Mica, feldspar, iron, copper, and even clay would be mined and sold here and abroad. Cotton fibers from the Piedmont and coastal plains and wool from mountain farms would be spun into threads and woven into fabrics on looms powered by coal-fired steam engines and hydroelectricity from low dams on the French Broad and Pigeon.

No matter what industry, no matter what product, all depended and still do on the watershed's strongest asset: its human capital. The work ethic and genuine hospitality of the men and women who lived in small farms tucked high up in its coves, in hamlets clustered around a stock stand, in villages of a handful of houses and a store, and in county seat towns with churches and courthouses were and are the region's greatest natural resource. From that day in 1791, when William Neilson opened his home to guests seeking to soak in his warm springs, tourism had been and would be the French Broad watershed's most enduring industry.

ROOM WITH A VIEW

Over the preceding century, Asheville had gained national repute as a destination for well-heeled vacationers. From virtually anywhere east of the Mississippi, this mountain town known for clean air, cool waters, and stunning mountain vistas was little more than a day or two's travel by train. As historian of the South Edward L. Ayers puts it, tourism offered "a way for places that had languished for years with unpromising agriculture to finally come into their own."[2] And come into its own it did. In the decade following the arrival of the railroad in 1880, Asheville's population increased four-fold, from 2,616 to 10,235, as the city in the mountains leveraged its antebellum gentility by erecting fine hotels catering to the wealthy.

Among the first and finest of Asheville's luxury resorts was the Battery Park Hotel. Built by Franklin Coxe in 1886 atop leveled earthworks of Confederate Battery Porter on the highest hill in town, it offered commanding views northward, down the river toward the far away gap in the mountains. To the south, Mount Pisgah dominated the horizon, and to the east, discerning eyes could pick out Mt. Mitchell. The first hotel in the region with elevators, its height captured every refreshing breeze no matter how slight. Refined ladies in long, light, and impossibly tight-waisted dresses and gentlemen in dark alpaca frock coats and bowlers strolled its veranda seeking those two perfectly situated rockers in which to recline and discuss those other guests whom they wished to avoid at dinner. In addition to carriage rides and elegant picnics in the mountains, the Battery Park offered golf, shooting galleries, fox hunting, bowling, and tennis. Cultured ladies and gentlemen enjoyed evenings of exquisite dining and dancing to the best orchestras of the day.

Four years later, the 250-room Kenilworth Inn opened, to be followed in 1913 by the Grove Park Inn.[3] Down river at Warm Springs, Neilson's modest inn had been inherited by his son, enlarged, and sold, eventually, ending up in

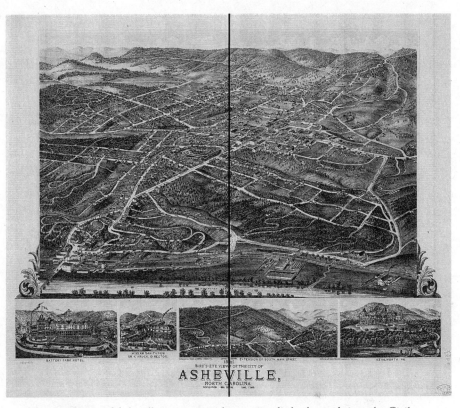

BIRD'S-EYE VIEW OF THE CITY OF
ASHEVILLE,
NORTH CAROLINA.

The population of Asheville in 1880 was about 2,600, little changed since the Civil War. After the arrival of the first train that fall, riverside industry, sanitaria treating respiratory diseases, and related small businesses quadrupled the population to 10,235 in 1890. (Ruger & Stoner, and Burleigh Litho. *Bird's-Eye View of the City of Asheville, North Carolina* [Madison, Wis., 1891].)

the hands of John and James Patton of Asheville. They opened the 350-room Warm Springs Hotel with dinner seating for 600 in 1837. Acquired by James H. Rumbaugh in 1862, the hotel's reputation continued to spread despite the Civil War. It burned in 1882, and the property was sold to a northern syndicate, which constructed the famed Mountain Park Hotel. Though containing just 200 rooms, it was known not only for its healing waters and sophisticated clientele but for its riding stables and nine-hole golf course. At the time the Mountain Park opened in 1886, the town's name was changed from Warm Springs to Hot Springs, a gambit perhaps to differentiate it from other towns named Warm Springs in Virginia and Georgia. In contrast, Gatlinburg and Pigeon Forge on the Little Pigeon were bucolic farming communities annually hosting no more than a few dozen tourists. How that would change.

POWER OF WATER

1886 was a banner year for Asheville hoteliers. A little ways up Hominy Creek, Edwin Carrier was rebuilding the ruins of the resort at Sulphur Springs. With his resort located five miles out of town, Carrier knew it would thrive with a streetcar connection, opened in 1889, to the center of town. There it met the Asheville Street Railway, which ran another five miles or so down to the depot in Best. Porters trundled arriving tourists' trunks across the platform to waiting streetcars across the street. To power his line, Carrier lay a low wooden dam across Hominy Creek, creating the first hydroelectric project in the upper watershed.

Hydropower was seen as the cheapest source of electricity to support industry. That meant tourism, but also milling of cloth and grain. On Richland Creek flowing through the Frog Level section of Waynesville, in 1900 Daniel Killian erected a low dam turning a waterwheel that generated power for his woolen mill. He sold surplus electricity to nearby White Sulphur Springs Hotel and ran a line up the hill to Main Street. It fed three streetlights and a few other hotels. Electricity generated by Killian's dam was DC, direct current, as opposed to today's all but universal AC, alternating current. During the day, when demand was low, extra DC was stored in glass batteries. In the evening, as demand peaked and drew down the batteries, the manager of the mill would pull the cord, giving two blasts on a steam whistle. At the hotel, lights would fade, the orchestra would cease playing, oil lamps would be lit, and dancers would stroll the wide porches waiting for the whistle signaling that power would soon come back on and the dance could begin again.[4]

Early power-generating dams on the French Broad are of the low-head, "run of river" type. In these, a river fills the impoundment behind the dam to its top and runs over its crest. The first dam on the upper French Broad was built by W. T. Weaver in 1904 to provide power to Asheville. Known as Craggy Dam, initially it was 13 feet high, made of granite masonry, and fed a small generator at the end of a short canal. During the flood of 1916, a portion of the dam was washed out. It was rebuilt into the structure easily seen from Riverside Drive, about four miles north of Asheville. Craggy dam was actually Weaver's second hydro project. His first, completed in 1901, filled a 120-foot wide gorge on the Ivy River a few hundred yards north of today's US 25 bridge. Rocks quarried on the site were cemented together to a height of 65 feet. Iron flumes 6 feet in diameter carried water from just below the crest of the dam to generators housed at its base. This dam was also breached in the 1916 flood and restored with concrete. Weaver's third dam, Redmon, is located about five miles downstream from Marshall. Completed in 1912, the dam is 30-feet high, built of concrete, and features a broad apron at its base to keep water cascading over the top from digging a hole under the dam.[5] Along with dams, he built the Elk Mountain Steam Plant on the river at Woodfin. Weaver was primarily responsible for developing electric power in the upper French Broad watershed.[6]

THE OLD MILL STREAM

So iconic is the image of grist mills like the Old Mill at Pigeon Forge. Water flows over a wheel, turning it slowly, powering gears first of wood later of iron that rotate heavy grindstones, which gently shush out meal that bakes into cornbread, the equally iconic vittle that nourished generations of pioneering families. Little tub mills were found on virtually every creek in the watershed. Where current was ample, it turned tall wheels, driving not just millstones but also thin sawblades up and down, in the manner of a pit saw. Such was likely the design of Maj. Davidson's sawmill in the Swannanoa Settlement at the mouth of Bee Tree Creek.

Side by side, railroads and water power fostered industrial growth along the French Broad. Farm families who had for generations grown corn to feed stock driven along the Buncombe Turnpike found a new and lucrative market for their grain. Grist mills were no longer driven by water wheels. Instead, the current spun turbines generating electricity. Among the companies along the French Broad that made the early transition from water power to electricity was the J. P. Robinson & Co. mill at Newport. Grinding corn as early as 1868, it was one of the first mills in the southeast to adopt hydroelectric power, pioneered in 1882 on Wisconsin's Fox River. By 1886, a low rock dam had been thrown across the Pigeon. Within a decade, the mill was producing 225 barrels of flour, 1,500 barrels of corn meal, and 50,000 pounds of feed per day. The plant also furnished electricity to the town.[7]

Further upstream, in 1895, the Marshall Milling Company was chartered and began building a rock and crib dam across the river, feeding a long race that spun turbines originally designed to grind grain into flour and meal. The mill itself was a brick building, highly unusual for grist mills of the era, which were

Newport's J. P. Robinson milling company converted its dam on the Pigeon
to generate electricity in 1886, among the first hydroelectric projects in the Southeast.
(Stokely Memorial Library, Photographer: John Glenn.)

usually wooden and barn-like. Could be that the company's owners patterned theirs after fabric mills of their native New England. Twenty years later, the mill and dam were acquired by Capitola Manufacturing. They built a new three-story factory to spin cotton into cloth.

Not long after shuttles began flying back and forth in its looms, Capitola became ensnared in the national child labor law controversy. In 1907, the same year Marshall's stunning Classical Revival courthouse opened with such great promise, a federal Department of Commerce agent, Thomas Robinson Dawley, Jr., was dispatched to investigate working conditions for women and children in the mill. He found no wrong doing. In part, his report read:

> As the cotton-mill had educated and improved those people whom it had called down from their mountain homes, so had the straggling old county-seat been improved by it. The earnings of the women and children in the mill enabled them to buy goods from the merchants, the merchants bought from the farmers, and the farmers got better prices for what they had to sell. Fathers who had rarely found work around their cabin homes at fifty cents a day, now got from a dollar to a dollar and a half with work all the time they wanted it. They had the money to pay their taxes without any necessity for the tax collector seizing their cow, and they had something upon which to pay the tax as well.[8]

Dawley's report of working circumstances of women and children at the Capitola Mill did not jibe with the wretchedly abusive conditions in urban factories and sweatshops held to be universal by Theodore Roosevelt's Commissioner of Labor. Dawley's observations were excluded from the commissioner's final report, and he was fired.

Capitola's was one of dozens of fabric mills that characterized early industry in the upper French Broad watershed. Among the earliest was John Cairns's woolen mill on Reems Creek just south of Weaverville. After immigrating from Scotland in 1868, he gathered wool from area farmers and fashioned it into rough-wearing cloth of "jean" weave, worsted for men's suits, and cloth of softer finish for women's skirts and coats.[9] By 1883 in Asheville, C. E. Graham was selling dry goods and shoes on Main Street. Four years later, he would develop a cotton mill on the river. Mountain families came to work its spindles and looms and shared large multifamily homes of classic Victorian stick style, a common bath house, and a clubhouse. The mill was acquired by in 1894 by the Cone brothers and renamed Asheville Cotton Mill. As part of their expansion, they constructed simple one-bedroom cottages for workers on the slope above the plant. Workers kept chickens, which often roamed freely giving the community today's name: Chicken Hill.[10]

TIMBER!

At the beginning of the watershed's age of heavy industry, mountain forests were quite different from today's. Other than acreage ravaged by hurricane, tornado, or fire, woods were largely free of entangling underbrush. What little lumbering occurred prior to 1880 was intensely local, restricted pretty much to lower slopes on the periphery of land cleared for farming. Many too steep to till had been stripped of trees for firewood, the primary source of heat until coal became readily available in the 1890s. Poplar, because it is light and easily worked, was a favorite for construction and everyday tables and chairs. Walnut, cherry, and occasionally chestnut were favored for fancier furniture. Oak was prized for flooring. Not until the arrival of Champion Fibre in Canton in the 1920s would pines and fir be felled for pulping.

The first planks were rip-sawed by hand. A pit deep enough for a man to stand was dug, then a floored frame with a cradle was erected over it. A log of 10 feet or so was secured in the cradle. Two sawyers, one standing on the floor and another in the pit, grasped handles of a saw, usually between four and six feet long. Up and down, up and down, they sawed vertically the length of the log. A typical log was about 20 inches in diameter and 10 feet long. It would yield 10 or so planks about an inch and a half thick. Sawing a dozen logs into lumber was a day's back breaking work. Water powered saws multiplied that output by 10. Most farmers owned two-man saws and could build a crude pit mill when they needed lumber for building.

Railroads triggered the boom in industrial scale logging. Thirteen years after the East Tennessee, Virginia, and Georgia's tracks reached Newport in 1867, Alexander A. Arthur was scouting stands of timber in the headwaters of the Pigeon River for the Scottish-Carolina Timber and Land Company. Arthur's vision was immense. Rising upriver were ridge after ridge covered by primeval hardwood forest. Each cleft in the mountains was drained by a creek, some naturally robust enough to float logs downstream during the rains of spring and fall torrents delivered by tropical storms from the South. Streams with flows too low were impounded by temporary log "splash" dams. On the resulting lake, timber was floated. When the pond was full, the dam was dynamited, releasing a raging cascade of tumbling logs down the stream into the river. Such floods scoured stream beds barren of all aquatic life, leaving them sterile.

Upon reaching the river, logs were corralled in "booms," essentially chains stretched across from bank to bank. When a boom was loaded, the chain was released and the logs allowed to float downstream. Among Arthur's loggers were French Canadian lumberjacks whose language was as foreign to Newport's townspeople as their ability to walk rafts of floating logs and bust up incipient jams with their pikes and peaveys. To fashion timber into lumber, he built two mills, one at Newport and the other at Knoxville. He reasoned that logs the upper boom failed to catch would be snagged by the boom at the second 70 miles downstream.

Old timers warned him: "Wait till the Pigeon gets on its big britches one of these spring freshets and you'll see how stout them little booms you're building will be. They'll never hold the Pigeon." The mountain men were not particularly prescient—they just knew ways of the river. And, in 1886, the river had its way. Intense spring deluges sent the normally tranquil Pigeon marauding out of the mountains, sweeping away the booms and scattering logs on floodplains for miles downriver. Arthur's mill at Newport folded soon thereafter, and his Glasgow-based company fired him for not heeding the locals' cautions.[11]

Owners of the French Broad Lumber Company at Asheville were more successful with their booms. Its mill was located next to the WNCR tracks, just below the mouth of the Swannanoa. During low water, masons built rock pylons from shoal to shoal every few hundred yards up the center of the river for a distance of 16,000 feet, or a little more than three miles. The boom's catchment area lay along the Biltmore side of the river. At the top of the boom, a heavy chain was attached. During periods of high water when logs were being floated downstream, the upper chain was stretched all the way across the river to capture them. When flows were low and in icy winter weather, the chain was secured on the Biltmore bank, closing the boom and protecting its timber.[12] The great French Broad flood of 1916 laid waste to the lumber company as it did to all industries built on the floodplain.

ALL THAT GLISTENS

Many western North Carolina state highways sparkle with flecks of mica, a mineral widespread among the metamorphic rock of the watershed. For ornaments and trade, prehistoric Indians dug mica in what is now known as the Sinkhole Mine near the hamlet of Bandana in the headwaters of the Nolichucky River. By far the greatest concentration of the mineral is found around Spruce Pine. Located on the North Toe River, this town sits in the middle of a 25 mile long, 5-mile wide mineral-rich *pegmatite*. This unusual volcanic formation is comprised of large crystals, including sheet mica, quartz, feldspar (moonstone), and beryl. Pure beryl is almost clear, yet the presence of chromium turns it into emerald, the official precious stone of North Carolina. Just over the mountain in Little Switzerland, the historic Crabtree Mine is open to the public for mining emeralds and other gems.

Of the several types of mica, the most valuable and commonly found in the watershed is *muscovite*. First commercially used by Russians as a cheap substitute for window glass, *muscovite* can be virtually colorless. Its unique horizontal atomic structure of silicon, aluminum, and potassium allows it to be split into ultrathin sheets for use in electron microscopy. Resistant to heat up to about 900°C, it was frequently used in peepholes to wood and coal stoves and later in radio tubes. Its flexibility gave it broad utility a hundred years ago in transparent roll-down curtains on carriages and early autos. Ground-up mica is still used in paints, shingles, hoses, sponges, cosmetics, and a host of other products.

The Spruce Pine pegmatite is one of the country's largest deposits of feldspar in which sheet mica is often imbedded. Feldspar weathers into soft kaolin, a major source of commercial clays. According to legend, clay from the region was exported to England in the mid-1700s for use in fine china such as that made by Josiah Wedgwood and Sons. In the early 1900s, it was discovered that adding finely ground feldspar to sand resulted in molten glass that flowed much more easily. As a result, glass bottles that had heretofore been mainly hand blown could now be molded by machine. Demand for industrial feldspar and mica heightened in the 1930s and 40s, triggering mining of low-grade rock. Thousands of tons of fine-grained waste or spoil were heaped in huge mounds. When it rained, the North Toe bled white. In the late 1960s, modern milling processes reclaimed valuable minerals in the spoil. Today, the river no longer runs chalky.[13]

DOWN IN THE VALLEY

For a decade in 1880s and 90s John Stokely's family had raised row crops on the rich bottomlands along the French Broad half a dozen miles west of Newport.

The soil was uncommonly productive, nourished every few years by humus deposited when the river flooded. The family prospered, as Wilma Dykeman Stokely tells it in her seminal book *The French Broad*. While the family sat around the table after dinner one summer's day in 1897, Wilma's father-in-law James said, "I've been thinking . . . about trying to can some of the tomatoes we grow around here on the place. Set up a little cannery."[14] That winter, they built a store at the crossroads hamlet of French Broad near their farm. Nearby, in an open 60-foot by 30-foot shed, they set up canning equipment, metal tubs, tables, peeling knives, and crates of cans and lids with solder and irons to seal them. The first summer they harvested tomatoes from 60 acres and produced 4,000 cases of cooked and canned tomatoes. By wagon, they hauled them down to the landing on the river and loaded them on the steamboat bound for Knoxville, 40 miles downstream.

Thus was born Stokely Brothers Canning Company, which bought Van Camp in 1933; together, they grew into one of the nation's major packers and suppliers of canned vegetables, with 60 plants worth $100 million by the 1950s.[15] Along the way, in 1904, they partnered with A. J. Bush of nearby Chestnut Hill. Four years later, Bush bought out his interest in the partnership and went on to establish Bush Brothers, Inc., known world-wide for its varieties of canned beans. Today, the Bush homestead attracts tourists on the road from Newport to Sevierville. Across the road is the firm's 200,000 sq. ft. plant, which offers tours.

COMETH THE COMMODORE'S GRANDSON

Mrs. William H. Vanderbilt, the daughter-in-law of Commodore Cornelius and mother of George Washington Vanderbilt III, was a slender lady of medium height, hazel eyes, "and a very sweet and refined expression," according to W. A. Crofutt in *The Vanderbilts and The Story of Their Fortune*. "Exceedingly simple in her mode of life," the author continues, "she rises early, devotes several hours to her household duties, and afterwards visits some of her grandchildren or has them brought to see her." Though her husband had been branded a worthless "blatherskite"[16] by the Commodore, William H. inherited $90 million (roughly $2.25 billion today), when the family patriarch died in 1877. Two years later, William H. initiated construction of a massive mansion on Manhattan's Fifth Ave., but his wife preferred life on their farm on Staten Island.

She suffered from chronic malaria.[17] After the death of her husband in 1885, it was thought that perhaps Asheville's healthful clime might bring her some

The Battery Park Hotel attracted health-seeking visitors, among them George W. Vanderbilt III and his mother, Maria Louisa Kissam, who sought treatment from Dr. Simon Westray Battle whose office was in the hotel. (North Carolina Room, Pack Memorial Library.)

relief. Just how she or her son first learned of the city in the mountains seems to be lost. Yet the physician whose treatment she sought in Asheville, Samuel Westray Battle, was a 1875 graduate of Bellevue Medical Hospital College in New York City. Unmarried, he treated crippled children there until being commissioned in the US Navy later that year.[18] Society matrons like Mrs. Vanderbilt, with three daughters of marriage age—her fourth, Eliza, was too young—no doubt discussed the prospects of the bright, young, and eminently eligible Dr. Battle.

After injuring his wrist in an accident at sea, the now-married Dr. Battle was placed on the navy's retired list in 1884. He moved to Asheville a year later and took up residence in the city's elegant Battery Park Hotel. While in the navy, he had become fascinated—as had so many of his peers—with the healthful benefits of climate. Perhaps based on Dr. Battle's writings on the topic and their probable prior acquaintance with him, Mrs. Vanderbilt and her son, George Washington Vanderbilt III, took the train to Asheville in 1888 seeking his treatment of her persistent malady. Both were so enamored of the soothingly bucolic views from the grand hotel that they decided to establish a residence there. Vanderbilt first attempted to buy Fernihurst, the stately hilltop, post-bellum brick mansion now surrounded by the campus of Asheville-Buncombe Technical Community College. When the owner refused to sell, Vanderbilt began acquiring small farms along the river that would become the core of Biltmore, his vast 125,000-acre estate.

EPITOME OF ELEGANCE

Nothing so epitomizes the height of the Gilded Age in the watershed than Biltmore House, Vanderbilt's 250-room mansion built in the style of a French chateau. He derived the name from the Dutch village of *Bildt* where the family heritage was rooted, and Americanization of *moor* after the gentle English countryside of which the surrounding terrain so much reminded him.[19] At 26, Vanderbilt had already developed a reputation as a scholar of fine art. His mother, concerned about his health, sheltered him and had him tutored at home. Frequent extended trips abroad with his parents deepened his interest in the arts, classic architecture, and agriculture. He admired vast European estates with manor houses surrounded by productive pastures and fields of grain and supported by stables, houses for fowl, creameries, smithies, and acre after acre of gardens for vegetables and flowers. This drove his vision for Biltmore Estate.

As he and his friend and attorney from New York, George McNamee, toured Asheville, they crossed the Swannanoa near Gum Spring, where Buncombe County had been founded nearly a century earlier. They rode up a low ridge to its nose, with its panoramic view not just of the river bottom stretching for miles north and south but of the western range of the Blue Ridge dominated by Mt. Pisgah. In *Lady on the Hill: How Biltmore Estate Became an American Icon,* author Howard E. Covington Jr. writes that before day's end, they "rode directly to the landowner's house and purchased it along with 10 acres of land."[20] Thence began the acquisition of several thousand acres along the river, the hills beyond, and in the village of Best, which contained the Asheville's only train station until 1905.

Along with McNamee, Vanderbilt engaged Richard Morris Hunt and Fredrick Law Olmstead. Hunt was responsible for the architectural design of the mansion and Olmstead, design of the grounds. As the first American admitted to the prestigious École des Beaux-Arts, then the world's finest school of architecture, "the subsequent importance of [Hunt's] influence on the architecture of his own country can hardly be overstated," observes historian David McCullough.[21] Though primarily known as the landscape architect for New York's Central Park, Olmstead had toured the South as a journalist on assignment from the *New York Times*. His book *A Journey in the Back Country in the Winter of 1853–4* is a powerful portrayal of antebellum mountain life. Hunt, too, had worked on Central Park. To his design for its main entrance, Olmstead objected strenuously. When it was approved, Olmstead resigned his commission and only returned when Hunt's plans were modified. Somehow, Vanderbilt fostered their collaboration with spectacular and enduring results.

Construction started in 1889 and, when completed in 1895, it contained 174,240 sq. ft. of floor space, 35 bedrooms, 43 bathrooms, 65 fireplaces, an elegant banquet hall beneath a towering 70-foot ceiling, an indoor swimming pool, a bowling alley, and a trove of sixteenth century tapestries, hundreds of paintings by such masters as Pierre-Auguste Renoir and John Singer Sargent, and Vanderbilt's personal library exceeding 10,000 volumes. More than 1,000 masons, stone cutters, carpenters, landscapers, electricians (Biltmore had its own steam power plant), and laborers were employed. Vanderbilt laid a three-mile railroad spur to bring materials to the building site from the train station at Best.

To house personnel, but more so to create a model, self-sustaining community

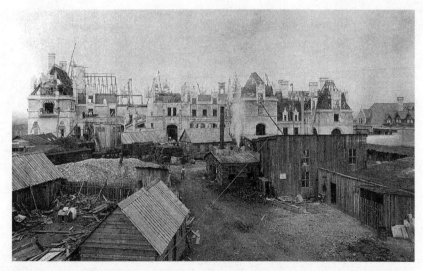

Construction of Biltmore house with its 225 rooms began in 1890 and was completed in 1895. To support its workers, Vanderbilt bought the town of Best and renamed it Biltmore Village. (The Biltmore Company Archives.)

In 1912, two years before his death, Vanderbilt began negotiations with nascent U.S. Forest Service to sell it 86,700 acres of cut-over mountain land (area in darker grey) which became the nucleus of Pisgah National Forest. (North Carolina Room, Pack Memorial Library.)

PISGAH PURCHASE AREA

like those adjacent to great manor houses in Europe, Vanderbilt purchased the village, erected scores of substantial gambrel-roofed stucco rental houses euphemistically called "cottages," buildings for stores, a hospital, and All Soul's Church,[22] enjoyed today as Biltmore Village. Of Biltmore Estate, Olmstead would later aver it to be "the most distinguished private place, not only in America, but in the world."[23]

While construction continued on Biltmore House and the estate, Vanderbilt initiated the age of conservation in the watershed. Guided by Gifford Pinchot, the twenty-something forester who would become the first to head the US Forest Service, and professor Carl A. Schenck, Vanderbilt would purchase some 125,000 acres of mountain lands. Much of it had been already logged, leaving a wilderness of stumps and tangled dead branches. A good deal of it, though, had yet to be timbered. Schenck's mandate was to log it in an ecologically balanced manner, feeding logs to the French Broad Lumber Company, which Vanderbilt had acquired. Schenck pioneered modern forest management. He opened the Biltmore Forest School, the first such school in America, now memorialized as the Cradle of Forestry in America near Brevard. Two years before his death in 1914, Vanderbilt opened negotiations with the new US Forest Service, which resulted in its purchase of 86,700 acres, which became the nucleus of Pisgah National Forest, among the first national forests east of the Mississippi River.

TEN

Hardwoods, Hides, and Over Here

The broad mountain slopes, gorge like coves lower down have a forest cover of truly virgin character. In some of the eastern border counties, where railways have yet to come, the silence of those somber forest depths is scarcely ever broken by the sound of a woodsman's axe. Primeval forests of centuries guard the cold crystal streams that flow throughout the year. Bear and deer slake their thirsts from the clear bubbling pools of these streams and somewhere in their hidden, winding courses the moonshiner brings life into the "mountain dew." Huge tulip trees (poplars), with ages numbered in centuries, crowd the deep coves and rich mountainsides with their gigantic forms.

The sugar maple, which we expect to find in perfection only in a northern forest, is represented here in great numbers and in the finest development. So, too, is the familiar beech. The little-known yellow buckeye is nowhere else surpassed in its great height and diameter growth. The cucumber magnolia, a rival to the tulip tree in the appearance and excellence of its timber, occurs plentifully and of large size in these forests, together with the much valued white ash, three to five feet in diameter and with 60 feet of clear trunk.

Here too the southern white-leaved basswood grows to fine diameters, scattered in small and large groups throughout the region. The abundance of big chestnut timber in this region makes the large chestnut of the coast region look small.[1]

So wrote George B. Sudworth, dean of American forestry, in *"Forest Trees and Forest Conditions of Eastern and Middle Tennessee,"* a paper he presented at the annual meeting of the American Forestry Association in 1897. Every year thousands of casual hikers stroll myriad trails through sections of Great Smoky Mountains National Park and Pisgah National Forest drained by the French Broad and its tributaries. They enjoy the gentle grades and marvel, perhaps, at cuts through low rocky ridges wondering how they came to be. They picnic in rumpled streamside flats, where, if they happen to spread their lunches in April or early May, they might see a patch of daffodils planted by a homemaker ages ago. Some discern shallow rectangular depressions and surmise, correctly, that these may have been root cellars where 'taters and turnips had been stored for winter. Here and there sprawl lines of rounded river rock, remnants of fences once topped with crossed rails.

Walk one of the gated forest roads. Listen carefully, and you may hear the whistle of small but utterly rugged all-wheel drive steam engines, an off-set Shay or a Climax, backing a dozen cars loaded with fifteen-foot-long butts of chestnut or oak down the mountain from switchback to switchback. On broad flats, now occupied by camp grounds or visitor centers, the cacophony of screaming band saws ripping logs into lumber, chuffing yard engines sorting loaded flatcars, and coarse shouts of men hollering orders and warnings can be overwhelming to imaginative ears. Educated noses are quick to pick up the ever-present wafting of wood smoke, the industrial odor of hot oil and grease, and maybe a hint of freshly baked bread cooling in open cookhouse windows. Up the hill, a school bell may ring, calling children with their writing slates to class while their mothers and grannies, grown gnarled as oaks from their labors and worries, boil the week's wash and hang it on the line to dry. Gentle evening breezes might pick-up Uncle Zeke sittin' on his porch scratchin' out a spritely rendition of *Flop-Eared Mule* or *Cabin Creek* on his fiddle.

Rivers and rails ignited a robust logging industry throughout the watershed. Wherever a mountain valley opened onto a broad floodplain, and the stream that laid it down was crossed by a road, manufacturing was likely to root. From it could spread a web of narrow gauge rails twisting like varicose veins up steep flanks onto little flats so isolated by their ruggedness that only the most sure-footed mule could navigate them comfortably. Lumber was their quest. By the early 1900s, great forests of the Northeast and the Midwest had been largely shorn of their timber, particularly of hardwoods. Pine and cypress forests of the lower Mississippi and the Gulf Coast were being cut. As America's population nearly tripled from 1870 to 1910, the country faced critical shortages of its most common commodity: wood. Reports from Sudworth, Arnold Guyot, and other early foresters focused attention on the last great primeval woodland in the East, the southern Appalachians.[2]

FOREST SEEDLINGS

In many ways, the first seeds for Pisgah National Forest were sown in Carl Alvin Schenck's native Germany about the time Vanderbilt and his mother were planning their initial sojourn to Asheville in 1888. The science of sustainable forestry was pioneered in the Black Forest. There Schenck was studying forest management and finance and carousing with other students. From his lady love, he learned to recite Shakespeare's *King Richard II*. His grasp of sylviculture and modest fluency in English brought him to the attention of Sir Dietrich Brandis, also a German but the pre-eminent forester for the British Commonwealth.

Broad mountain slopes and gorge-like coves covered with truly virgin timber yielded trunk after trunk into the insatiable maws of riverside lumber and paper mills throughout French Broad country. (Great Smoky Mountains National Park Archives.)

Brandis's work was known by Olmstead and Pinchot. Through those connections, Vanderbilt learned of Schenck and, on Pinchot's recommendation, cabled the young German in 1895 asking, "Are you willing to come to America to take charge of my forestry interests in Western North Carolina?" After checking with Brandis, Schenck accepted the offer.

About the time of Schenck's arrival, Vanderbilt acquired roughly 100,000 acres, stretching up to the crest followed by today's Blue Ridge Parkway. As Schenck toured the estate with Pinchot, they conversed mostly about hunting and fishing.[3] They rode horseback up Big Creek, a tributary of Mills River, which Vanderbilt planned to log. Oak predominated. Schenck also reported seeing fungus-ridden shortleaf pine and "remnants of chestnuts which, in earlier times, must have been the leading hardwoods in the stands." He wondered how they died and was told they were killed by farmers who set fires to clear brush so they could plant crops. The chestnut blight had yet to devastate Southern Appalachian forests. Pinchot showed him the location of a planned 22-foot-high splash dam on Big Creek, designed as a permanent structure. Logs would be towed by horse to the lake, and when it was full, the gate would be opened, and timber sluiced down the Mills into the French Broad. To augment the man-made flash flood, a second dam was planned further upstream. Schenck had seen splash dams in the Black Forest, felt they were most inefficient, and thought that roads were much more practical.[4] When the dams were completed and the first load flushed downstream, he was proven correct. The lumber-laden torrent washed out bridges and scattered jumbles of large logs in farmers' fields. Some were so angry they sued.

Schenck was convinced that forests were best utilized as nurseries for producing marketable timber. He advocated and practiced selective cutting, clearing out species of limited commercial value, and providing space to grow hardwoods in high demand. On the estate's vast former farmlands, then overtaken with sedge, he planted bushel after bushel of acorns in hopes of growing forests of oaks. When none sprouted, he discovered he had been thwarted by scavenging mice and squirrels. With seedlings of white pine, he was far more successful. And he found that by pushing acorns deeper into soft humus where they had fallen with the toe of his boot and fertilizing them with handfuls of manure, oaks would develop. In many ways, Vanderbilt provided him with a forest laboratory of thousands of acres. What he learned he would begin teaching in 1898 at the Biltmore Forest School, now the Cradle of Forestry in America.

Despite their best efforts, Biltmore's forest efforts were never self-sustaining.

Only the rush of brawling rapids and laughter of picnicking families break today's silence in Big Creek Camp Ground, once the bustling lumber town Crestmont and "a gay, social place with weekly dances, a movie theatre, and other forms of entertainment," wrote Pauline Walker who grew up there. (Great Smoky Mountains National Park Archives.)

Tension escalated between Schenck and Vanderbilt. Schenck was fired in 1909 and the school closed, but he continued to offer instruction from 1910 to 1913 across the mountain at Sunburst, Champion Fibre's model logging community on the Pigeon's west fork. Much of Vanderbilt's forest holdings, eighty-six thousand acres, were purchased by the United States in 1914 to create Pisgah National Forest. Today's towering stands of tulip poplar, oak, hickory, and pine are testimony to both of their visions.

HIKING THE RAILS INTO THE BACK OF BEYOND

The history of logging in the Pigeon River watershed is perhaps most visibly written by trails, campsites, and picnic areas up Big Creek from the powerhouse at Waterville near exit 451 on I-40 just west of the Tennessee-North Carolina border. Eloquence like Sudworth's description of East Tennessee's forests no doubt caught the eyes of Jacob Holloway and John B. Hart, partners in the North Carolina Land and Lumber Company. Headquartered in Jersey City, N. J., the company paid $60,000 in 1898 to purchase 54,876 acres in the Big Creek–Cataloochee Creek watersheds, which became, in 1934, the northern most section of Great Smoky Mountains National Park. To move lumber to markets, they laid rails from Newport, 19 miles downstream. By 1902, their line, officially the Newport Division of the Tennessee & North Carolina Railroad, was completed. At the time, Hart planned to extend the route to Waynesville, but a bitter winter snow storm blanketed the region and he dropped the idea.[5]

Holloway and Hart speculated in forest lands. As they finished the railroad into Big Creek, they sold it and their acreage to the Cataloochee Company located in Waynesville. The selling price was $675,000, a profit of ten times their original investment four years earlier.[6] Around 1903, the company established the sawmill village of Crestmont on the flats now occupied by Big Spring Creek campground. It was a real town with two streets of one-story houses for workers, larger ones for management, a school, a hotel, theatre, commissary, workshops, and of course the mill with its log pond and company offices.

"Crestmont was a gay, social place with weekly dances, a movie theatre, and other forms of entertainment," remembered the late Pauline Shields Walker, long-time Cocke County librarian and daughter of the physician who lived in the village for three years. "There were people from other parts of the country which made it seem a bit cosmopolitan." Every day but Sunday, the T&NC ran round trips to Newport. Fare was 80¢. Upon returning, decades after the coming of the park, she reported, "nothing remains of the town except the great towering stone fireplace that once graced the Club House. The roar it [Big Creek] makes is the same that it made 75 years ago when we lived on the bluff above it and it roared over the huge boulders in its bed."[7]

From the T&NC depot at Crestmont, more than 20 miles of narrow gauge logging railroad climbed more than 4,000 feet up flanks of mountain ridges defining the cove. The run up Shallow Fork from the mill at Walnut Bottom to just beneath the summit of Big Cataloochee Mountain zigzagged through nine switchbacks. Camps, some comprised of single room huts that could be hauled from place to place on flat cars, were set up for loggers along the tracks.

In 1910, Schenck and students from his forest school then located at Sunburst, toured Crestmont to study how logs were transported from where they were cut to the mill. They observed clutches of logs swinging down aerial cables, which ran much like zip lines from a tall tree on a flat at the top down to another, shorn of all its limbs, by the tracks. Attached by similar cables, logs were snaked out of the woods by steam donkeys (winches). At the time of their visit, the mill with its double band saw was turning out 80,000 board feet of lumber per day. After a stint in a drying kiln, fresh-cut boards were stacked in the drying yard to cure. Raw lumber from Crestmont would be carried by rail to mills in Newport and beyond, there to be finished for use in construction and furniture.[8]

SUNBURST ON THE WEST FORK

In the early years, bankruptcies and reorganizations were common among mountain lumber companies. Ultimately operations in Big Creek and later neighboring Cataloochee Cove were acquired by Champion Fibre Company of Canton. The hamlet had been formerly known as Pigeon, Pigeon Ford, Ford of the Pigeon, and Pigeon River, all names utterly despised by one group or another of its residents. There, in 1893, the Wrought Iron Bridge Company of Canton, Ohio erected a steel truss bridge over the Pigeon. At a meeting soon thereafter, when the community's name was again being hotly debated, someone suggested Canton from the company's sign on the bridge.[9]

That same year, Peter Thomson, a retired Hamilton, Ohio, printer, founded Champion to produce ultra-smooth paper especially suited for rotogravure reproduction of photographs in magazines and books. He quickly recognized that he needed a reliable supply of pulpwood. His requirements were simple: (1) a consistent supply of clean water, (2) railroad access, (3) reliable, inexpensive workers, and (4) inexhaustible balsam and fir forest. After touring Western North Carolina from Asheville down to Murphy, he settled on Canton.[10] His mill there would become one of the world's largest suppliers of book paper and the source of angry, dark brown, cancer-causing pollution that foamed and fouled the Pigeon for more than a century.

Champion owned most of the northeast half of the Great Smokies stretching from beyond Clingman's Dome and Deep Creek to the mouth of Big Creek on the Pigeon. Lumbering was incredibly intense in 64,000 acres of the upper Pigeon's watershed. To log the region, Champion developed a community in 1906, where the West Fork's Right Hand, Middle, and Left Hand prongs come together close to today's Forest Service campground on NC 215. Like Crestmont, it was vibrant with scattered homes, and a community center that also served as a school, church, dance hall, and commissary. As Thomson was

Now submerged by Lake Logan, picture Sunburst, a community of 500 or so surrounding Champion's sawmill which in the 1920s could turn out as much as 250,000 board feet of lumber in a day. (*If Rails Could Talk, Sunburst, and Champion Fibre, Vol. 2,* Ronald Sullivan and Gerald Ledford. Photography: Gerald Ledford Collection.)

planning the little town, early one morning he saw the sun burst over the mountain crest and so the town was named.[11] For the 100 African Americans employed at Sunburst, about 20 percent of its population, work represented dawn of another kind. Throughout the South, racial oppression was reaching heights unseen since the Civil War. Yet in Sunburst, remembers Lewis Oats Jr., whose grandfathers belonged to its African American community, everyone was judged by what they did, not by the color of their skin.[12]

That was the first of two Sunbursts. New investors joined Thomson in 1910, creating a new firm, the Champion Lumber Company. They moved the original Sunburst four miles down the West Fork to a much broader floodplain. By 1912, the site swarmed with carpenters building houses, a commissary, a school, a church, a 40-room hotel, and mill buildings. Chuffing steam engines, echoes of sledge on steel spike, the rattle of boards in hurrying wagons, the pace must have been frantic, for all was finished by March 1913. For the next four years, Sunburst thrived as war in Europe increased demand. But the entry of the United States into the conflict and the resulting draft in 1917 depleted the company's work force. WWI demonstrated the critical importance of military aircraft. Frames for wings and fuselages were fashioned from spruce, which is strong, light, and easily steamed and bent into shape. To fill the need, the

Army Corps of Engineers dispatched soldiers in the spring of 1918 to augment Sunburst's beleaguered work force and log high mountain tracts.[13]

By the 1920s, the headwaters of the East and West Forks of the Pigeon were pretty well swept of standing timber, and in late 1925 the watershed was left smoking and charred by a massive forest fire. But the Twenties were roaring, and thirst for summer mountain retreats was seemed unquenchable. Tracts around Sunburst were sold to developers, and the town itself was purchased privately by Thomson's son-in-law, Reuben, then president of Champion Fibre Company. Equipment was removed, lumber from buildings salvaged, and a concrete arch dam plugged the valley's outlet in 1932. During droughts, Lake Logan, named for Thomson's son, would provide a reliable water source for the mill in Canton. Deer abounded, browsing on new growth on timbered slopes. Millions of rainbow trout were stocked in the lake and the West Fork and its tributaries.

For 60 years, the lake and surrounding mountains served as a private hunting and fishing retreat for Champion executives and their guests, including presidents Richard Nixon and George H. W. Bush.[14] Late in the 1990s, Champion sold its assets to its employees, who in turn formed Blue Ridge Paper Products, now Evergreen Packaging. They transferred ownership of the lake property to the Episcopal Diocese of Western North Carolina for use as a retreat and conference center.

HIDE BOUND

After the Buncombe Turnpike was completed in 1828, East Tennessee and Western North Carolina became known as the land of hogs and hominy. With the arrival of railroad and the advent of the refrigerated rail car in the 1880s, the market for beef and pork opened for small farmers. They could drive their livestock to stations there to be loaded onto cattle cars and transported to Swift & Co. and other large slaughterhouses. Hides from butchered carcasses were packed in boxcars and freighted to large tanneries located near sources of abundant water and readily available oak, hemlock, and chestnut bark. Bark was the deciding factor. A waste product from the robust lumber industry, it was also a natural resource of tannins that could be gathered by farm families. When dried and then soaked, bark produces an astringent acidic liquor that preserves hides and makes them more supple. Production of tannins ranked among the top chemical industries in North Carolina in the early 1900s.

Lovers canoed and swam in Riverside Park's lake unaware of pollution from seepage from Hans Rees' tannery a mile upstream. (North Carolina Room, Pack Memorial Library.)

Like lumber, leather was also in high demand in the first quarter of the 1900s. Well-tanned leather was essential for shoes, clothing, and furniture. In addition, most factories used heavy leather belting to transfer power from huge steam, and later electric, engines to pulleys that rotated long shafts hung beneath ceiling rafters. From these shafts, smaller belts dropped down and spun gears of milling and weaving machinery. Among the earliest industrial producers of commercial leather in the watershed were the Toxaway Tannery in Rosman, the Junaluska and the Hazelwood tanneries in Waynesville, and the Unaka Tannery in Newport. The last three were absorbed by A.C. Lawrence Leather Company of Peabody, Mass. The Hazelwood operation was forced to shutter its doors in 1982 over increasing competition from synthetic leathers and growing concern over pollution of the Pigeon. The Unaka Tannery and related Chilhowee Extract Plant on the Pigeon in Newport were employing 400 people by 1928. In 1991, bowing to competition from overseas, A. C. Lawrence went out of business as did many of its smaller operations.[15]

Hans Rees, one of world's largest manufacturers of industrial leathers, located a plant in Asheville in 1898 on 22 acres on the French Broad. Behind it ran the Southern Railway. Some of the hides tanned there were of local origin, but the bulk of them were delivered by train from slaughterhouses in Chicago. Working conditions in tanneries could only be described as most foul. Box cars, stuffed with fully haired hides salted to keep them from rotting had to be unloaded by hand winter or summer when temperatures could reach 100°F. Spread over frames, hides were scraped to remove hair and flesh, immersed in putrid-smelling chemical vats, retrieved, and scraped again and again until they were clean. That was just the start. For weeks, hides soaked in various tanning acids depending on their ultimate purpose. Then came stretching and drying, perhaps shaving and dying, cutting, bundling, and shipping.[16] Exhausted tanning liquor flowed into the French Broad, ironically less than a mile upstream from popular Riverside Park. The park featured a lake no doubt filled by river water. Picnickers spread their blankets along the lake shore and, perhaps, cooled off with a swim unaware of the lake's toxicity. After dusk, couples courted in canoes while they watched silent movies on the big screen ashore.[17]

RIVER ON THE RAMPAGE

On the Fourth of July 1916, a low-pressure cell was brewing in the Caribbean. The resulting tropical storm drifted slowly northwestward, coming ashore near Charleston a few days later. A high-pressure ridge to the west was slowing it to a crawl over the upper French Broad watershed and, on July 8 it began to rain, hard. By the 10th, nearly six inches had fallen, saturating mountain soils, filling resort lakes above Hendersonville, and raising the river at Asheville by four feet. A day later, the river began to fall. But another storm was following the first. A week later, that storm also stalled over the Blue Ridge. In 24 hours on July 16, it dumped 12 inches of rain on Hendersonville and nearly 15 inches on Brevard. At Altapass near Grandfather Mountain, 24 inches fell in as many hours. Resort dams at Kanuga and Osceola burst, their waters surging into the already-rampaging French Broad. At Asheville, the flood crested at 23.1 feet, 19 feet above flood stage. At its height, the flood traveled at 110,000 cubic feet per second, seven times its average annual maximum.[18]

> At Riverside Park again the river found a broader expanse in which to vent its fury, but in the section of the city occupied by the lumber yards, wholesale houses, oil storage and freight yards, the banks were more confined, and the rush of waters far more terrific.
>
> Great warehouses, a hundred feet and more in length, and possibly fifty to sixty feet high, were picked up like playthings by the flood and tossed into the middle of the stream. Moving at first slowly and majestically the structures were swept with

Twin storms stalled over the watershed in July 1916 producing a record French Broad flood that devastated industry, business, and residences along the river. (North Carolina Room, Pack Memorial Library.)

increasing speed down the river, and then crushed with a horrible, dull grinding boom, against the concrete bridge.

The shock was terrifying. . . .[19]

So reported the *Asheville Citizen* on the morning of July 17. Eighty persons were killed. Floodplains of the French Broad and Swannanoa were swept virtually clean. At Marshall, 53 homes were floated off their foundations and dashed in the rapids below the town. Thirty miles of the Southern Railroad's track, the industrial lifeline of the upper watershed were washed out or buried in landslides.[20] Damages were estimated to exceed $500 million in today's dollars. Of human suffering, there could be no measure, but a front-page headline on July 18 proclaimed community resilience: *"CITIZENS, AT MASS MEET-ING, RAISE FUNDS CLOSE TO $10,000 TO CARE FOR THOSE MADE DESTITUTE BY FLOODS."*

CRAFTING THE FUTURE

Mountain women, masters at making do, may have had a slightly easier time during the deluges of 1916. Few farmsteads lacked hand looms. Clothing was cut and sewn. Baskets and chair seats were woven from cane and split saplings. Brooms were fashioned from wild grasses. Pottery could be made from local clays. Neighbor ladies gathered around quilting frames trading gossip with every stitch. They took as much pride in their crafts as men took in their prowess with their squirrel rifles and stills hidden deep in laurel hells. As railroads brought tourists into the watershed, many of them sought mementos of their visit, something to remind them of the tranquil beauty of the mountains and the quiet hospitality of people who lived up its coves. Some wanted something more substantial, more useful than a knick-knack for fireplace mantle, bookshelf, or window sill. And perhaps they were seeking a bit of nostalgia, something that reminded them of the homes of their grandparents, of an earlier and simpler time.

As the 1800s evolved into 1900's, the Southern Highland craft tradition began to take root. Teacher Lucy Morgan arrived at the Appalachian School in Penland on the North Toe River and began laying the foundation for the Penland School of Craft which she would establish in 1929. Across the mountains in Gatlinburg, Pi Beta Phi women's fraternity had opened a settlement school in 1912 to teach women more healthful ways of cooking and caring for their families. Their initiative grew into Arrowmont School of Arts and Crafts, internationally known for utilizing natural materials in weaving, pottery, sculpture, furniture, and pictures. However, no single individual would have greater influence in expanding the mountain craft tradition than Frances Louisa Goodrich.

Her father was a reverend whose declining health carried the family to France in search of recovery. After studying art there, she returned to America and continued her education at Yale's School of Fine Arts while trying her hand at selling paintings in New York. Her work, evidently, was not fulfilling, and she welcomed the opportunity to come to the mountains in 1895 to live with a friend teaching school near Riceville about five miles east of Asheville. Shortly thereafter, she and her friend relocated to Brittain Cove, just east of Weaverville. She built a house and soon nearby a school and a church, honoring her father.

In 1897, she moved again, this time to Allanstand, not far from Shelton Laurel in the heart of Madison County. There she made her home until her death in 1944. Enthralled by the natural beauty of the handiwork of her neighbors and seeing how they suffered from persistent shortages of money, she considered it her missionary duty to help them. She established Allanstand Cottage Industries and, to sell their handicrafts, she opened a small shop in Asheville in

Coming to Asheville to do missionary work, Frances Goodrich discovered mountain women weaving and spinning in traditional ways. She founded Allanstand Cottage Industries in Madison County, N.C., in 1897 which she and Dame Olive Campbell, founder of the John C. Campbell Folk School, nurtured into the Southern Highlands Craft Guild. (Hunter Library Special Collections, Western Carolina University.)

1908. Her collaboration with others, including Lucy Morgan at Penland and Olive Dame Campbell and John C. Campbell at Brasstown, N.C., led in 1937 to the establishment of the Southern Highlands Craft Guild.[21]

BLUEGRASS ROOTED IN THE MOUNTAINS

Scots-Irish who settled in the mountains not only brought with them their native penchant for making whiskey but also their music. So isolated were they in their coves that their music, rich with lore from their native highlands, yet so evocative of yesterday's happenings, sometimes haunting and other times spritely, thrived from generation to generation. Traveling the Southern Appalachians with her husband, an educator surveying social conditions with an eye toward reform for the Russell Sage Foundation, Olive Dame Campbell gathered country folk music. She collected more than 200 songs, which she published in *Songs and Ballads of the Appalachians* in 1915. The book attracted the attention of British music teacher and composer, Cecil Sharp, and the two met while she was in England. The following year, he traveled to America to explore English folk music's influence on American music. He'd made arrangements to meet Campbell in Asheville. Both were concerned that the rising tide of modernity would eradicate mountain music.

For three summers, 1916, 1917, and 1918, Sharp, accompanied by Maude

Karpeles, who was deeply interested in the roots of English folk dancing, journeyed through the Southern Appalachians. She wrote down lyrics while he, the music. Their first stop was the Campbell's Asheville home. A few days later, Mrs. Campbell drove them to Allanstand to meet Frances Goodrich. Among the first singers they heard was Aunt Polly Shelton, a member of the clan for which the infamous Civil War Shelton Laurel massacre was named. For them she sang *Earl Brand*, a ballad with roots dating back to the mid-1600s. The next day, Mrs. Shelton took them deeper into the mountains where other members of her family performed for them. In four days, Sharp and Karpeles collected 50 ballads, the first of hundreds they would gather. In August, they were rowed across the French Broad to Hot Springs; the bridge had been washed away by June's rampaging great flood. There, they met Jane Gentry who sang them 70 songs, the most collected from anyone.

Their ensuing travels took them into Tennessee, Kentucky, and Virginia. There, in April 1918, in the community of Nash near the northern end of the future Blue Ridge Parkway, they were taken for German spies. By then the United States had been at war for a year, and to the mountaineers, the ways of this "furrin'" couple were strange. They were always taking notes. They were vegetarians and ate no meat. Some folks were convinced their professed interest in old songs was clearly a "dodge" to hide their true and nefarious purpose. Their loyalties were hotly debated at Wednesday-night prayer meetings. Even though suspicions lingered, they were always cordially welcomed to stay, sit a while, and hear a song or two.[22] The hospitality of all who sang for Sharp and Karpeles fertilized seedlings that grew into America's 1960s folk music culture.

OVER HERE

As Sharp and Karpeles roamed the watershed, newspapers were heavy with black headlines announcing the Somme, Marne, Verdun, and other great battles of World War I. Patriotism and the draft had called thousands of young men from the mountains to trenches zigzagging along the French frontier. Among the first to volunteer in 1914 was Kiffin Rockwell. Born in Newport and reared in Asheville, his grandfathers had regaled him with stories of their marches and battles during the Civil War. Eager to serve, he studied briefly at the Virginia Military Institute and the US Naval Academy before enlisting in the French Foreign Legion. Seriously wounded in 1915, upon recovery a year later, he wanted to fly and transferred to the Lafayette Escadrille. On May 18,

Because it was served by the railroad and far from anywhere else, 2,200 German
sailors were imprisoned in Hot Springs during WWI. Officers were quartered
in the Mountain Park Hotel, and sailors in rude barracks built on what had been
the golf course. (*The German Invasion of North Carolina*, Jacqueline Burgin Painter,
Overmountain Press.)

he became the first American pilot to shoot down a German aircraft and,
four months later, the first American pilot killed in aerial combat in World War I.

Industry throughout the watershed thrived during the war as did some of
Western North Carolina's resorts. Less than two months after war was declared
on April 6, 1917, the federal Department of Labor leased the stately Mountain
Park Hotel in Hot Springs to house about 2,200 German merchant sailors.
They were the crews of grand passenger liners like the *Kronprinzessin Cecile*
and *Vaterland* impounded in New York harbor. They were joined by members
of the German Imperial Band, which had been captured in China. Officers
were quartered in the hotel and crewmen in barracks built across the highway,
now the site of the Hot Springs Campground. In addition, about 30 members
of their families were also sent to Hot Springs, where they boarded in town.
Children attended public schools and became friends of their classmates. Some
of the wives worked, among them a seamstress who boarded with the Jane
Gentry. She, and perhaps other Germans, likely met Sharp and Karpeles on
their collecting trip in July 1917.[23]

On Sunday afternoons, the band gave concerts enjoyed by townspeople who
brought their chairs and sat outside the prison camp's fence. From scrap wood
washed up from the great 1916 flood, sailors built a charming little Bavarian
village of single-room cottages with gardens and gazebos. With mixed emo-
tions, in June 1918, residents of the community bade good-bye to their German

guests, who were ordered transferred to the prisoner-of-war stockade in Fort Oglethorpe, Georgia.[24]

German interns, too ill to make the trip to northern Georgia, were transferred to Biltmore Hospital operated by nearby All Souls Church in Biltmore Village. Not far away in the village of Azalea, the War Department, overwhelmed by the need for beds for casualties of war, illness, and accident, began construction of General Hospital #19 providing 1,000 beds in 60 frame buildings for tuberculosis patients. Later that year an additional 200 buildings housing 500 more veterans were authorized. Together, they formed the foundation for today's Charles George Veterans Administration Medical Center

With the completion of the hospital, the U. S. Post Office opened an adjacent branch which took "Oteen" as its name. The name originated with the hospital's first commanding officer, Col. Henry Hoagland who claimed that "Oteen" was the Indian word for "Chief Aim." In the first edition of the hospital's newsletter The OTEEN, the colonel wrote: "Our Chief Aim, broadly stated, should be the giving of our best for the honor and services of our country."[25]

In addition to thousands of cases of tuberculosis, Army camps and Navy bases throughout the country were overwhelmed by a new and viciously lethal pandemic that came to be known as Spanish Influenza or The Spanish Lady though its origin had nothing to do with Spain. According to the newsletter, "The Surgeon General, after the ravages the flu made all over the land, acknowledged that Oteen had less influenza per capita than any other military organization in the country."[26]

As soldiers will, patients made light of their plight. Dances sponsored by Asheville's Knights of Columbus had been hugely enjoyed. After their cancellation, a jester reported in The OTEEN: "A new dance called "Flu Flitter" has been invented. To dance it, you take one step forward, then sneeze twice, pivot and swallow two quinine capsules, swing your partner, then cough in unison, take two steps backward and blow your noses. . . ."[27]

Spanish flu was not taken so lightly by Ashevillians. Schools, churches and theatres were closed. Many wore masks. Mouthwash instead of whiskey filled pocket flasks. Some sprinkled sulphur on their shoes. The Army hospital donated 100 beds to an emergency ward established in the Masonic Temple. Debate raged over whether officials reopened businesses in the city too soon. Overall, about 3,479 Ashevillians came down with the disease and locally, by February 1919, 127 had died.[28]

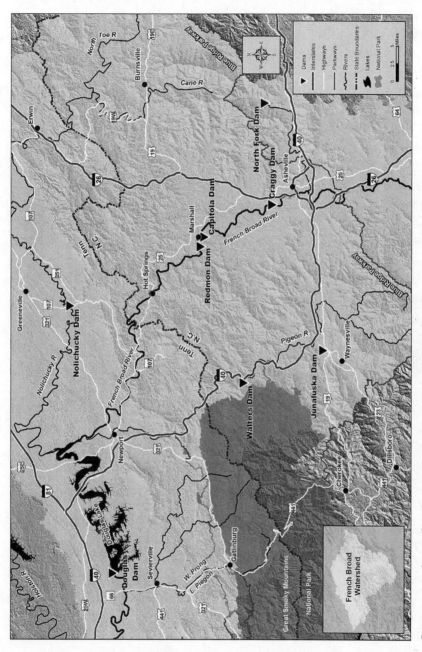

Starting around 1900, four dams were erected in the French Broad, two on the Pigeon, and one on the Nolichucky. (Cartography: Greg Dobson.)

ELEVEN

Promise and Peril

On November 11, 1918, at 11 a.m., church bells rang throughout the world. The war to end all wars was over. Joyous throngs gathered in every town to celebrate victory. America had turned the tide. Timber, hides, ores, mica wrested from the hills; months of over-time labor in sweltering factories; meatless Tuesdays, wheatless Wednesdays; a bucket of coal scavenged along railroad tracks; and thousands of men and scores of women who had answered their country's call, all contributing to victory. That gnawing worry whether Johnny would come marching home now seemed worth it. Peace and prosperity would prevail. One concern warbled from the Victrola: *How ya gonna keep 'em down on the farm (after they've seen Paree)?*

Ragtime reigned. "There's a good play in Asheville, a play of a town which never had the ordinary, healthy, industrial life of a town ought to have but instead dressed itself up in fine streets and stuck hotels in its hair in order to vamp the tourist populace," wrote Thomas Wolfe to his brother in 1921. "There's a good play in the boy who lets the town vamp him, who sees the rich tourists and mode of life and thinks he must live that way. . . ."[1]

There was no other town like it in the watershed, and there never would be. Flappers and fellas raced in top-down Fords from watering holes at the Grove Park Inn over to the Battery Park and down to the Glen Rock across from the Southern Railroad station on Depot Street. Hooch, bootlegged bourbon or squeezed from local corn, lubricated every dance. These were high-flying days for the affluent. Businesses prospered. Investors arrived daily by train invited by friends like Vanderbilt and Edwin Grove, sire of the Grove Park Inn in 1913,

At the height of the Roaring Twenties in Asheville, the fifteen-story Jackson building, topped with an 18-million watt searchlight to attract attention to the city, was erected on the site where Thomas Wolfe's father carved his famous angel. (North Carolina Collection, Pack Memorial Public Library, Asheville, North Carolina. Photography: George Masa.)

who made millions from Grove's Tasteless Chill Tonic, which, according to its label, "Makes Children and Adults Fat as Pigs."[2]

From 1910 to 1930, Buncombe County's population nearly doubled, from 49,798 to 97,937. In this, the "Land of the Sky in the Heart of the Blue Ridge," enthused a 1921 Chamber of Commerce publication, "The Earth is so Kind, that just Tickle Her with a Hoe and She Laughs a Bountiful Harvest." The county boasted of seven new buildings and 54 rural libraries. Leading out from Asheville's 50 miles of paved streets were 150 miles of asphalt surfaced concrete highways with an average width of 18 feet. Boosters of Buncombe claimed theirs was the "best paved county in the South."

Building boomed. In Asheville's center, developer Lynwood B. Jackson erected Western North Carolina's first skyscraper in 1924. The 15-story Jackson Building was topped by an observation tower equipped with a 400× telescope and an 18 million candle power search light to attract tourists. For the building, Jackson chose the tiny 27-foot by 60-foot lot where Thomas Wolfe's father, William Oliver, likely carved his famed angel. Across the way and down the hill to the east, the county was constructing its new 17 story courthouse, which would be completed in 1928. Next door, a fine new city hall, a classic example of art deco architecture, would open the same year. Four years earlier, the new Battery Park and George Vanderbilt hotels opened within shouting distance of each other. And in 1926, Grove began construction on his Arcade, possibly Asheville's most ambitious commercial structure. Occupying a full city block across the street from the Battery Park Hotel, Grove planned a grand Tudor-esque structure housing scores of shops and offices for small businesses. The mall would be roofed with a pedestrian terrace surrounding a 14-story residential skyscraper. Grove died before its opening, and the 1929 stock market crash scotched plans to build the tower.

As Thomas Wolfe recalled in *Boom Town*: "It was fantastic! Everyone was a real estate man . . . barbers, lawyers, clothiers. . . . And there seemed to be only one rule . . . buy, always to buy . . . and to sell again within any two days at any price. . . . When the supply of streets and houses was exhausted, new streets were . . . created in the surrounding wilderness; and even before these streets were paved or a house had been built upon them, the land was being sold, and then resold, by the acre, by the foot, for hundreds of thousands of dollars."[3]

WATER AT WORK

In his report to his client, the Asheville Chamber of Commerce, in July 1929, Charles F. Waddell, a prominent engineer and industrial consultant, recounted a call he and Fred L. Seely, Grove's son-in-law and business manager, made on Firestone Tire and Rubber Company in Akron, Ohio. Asheville was one of a number of cities in the South that was in the running to become the location of a new plant to produce 5,000 tires per day. The availability of "white and negro labor . . . suited to the tire industry," a 100-acre site, and an airport "for landing Ford three-motor, twelve passenger planes" were critically important. In addition Firestone stated "7,200,000 gallons of water will be required per day, of which 10% must be clean and is used for process work, and the balance can be of almost any quality, being used for cooling purposes." The temperature of the water was also a concern.[4]

Though the stock market crash prevented Firestone from choosing a site in the South, in the 1920s the availability of fresh water, flat floodplains framed by gentle hills, reliable labor, and lack of unions lured three textile plants of 1,000,000 square feet or more. Opened in 1927, Sayles-Biltmore Bleachery and its workers village sprawled along the Swannanoa, now the location of Walmart. Sayles bleached raw cotton fabric known as "grey goods" with tetrachloroethylene, also known as PERC. Used in dry cleaning and to degrease metal in manufacturing, after long and heavy exposure, PERC poses severe risk to human nervous system, liver, kidneys and is likely to cause cancer.[5]

Upstream a few miles, Beacon Manufacturing opened its plant in 1925. Beacon was among the world's largest blanket makers. Its owner, Charles D. Owen, was known for his civic benevolence. Its workers' village enjoyed congenial community life. At its peak, 2,200 were employed, and it was the mainstay of Swannanoa. After it closed in 1991, its 42-acre site was declared a brownfield due to toxic pollution of soil and groundwater.[6]

On September 23, 1928, subscribers unrolling their *Asheville Sunday Citizen* could not help but read the frontpage headline blaring, "American Enka Locates Great Plant Here" The company had chosen 2,000 acres along Hominy Creek not far upstream from where Capt. William Moore had received the land grant for his "Eden" in 1784. Enka selected the site because of the ready availability of fresh water essential for the manufacture of artificial fibers. Adjacent ran the Southern Railroad with connections to textile mills relocating to the South to avoid labor issues up north and for delivery of coal from Tennessee and Kentucky to fire the plant's boilers. The plant would contain two massive buildings, each 1,000 feet long. Its management anticipated building a village in the hills above the plant to house 25,000.[7]

Along the French Broad, industry was thriving. In 1929, Asheville Knitting Mills doubled its capacity. Hans Rees Tannery was now recovered from the 1916 flood and running at full tilt. Making furniture downriver in Woodfin, Carolina Wood Products employed 500 with a payroll of $350,000. Of the future for more furniture factories, I. E. Monk wrote: "The wonderful forests of Buncombe county and vicinity together with the four hundred thousand hydro-electric horse-power in the mountain streams within a forty-mile radius of Asheville certainly are inducements. . . ."[8]

LANDS NOBODY WANTED

Stand on the terrace outside the library of Vanderbilt's grand chateau and gaze across the estate. Below the gardens and down the hill along the French Broad stretch verdant fields. Beyond, roll vineyards and woods hiding shotgun sports courses. In the distance rises the Blue Ridge capped by Mount Pisgah. Beneath it on a grassy knob sprawls the site of his beloved mountain hunting retreat, Buckspring Lodge. When Vanderbilt scanned his cherished highlands, what met his eye was quite different from today.

Rather than a carpet of consistent loden, an irregular patchwork quilt spread up the mountains. Mostly drab and brownish grey in winter except for patches of spruce and fir and when covered with snow, recently cut-over tracts glowed with spring's new growth. Unlogged parcels stood dark with mature foliage. Up-close detail emerged. Historic photos present his woods as a broad sepia wreckage of jagged stumps erupting from a welter of jumbled logs and withered limbs. Had color film been available in Vanderbilt's day, pictures would have revealed thousands of seedlings with their oversized apple green leaves struggling up from the forest floor. As he had learned from Schenck and Pinchot, Vanderbilt no doubt could see future woodlands towering in his mind.

To many, mountain slopes were nothing but barren wastes, or as William E. Shands and Robert G. Healy put in their landmark 1977 book, *The Lands Nobody Wanted*. Because they had been cut over or burned, they were thought in the 1890s to have very little value. Generations would pass before their timber could be harvested. As the mountains were generally too steep to till, rains washed away what little soil covered their slopes, turning cold, clear streams into raging, dirty brown cataracts. Until passage of the Weeks Act in 1911, most national forests were established on land already owned by the government. The new legislation permitted the government to purchase private tracts. In 1914, the act allowed Edith, Vanderbilt's widow, to sell 86,700 acres, roughly 135 square miles of the estate's mountain lands, to the US Forest Service in 1914. The Forest Service's mission in those years was to ensure that the nation would never exhaust its stocks of timber for construction and other commercial purposes. Half a century later, the service would broaden its mission to include recreation.

At the time of the sale, the Vanderbilt tract was known as Pisgah Forest. It was adjacent to the smaller Burke-McDowell tract near Marion, which was the first parcel acquired to form the core of today's 512,758-acre Pisgah National Forest. When combined with Cherokee National Forest, Nantahala National Forest, and Great Smoky Mountains National Park, they constitute the largest environmental reserve in the Southeast. Together, they provide the sources of fresh water for many of the region's major metropolitan districts, including Atlanta and Charleston. Tourists and retirees drive the economies of scores of small towns on their flanks—none more so than those on the West Prong of the Little Pigeon River. But into the end of the 1920s, Gatlinburg, Pigeon Forge, and Sevierville largely escaped the exuberant growth of Asheville and other communities on the upper French Broad. It seems supremely ironic that the implosion of the stock market in 1929 and the onset of the Great Depression triggered the economic explosion of those three towns.

HIKING AND HANDICRAFTS

When the Pi Beta Phi's arrived in Gatlinburg to establish their settlement school in 1912, they found a crossroads store, a sawmill, a blacksmith, a Baptist church, and half a dozen houses scattered on the fertile flats separated by a low ridge and drained by a pair of creeks that emptied into the Little Pigeon. Though a railroad had been planned to come up the river since 1907, it never made it past Sevierville. Beyond Pigeon Forge, the route would have had to wind through a narrow gorge following the main dirt road. Anybody trying to reach Gatlinburg by car usually had to leave it in Pigeon Forge and take a wagon. It was not until 1925 that Sevier County approved a $100,000 bond issue to build a road through Gatlinburg to the Sugarlands at the base of the Great Smokies. Rural postmen, riding about 25 miles a day, delivered mail, including the Sears & Roebuck catalog. That thick book, a staple of outhouse reading, was one of the ways mountain folks kept in touch with the outside world. But they were very heavy. The draining of one pond in Gatlinburg revealed where one mailman had been delivering his catalogs.[9]

Though forests rising above Gatlinburg were wealthy with oak, chestnut, and poplar, the region's inaccessibility by railroad limited logging. Around the opening of the 1900s, portable steam sawmills made their appearance in the headwaters of the West Prong of the Little Pigeon as far up stream as the Sugarlands and the Chimneys. Often mounted on a chassis with four iron wheels, they could be dragged to a suitable site by a team of mules. Once set up, they were particularly efficient at reducing logs into lumber suitable for furniture. In 1910, Andy Huff located his mill on Roaring Fork close to where it flowed into the West Prong. As the Little River Lumber Company intensified, cutting on the 76,000 acres it owned over Sugarland Mountain to the southwest, more and more timber buyers arrived in Gatlinburg to scout the forest's potential on the flanks of Mt. Le Conte. Huff opened a small hotel—The Mountain View—near his sawmill in 1916 to accommodate them and a trickle of tourists. Three years later, he added indoor plumbing.[10]

As railroad travel to Sevierville improved and roads became hard surfaced

Andy Huff opened the first of Gatlinburg's great hotels, The Mountain View, in 1916. By the 1920s, it had become the jumping off point for Smoky Mountain hikers, anglers, and hunters. (Great Smoky Mountains National Park Archives.)

over the following decade, travel into Gatlinburg became less arduous. Hiking drew so many that Huff's son Jack established LeConte Lodge in 1926 atop the high peak that towered over the rapidly growing town. That same year, the Pi Phi's opened Arrowmont Shop to sell local handcrafts. Before they arrived in 1912, the hamlet had no school and no medical clinic. The sorority's teachers and nurses often were given baskets, quilts, and woodcarvings as expressions of appreciation by their students, patients, and their families. Recognizing the growing popularity of items made by hand rather than machine and offering courses in marketing, Arrowmont added a new source of income for mountain families and another reason for tourists to visit Gatlinburg. Hiking and hand-icrafts pointed to a brightening future for residents of the upper Little Pigeon watershed. And the hoped-for arrival of the railroad from Sevierville would bring accelerated growth from large-scale logging just as it had to Waynesville and Canton. In the final years of the 1920s, few thought America could not keep living high on the hog.

Most families living in the French Broad watershed enjoyed, if one could call it that, a natural protection from the collapse of America's financial system in 1929. Small farms dominated the countryside. Towns had yet to swell with retirees and tourists and businesses that supported them. Few outside of the very wealthy speculated either by purchasing shares in local companies or in corporations whose futures were reported on ticker tape. Though local news-papers and newfangled radio stations like WNOX down in Knoxville reported the national debacle, news of the Great Depression was slow to filter into mountain communities. Those with subscriptions to nearby weeklies got the word in the mail. Others heard it from traveling agents looking to buy timber and from drummers, those salesmen who peddled their wares house to house on county back roads.

Large-scale logging had yet to develop in the Little Pigeon drainage. Yet in the next watershed over, it was booming. A number of Sevier County farmers stabled their mules when harvesting was done, stuffed a few clothes and other gear into saddle bags, and rode across the divide at Sugarland Mountain to work the "leisure season" for the Little River Lumber Company until it was time to come home and plant spring crops. Some may have stayed a while longer and worked at the Wonderland Hotel in Elkmont, a popular destination for hikers, hunters, and anglers. Cash money grew ever tighter. In 1925, a bushel of corn brought $1.26. By 1932, it had fallen to 29¢. Tobacco, for 50 years a staple crop across the mountains in North Carolina, became increasingly popular. Not only did it require less cultivation than corn, but it also paid handsomely just in time for Christmas. Free time, after crops were sown and taken in, was increasingly devoted to weaving, wood carving, and furniture making to be sold at Arrowmont.[11]

Summer and fall, hikers from the city continued to arrive. They paid cash for room and board at many a mountain home. The word about the natural beauty of the Blue Ridge Mountains had been spread by scores of articles in national magazines, none more influential than the writings of Horace Kephart. A Yale-educated bibliographer, noted for his work on the fourteenth century Italian poet, Petrarch, while director of St. Louis's Mercantile Library, he longed for the simpler life of his Iowa upbringing. His increasing sojourns to hunt and fish in the Ozarks and bouts with the bottle cost him his job and marriage.

Recovering at the home of his father in Dayton, Ohio, he sought a land where contours were close together and the people were not. In October 1904, he washed up in a cabin on Little Fork of Sugar Fork, a tributary of Hazel Creek across from today's Fontana, N.C. He was enthralled by the wilderness around him and the frontier-like lives of his widely scattered neighbors. Meticulously recording what he saw in card files he kept under his bunk, he would write numerous articles for national magazines and, in 1913, *Our Southern Highlanders*. Though panned for his exaggerations of moonshining, which he knew all too well from personal consumption, the book was pivotal in galvanizing regional and national interest that led to the creation of Great Smoky Mountains National Park. Wrote Kephart: "I owe my life to these mountains and I want them preserved that others may profit by them as I have."[12]

After leaving Hazel Creek, Kephart took up residence in a Bryson City boarding house, did his writing in a small office over Bennett's Drug Store,[13] and served on the town's Chamber of Commerce and Board of Aldermen which he chaired. He traveled frequently to Asheville to conspire with his friend, photographer George Masa, on establishing the Great Smokies. No doubt they felt the first economic tremors that would hobble Asheville for half a century. Owing to retirees and tourism who summered here and wintered there, the city's burgeoning economy was closely tied to South Florida's. When the market for real estate collapsed there in 1925 and was left for dead after massive hurricanes of 1926 and 1928, Asheville's soon followed. Depression saddled Asheville with $56 million in debt, among the largest debt per capita of any city in the United States. Money was so tight, remembered Frank Coxe, grandson of the founder of the Battery Park Hotel, "You couldn't sell a dime for a nickel, because no one had a nickel to pay for it."[14] Rather than declare bankruptcy, the city made payments for nearly 50 years on its Depression-era bonds until they were fully retired in 1976.[15]

FROM VANDERBILT'S FOREST TO NATIONAL PARK

About the same time that Vanderbilt was contemplating seeking healthcare for his mother in Asheville, one of its physicians, Chase P. Ambler was thinking about creating in the Southern Appalachian an equivalent to Yellowstone, the first national park established in 1872. While on a fishing trip in the Western North Carolina Mountains in 1899, he and his friend William R. Day discussed the idea. Day was in a position to help. Earlier that year, President William

Authorized by Calvin Coolidge in 1926 and dedicated by Franklin Delano Roosevelt in 1940, the 522,000-acre Great Smoky Mountains is the country's most heavily visited National Park and a mainstay of the watershed's economy. (Great Smoky Mountains National Park Archives.)

McKinley had appointed him to the US Sixth District Court of Appeals, and in 1903 he was named to the Supreme Court by President Theodore Roosevelt. While their efforts gained little steam, similar conversations were being held across the mountains in Knoxville. They did not catch fire until 1923, when Mr. and Mrs. Willis P. Davis went west to visit national parks. While admiring their snow-capped grandeur, Mrs. Davis asked her husband, "Why can't we have a national park in the Great Smokies?" Later that year, Davis met with Hubert Work, secretary of interior. By that time, pressure to create a national park in the South was mounting and Secretary Work authorized the establishment of the Southern Appalachian National Park Committee.

The Great Smokies would be different from the 18 national parks established before 1924. Most had been formed from land already owned by the federal government. The 515,256 acres considered for this one were divided into 6,600 separate tracts. The largest share, about 85 percent, was owned by 18 different logging companies. Another 1,200 parcels were small farms. And, complicating issues further were some 5,000 tiny plots occupied by summer homes and lots.[16] Logging companies were, generally speaking, willing to sell. They had stripped the land of marketable timber. Given plummeting real estate values as the Great Depression deepened and corporate need for cash skyrocketed, sale for a national park was very attractive.

The Department of Interior had no funds with which to acquire park lands or prospects for securing any from Congress. Coffers of Tennessee and North Carolina were strapped as well. A new national park would rekindle prosperity stifled by the Great Depression. "Asheville has come out flat-footed for the park and one of its most ardent boosters is Mrs. Vanderbilt," Kephart wrote Knoxville's David Chapman, president of the Smoky Mountains Conservation Association. "Our hardest job was to convince our own folks in and around Bryson City that the Park would be worthwhile. They could not see what the coming of hundreds of tourists daily through the park in Swain County would mean for Bryson City."[17]

Truer words about the coming of the park were never written. With axe and hoe, from the wilderness many had wrought a home place to live pretty much as they pleased, to raise their children as they saw fit, and to earn the satisfaction of providing for themselves. They knew without a doubt they would be forced to move. "This is not true," Chapman said in December 1925. "They will be permitted to remain in their cabins and in a number of cases will find employment in taking care of the park." A few months later in 1926, he reiterated: "Let's have an end to this constant talk about dispossession of the mountain people. They ought to be . . . eager for consummation of a project that is going to mean to many of them real independence for the first time in their lives."[18] Their fears were fully realized. As the park was being established, thousands were evicted from their farms, which were taken by eminent domain. They struggled to find work in nearby communities, but with the onset of the Great Depression, their lives were difficult indeed.

In the spring of 1926, the Southern Appalachian National Park Committee recommended to Secretary Work that funds be appropriated for Shenandoah National Park on the northern end of the Blue Ridge. Less than 100 miles west of Washington, D.C., the region was similar in many ways to the Great Smokies and more attractive because of its proximity to much greater population and political power. Chapman and his allies in North Carolina would not be stayed. They lobbied and eventually preliminary funding for the Great Smokies and Mammoth Cave were also included. Surveyors begin defining the park's boundaries. The bill triggered efforts by legislatures in North Carolina and Tennessee each to raise $2 million to acquire properties. Public campaigns flourished as well. More than 4,500 school children contributed their pennies, raising $1,000. When these efforts fell short and the project teetered on the brink of failure, John D. Rockefeller, Jr. stepped up in 1928 and contributed $5 million through the Laura Spellman Rockefeller Memorial "in the beautiful spirit of my mother."[19] Creation of the Great Smoky Mountains National Park was formalized in June 1934 by President Franklin Roosevelt.

THREE SQUARES AND A DOLLAR A DAY

From mile marker 318 near Linville Falls south to Mile Marker 458 and the junction with the road to Heintooga Overlook, the Blue Ridge Parkway provides spectacular views framing the heights of the headwaters of the French Broad watershed. The route crosses the probable path of de Soto's 1540 expedition near Linville Falls; passes the Museum of North Carolina Minerals above Spruce Pine; runs below Mount Mitchell, at 6,684 feet the highest peak east of the Mississippi, and drops down to cross the French Broad at Asheville. Near Mt. Pisgah at mile 406.7, it swings past the site of Vanderbilt's hunting lodge, and then continues by Devil's Courthouse, where Judaculla sat in judgment of the Cherokee. From its peak to the northwest, one can see Shining Rock, the birthplace of Selu and Kaná ti, the first Cherokee couple. A little farther to the northwest rises the Cold Mountain of Charles Frazier's Civil War novel.

Touring the recently opened 105-mile-long Skyline Drive atop Shenandoah National Park in Virginia in 1933, the commonwealth's former US senator, Harry F. Byrd, suggested to Roosevelt how wonderful it would be to connect the parks with a mountain highway interspersed with areas for recreation. Thus evolved the 469-mile-long Blue Ridge Parkway, stretching from Rockfish Gap, Va., to Great Smoky Mountains National Park at Cherokee. Construction was authorized on November 24, 1933, and the final section, the 7.7-mile Linn Cove Viaduct, was completed in 1987. The route spawned incessant controversy; Asheville leaders insisted it had to pass through the city rather than around it. One cannot drive the parkway without thinking of the Civilian Conservation Corps, a pillar of Roosevelt's New Deal. Established in 1933, the CCC employed young men, out of work and often unskilled. They were paid $1 a day, given three square meals, military surplus uniforms, and housing. Of their $30 monthly pay, roughly $600 today, $25 was sent home to their families.

Originally called the Appalachian Scenic Highway and running 469 miles from Shenandoah National Park to the Great Smokies, work began on the Blue Ridge Parkway here at Cumberland Knob in North Carolina on September 11, 1935. (National Park Service. Photography: Abbie Rowe.)

Along with the CCC, thousands of men and women in the watershed survived the Great Depression employed by the Works Progress Administration and the Federal Emergency Relief Administration. Along with the parkway's gentle grades, tunnels, bridges, stout stone retaining walls, and countless overlooks, the handiwork of these workers is visible in scores of local schools and a handful of municipal buildings. Were it not for the worst depression in modern American history, would the Great Smoky Mountains National Park and Blue Ridge Parkway have been established? Together they, with neighboring national forests and state parks, annually draw more than 16 million visitors, who spend billions in cities and towns throughout the watershed. They sustain thriving economies in Western North Carolina and East Tennessee and are a major lure for new industry. And perhaps of even greater importance, they foster a thriving community committed to sustained conservation.

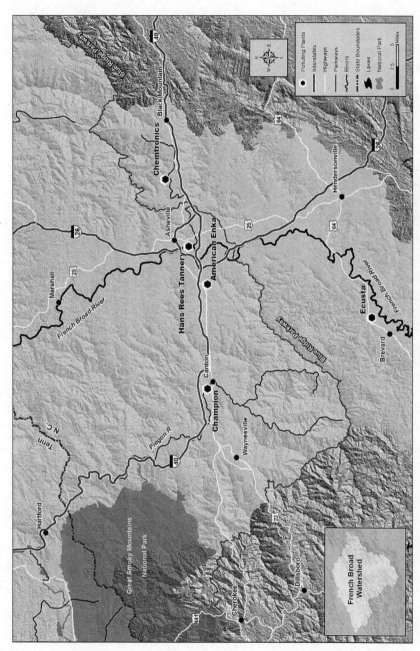

Huge forests, reliable and inexpensive labor, and good rail and highway transportation attracted industry dependent on ample supplies of pure cold water. (Cartography: Greg Dobson.)

TWELVE

Rivers of Resilience

Rivers are resilient. Left alone, they usually clean themselves naturally. Sun shining on long, shallow pools and riffles and oxygen replenished by turbulent rapids mitigate most bacterial and much chemical pollution. Yet rivers, their tributary streams, and ground water seeping in along their banks are also critical elements in the evolution of human endeavor. For millennia, their waters have slaked our thirst, grown our crops, watered our livestock, been our highways, powered our industry, and carried away our waste. Taken together, at the most basic level, they fuel our very livelihood as they have since the first Paleo Indians set foot in the French Broad watershed some 14,000 years ago.

Inexpensive mountain terrain, mostly denuded of marketable timber but laced with hundreds of miles of exuberant streams carving endless striking vistas, led to the creation of Great Smoky Mountain National Park and Blue Ridge Parkway in the 1930s. They became the watershed's primary economic drivers. Similarly, cheap land and apparently inexhaustible pure freshwater along with a reliable, underemployed work force and nearby railroads attracted major manufacturing industry. Every dollar earned in the watershed was spent largely in the watershed. As the decade wore on, small businesses began to thrive as did their surrounding communities.

Entry of the United States into World War II accelerated the opportunity for industrial development. Wartime demand for electricity fostered impoundment of the French Broad by Douglas Dam. It is said that an army travels on its belly. Not completely so. It travels on ream after ream of paper from firms like Ecusta in Brevard and Champion in Canton. Pure water was essential for manufacturing rayon for parachutes and milling and dying cotton and wool for uniforms and equipment. Hides were tanned into leather for everything from boots to helmets for pilots. Mills ground grains into flour and meal that found their ways into rations. Impurities were flushed from ores mined from mountain slopes. To carry increased freight tonnage, railroads double tracked some of their lines. At Asheville, routes from the Piedmont to Atlanta and Knoxville to Greenville crossed in the massive rail yard, with its extensive service shops and classic roundhouse, now razed, on the French Broad. Prosperity reigned, though at a horrible price in men and women maimed and killed by the war and industrial accident and by disease from degradation of the watershed's life-giving rivers and groundwaters.

ECUSTA'S ENDLESS BELT

Look at any slick magazine of the 1930s. There was Jean Harlow, that marcelled blonde temptress, begowned in slinky red, head thrown back with no care in the world, right hand raised with fingers beckoning "None so good as LUCKIES." Smoking became all the rage. No matter how down and out, one could live like the stars, cigarette intimately shared by lovers or dangling from a tough guy's lip. German-born importer of endless belts for fine paper making, Harry Straus of New York was no novice to cigarette manufacturing. Among his clients was American Tobacco, which owned a French mill that produced fine cigarette paper. As demand for it grew, Straus formed the Champagne Paper Corporation in 1930 with funding from American Tobacco, P. Lorillard, Liggett & Meyers, and Phillip Morris. Champagne Paper owned mills in France. Ever practical and with an eye to the probability of war in Europe, in early 1937, Straus began looking for a place to build a mill "in the South, preferably North Carolina." His requirements were straightforward:

1. No less than 10,000,000 gallons of pure water a day
2. Proximity of railroad
3. Availability of high type labor
4. We prefer a locality not in the vicinity of a manufacturing center,
5. We do not want any interference on the part of the State in the disposing of our waste water.[1]

Among locations considered for the new plant were Old Fort on the headwaters of the Catawba; Horse Shoe on the French Broad; and sites on the

Ecusta, one of the world's largest manufacturers of cigarette papers and cellophane, located near Brevard in 1939 because government placed no controls on polluting the French Broad. (Local History Room, Transylvania County Library.)

Mills, Nantahala, and Davidson rivers. Others included the headwaters of the Yadkin, Spruce Pine on the Nolichucky, and Murphy on the Hiwassee. The Davidson site was initially rejected because of concerns that the river could not provide enough water during periods of low flow and that it was a source of water for Hendersonville. Yet when Straus visited the Davidson, he was impressed by the huge, flat site, well-paved roads to Asheville, adjacent rail line, and good schools, including a college potentially benefiting employees. Transylvania County's Board of Commissioners offered to tax the corporation no more than $1,500 per year for the first three years after production began and $2,500 per year for each of the seven years thereafter ($27,000 and $45,000 respectively in today's dollars). That was good enough for Straus. A subhead in the *Transylvania Times* announcing the purchase reported: "Pure Mountain Water Was Deciding Location Factor."[2]

Preliminary estimates placed the cost of acquisition of 225 acres, erecting and equipping 13 buildings, and other site preparation would cost $3.6 million ($65 million). Though Straus blanched at the cost, he gave the go-ahead, and construction started in June 1938. The plant would be named "Ecusta," thought to be the Cherokee name for the Davidson River that flowed by the site just before joining the French Broad. A year later, the *Transylvania Times* trumpeted

"Whistle at ECUSTA Blows First Blast." Nearly complete were a 225-foot smokestack and the first 18 buildings at the plant.[3] Among the buildings was one that would filter 25 million gallons of water every 24 hours.

On September 2, 1939, Ecusta began production. The day before, Germany had invaded Poland igniting World War II. In the early 1940s, the plant became a community, though it did not, as many huge factories in the watershed did, provide housing for employees. In 1941, Straus opened a cafeteria for employees. Steaks cost a quarter and milk, a nickel, and one would be hard pressed to spend more than 50¢ for dinner. The company and its employees contributed about 25 percent of the cost of building Brevard's new hospital. Its baseball team won first place in the North Carolina Industrial League and plots and advice were provided for employees growing Victory Gardens. War Bond, Red Cross, and USO fund drives were enthusiastically supported. Shortages of wood pulp led to the use of flax stalks for making airmail, carbon, and other lightweight papers—all essential for the war effort.[4]

Frantic production slowed dramatically with war's end, and Ecusta was purchased by Olin Corp in 1949. Cellophane was added to the product line, with much of it sold for wrapping packs of cigarettes to keep them fresh. X-ray film was also manufactured at the plant. Senior management and other investors bought the mill from Olin in 1985 and resold it in 1987 to P. H. Gladfelter Company. Faced with accelerating improvements in paper-making technology, an increasingly outdated plant and equipment, foreign competition, and declining markets, Gladfelter sold the mill to Nathu Puri, head of international paper manufacturer Purico in 2001, known for purchasing distressed properties that had outlived their productivity. Puri placed Ecusta in bankruptcy in 2002, and approximately 700 employees were terminated. In 2007, Renova Partners, a firm specializing in redevelopment of brownfield sites and local investors, purchased the site.

Under U.S. Environmental Protection Agency (EPA) and North Carolina's Department of Environmental Quality (DEC) direction, clean up began in 2008. Buildings were razed. Excavated and removed from or stabilized on the site were 3,200 tons of mercury and lead-contaminated soils, along with another 5,600 tons from beneath building slabs. Wells were drilled to treat ground water. In a trench inside one of the buildings, eight gallons of extremely poisonous liquid mercury were recovered and 525 drums of intensely toxified soil were sent off-site for disposal. A Human Health and Ecological Risk Assessment concluded in

2009 that contaminant levels on the site and in neighboring stretches of the Davidson and French Broad were within EPA acceptable ranges. Removal of severely compromised soil was completed later that year. The property and its groundwater continue to be under constant EPA and DEQ monitoring. Ultimately, Renova plans to transform the property into a mixed-use development,[5] with room for 1,000 housing units and 1,250,000 sq. ft. of commercial space.[6] As this is being written in 2020, the property is still on the market.

Ecusta's saga is typical of all but one of the major manufacturing industries that relied on water from the French Broad and its tributaries. All fell prey to aging equipment, processes, and buildings; rapidly improving technology; and increased domestic and international competition. Some, like Ecusta and American Enka's plants in Asheville and in the Nolichucky watershed near Morristown, Tenn., and Beacon Manufacturing in Swannanoa appear to be in the final stages of remediation and awaiting redevelopment. Champion Fibre, once considered the nation's largest paper manufacturing plant, would be pilloried for polluting the Pigeon with cancer-causing dioxins and ricochet through a series of owners.

Others, like Chemtronics's former factory on Bee Tree Creek in Swannanoa, face a more checkered future. Located just upstream from Maj. Davidson's original settlement in the 1790s, the 1,027-acre site was purchased in 1951 by Oerlikon Tool & Arms Corp., a Swiss manufacturer of rockets and other weapons. The onset of the Korean War was forcing the US armed forces to modernize. The Cold War was beginning to boil. War with Russia loomed in Europe and the Middle East. The world lived under the threat of annihilation by nuclear warfare. To augment conventional high-explosive and armor-piercing ammunition, the United States and other nations were exploring chemical and biological weapons, among them nerve and other toxic gases that would be produced along Bee Tree Creek.

In 1959, Oerlikon sold the plant to the Celanese Corp., which in turn sold it to Northrop Carolina in 1965. Six years later, it was bought by Chemtronics, which continued manufacture of toxic chemicals. Placed on the first list of Superfund sites in 1982, the plant began installing remediation practices in 1991. It closed in 1994. Today, the site has been divided into two sections. The upper 526 acres adjoining Pisgah National Forest were deemed free of pollution and placed under conservation easement held by the Southern Appalachian Highlands Conservancy in 2018. The other 501 acres remains a Superfund site.[7]

The outbreak of World War II ignited industrial development that would forever alter the French Broad watershed. England's declaration of war in response to the Nazi invasion of Poland in 1939 dramatically expanded markets for paper, wood products, textiles, metals, and minerals. The following year, President Roosevelt called for the production of 50,000 new planes for Army and Navy air forces. They would wear aluminum skins from Alcoa's smelter and rolling mill 15 miles southeast of Knoxville. Cheap hydroelectric power, principally from dams on the Little Tennessee and its tributaries, enticed Alcoa's directors in 1914 to locate what became one of the world's largest manufacturers of aluminum sheeting in North Maryville, renamed Alcoa in 1919. The Japanese attack on Pearl Harbor on December 7, 1941, triggered almost universal urgency to arm and strike back.

Ten months later, a seven-mile-long valley framed by two ridges on the Clinch River was selected as the site for America's secret city, Oak Ridge. There, fuel would be made for the atom bombs that would end the war. The isolated valley was chosen because the ridges that hemmed it in could possibly contain an accidental nuclear explosion "like firecrackers on a string"[8] if untried manufacture of fissionable material went awry. Oak Ridge would also benefit from electricity generated by Norris Dam. Built by the newly established Tennessee Valley Authority in 1934, primarily to provide inexpensive electricity and flood control to depression-ravaged East Tennessee, Norris was TVA's first impoundment. Current from Norris's generators would be augmented by that from Cherokee Dam on the Holston River about 50 miles upstream from its confluence with the French Broad at Knoxville, forming the Tennessee. Cherokee was authorized in August 1940 and completed two days before Pearl Harbor.

A sibling dam had been considered on the French Broad since 1939 to control devastating flooding in Chattanooga. At Douglas Bluff, 32 miles above Knoxville, the river bed narrowed to about 500 feet. Above it stretched 15,000 acres of unbelievably rich floodplain surrounded by 18,000 acres of less productive fields and woods. The bottoms were intensely farmed by Stokely Brothers and Bush Brothers. Dividing the river were a number of large islands, including Zimmerman's, the site of the ancient Indian town, Chiaha, where de Soto paused in June 1540 and rested after crossing the Blue Ridge. Scattered up the river were numerous prosperous farms, many with family cemeteries dating back to the early 1800s. They, several crossroads hamlets, and a section of the Southern Railway's main line up the French Broad from Knoxville to Asheville would be flooded by Douglas Lake, stretching 43 miles upstream to the mouth of the Pigeon.

Such was the urgency to build the dam that enabling legislation flew through Congress. The bill authorizing $30 million for the project was approved by the House on January 27, 1942; the Senate, on January 28; and by President Roosevelt on January 30. The following Monday, construction began. A year and two weeks later, on February 19, 1943, the lake began filling. By March 21, its generators were producing commercial electricity. TVA had known the dam was going to be approved all along. Plans used in the construction of Cherokee Dam had been quickly adapted to Douglas's site. Since they were only about 20 miles apart, equipment used in building Cherokee could be easily moved to the French Broad. And the Smoky Mountain Railroad ran a line to bring construction materials up from Knoxville.[9]

FRACTURED AND FAULTED, I-40 ALONG THE PIGEON

Soon after President Dwight D. Eisenhower took office in 1953, he began planning America's interstate highway system. As the former supreme commander of Allied forces in Europe during World War II, he had been deeply impressed by how German Autobahns had facilitated movement of tanks, troops, and supplies. Three years later, in 1956, Congress approved construction of the Dwight D. Eisenhower National System of Interstate and Defense Highways, and planning began in earnest for I-40 through North Carolina into Tennessee.

For 20 miles, Interstate 40 swerves along the Pigeon River as it drops through its gorge from North Carolina into Tennessee. The rocks are some of the oldest in the Blue Ridge. Extensively folded, faulted, and fractured, when their natural terrain is disturbed by human engineering, they can become excessively unstable. The location of the highway following the eastern bank of the river, where steep rock slopes have been undercut by construction make it quite prone to road-closing rock slides.

Interstate 40 was to stretch from Wilmington, N.C., to Barstow, Calif. Steep and twisting two-lane road grades through the Blue Ridge were the greatest impediment to highway travel between industrialized North Carolina and Tennessee. According to plans, east-west running I-40 and north-south I-26, were to cross in Asheville. Two routes for I-40's stretch through the mountains were under consideration. One more or less followed the old Buncombe Turnpike down the French Broad to Marshall, thence to Hot Springs and on to Newport, Tenn. The other ran down the Pigeon from Canton, past Waterville, before reaching Newport. Both sides had their advocates. Champions of the French Broad option insisted it was shorter and would cost less. On the other hand, fans of the right-of-way through the Pigeon gorge staunchly maintained that I-40 would provide great economic benefit to Haywood County, which unlike Buncombe and Madison counties, was not well served then by east-west running federal highways.

There was another reason to bring I-40 down the gorge. As the interstate system was being developed, the National Park Service was embarked on Mission 66, a campaign to prepare for its 50th anniversary. The plan called for updating park infrastructure, particularly roads and bridges. Long envisioned had been a paved road that would connect Cataloochee Cove in the northeast quadrant of the Great Smokies with Cherokee at its waist. The route would follow Cataloochee Creek up the cove and connect with the Heintooga Road down into Qualla Boundary and Cherokee. While the idea had its advocates, its adversaries feared that a well-maintained highway of the caliber of US 441 from Cherokee to Gatlinburg and running almost exclusively through the park would rob Waynesville and Maggie Valley of the substantial economic benefits of tourism.[10]

Those promoting the Marshall–Hot Springs route lost out to those favoring traversing the gorge. But only five miles of the road through Cataloochee Cove was ever built. Getting to it can be a challenge. Narrow Cove Creek Road switchbacks up from US 276 near Exit 20 on I-40 in North Carolina before becoming gravel as it following the course of historic Cataloochee Turnpike over a ridge. A similar narrow gravel road with turnouts runs up from Waterville on the other side. First-time visitors to Cataloochee are astounded when they drop down into the valley and find the modern well-paved park service road. A trip into the cove presents the best view of a Smoky Mountain farm valley as it might have looked pre-park days. Early morning visitors in November may well see elk bulls defending their harems during their rut. Once native to the Blue Ridge, elk were reintroduced in Cataloochee in 2001. The herd has grown and is spreading throughout the park and surrounding countryside.

Draining 704 square miles, the Pigeon River rises in the steep western slopes of Cold Mountain, Shining Rock, Devil's Courthouse, and the Balsams. The river exits the mountains above Canton into a long, wide valley, well known by archaeologists for its extensive collection of pre-historic Indian villages. Flowing through Canton, the Pigeon River provided fresh water for what was the largest remaining pulp and paper mill in Western North Carolina. Downstream it rushes into an increasingly narrow valley, is impounded by Walters Dam, and below it dashes through class 1-4 rapids above Hartford, before joining the French Broad downstream from Newport. Of the French Broad's tributaries, the Pigeon is the second largest behind the Nolichucky.

The Pigeon and the French Broad are intensely prone to flooding when tropical storms stall over the mountains. Great floods occurred in 1791, 1876, 1901, 1916, 1928, and 1940. In September 2004, hurricanes Frances and Ivan delivered deadly back-to-back deluges that killed 11, destroyed 140 homes, and caused $200 million in damages including $87 million from lost tourism.[11] In planning for flood control in the 1950s, TVA tended to focus on saving Chattanooga, where the agency estimated that 86 percent of flood-related damage occurs.[12]

In the late 1950s, TVA and North Carolina began looking at the headwaters of the Pigeon and French Broad for sites for flood control dams. In 1967, TVA proposed a massive plan for 14 dams. Impoundments would cover 18,255 acres, comprised mainly of little family farms on floodplain coves high in the mountains. Approximately 600 families would be displaced. Also included in the proposal were 74 miles of stream channelization, which was then in vogue. Meanders would be straightened; banks, armored with riprap; and levees, built to protect industry along the river in Asheville.[13]

TVA and regional economic councils justified the proposal by claiming, in part, that the impoundments would increase tourism with additional opportunities for swimming, boating, and fishing and businesses that supported them. However, the proposed dams were unlike massive Douglas, which retains much of its pool throughout the year. Instead, those planned for the upper watershed would detain water from mountain deluges in small lakes. It would be released slowly leaving, opponents claimed, small ponds with broad muddy weed-choked banks until a new downpour, maybe months in the future, filled the lakes again.

Citizens of Transylvania and Henderson County objected vehemently. Under the leadership of retired professor of horticulture, Jere Brittain, the Upper

French Broad River Defense Association challenged TVA's assertions of economic benefit. A seventh-generation descendant of Gillespies and others who settled in the Mills River valley shortly after the Revolutionary War, Brittain was deeply steeped in the natural and cultural history of the French Broad. He was well known to community groups as a frequent speaker on improved agricultural practices. And perhaps Wilma Dykeman's landmark environmental history of the watershed, *The French Broad,* released little more than a decade earlier, helped whet awareness by region's residents of TVA's threat to their beloved mountains and their waters.

On November 14, 1972, TVA shelved the project, noting the growing concern for environmental protection as well as economic concerns. Citizens had secured victory through an aggressive campaign of meetings with elected officials in county, state, and national government; vocal attendance at public hearings; continuing briefings for area news media providing facts and personal stories about the impacts of the plans; scores of letters to the editor; and enlistment of national organizations like the Sierra Club in the cause of protecting the upper French Broad and Pigeon watersheds.[14]

POLLUTION, THE PIGEON, AND WIDOWVILLE

In his book *Troubled Waters: Champion International and the Pigeon River Controversy,* Richard Bartlett chronicles a story all too common throughout the America's history, that of looking upon small rivers to carry away human and industrial waste. The story of the fouling of Pigeon River is the story of almost any river in the country whether it waters an industrial city or not. The Pigeon's significance lies in the fact that determined downstream residents, upon learning the depth of Champion's egregious pollution of their river, went to war with company, local, state, and federal officials. For more than a generation, they demanded answers of fact not bromide. And in the end, they won the battle, but not yet the war.

In 1908, Champion opened its plant astride the Pigeon in Canton. Passengers on nearby I-40 either first notice huge billowing clouds of steam or the smell of rotten eggs that emanates from the process of cooking wood chips under high heat and pressure to produce pulp from which paper is made. The process of turning pulp into paper requires millions of gallons of water drawn from the river upstream of the town and discharged downstream. In the mid-1950s, Champion's pollution of the Pigeon turned Waterville Lake as dark as strong

Champion Fibre Company, one of the world's largest pulp mills, released dioxin-laced wastewater into the Pigeon turning the river dark as coffee and spiking cancer-related deaths downstream in Hartford, Tenn., which became known at "Widowville." (Canton Area Historical Museum.)

coffee. Below Walters Dam, the river's rapids brewed batts of dirty tan foam that littered the banks for more than 30 miles downstream past Newport. Though it stank badly, few who saw the river then had any idea of the sickness and death it carried.

Those living in the tiny riverside hamlet of Hartford, just downstream from the Tennessee line, suspected the river was killing their neighbors. "We've had 167 deaths from cancer in the past 20 to 30 years," postmaster Mary Woody told David Treadwell who was writing for the *San Francisco Chronicle* in 1989. He noted that local residents call the town "Widowville" and went on to report that Margaret Jenkins, 81, told him that her husband had died from cancer in 1977, "and I can look out my kitchen window and see half a dozen other homes where there's been cancer deaths. It's a tragedy." Residents of Hartford relied on water drawn from wells drilled into highly fractured rock. Those cracks were filled with water that seeped in from the river.

Noticing scores of dead fish rancid with putrid sores floating down the Pigeon, residents of Newport took water samples and had them analyzed.

Whitewater fans now ride the Pigeon below the Tennessee/North Carolina border thanks to two citizens' action groups who secured help from then Vice President Al Gore and the state of Tennessee which forced Champion Fibre to clean up its wastewater. (Photography: John E. Ross.)

The culprit was dioxin produced in the process of bleaching paper pulp. Their discovery occurred about the same time that the EPA identified dioxin as the carcinogen responsible for massive mortality in Love Canal, N. Y. and Times Beach, Mo. Subsequent studies confirmed the presence of dioxin in the Pigeon, but just how much was a matter of conjecture. State officials in North Carolina sided with Champion, concerned that if they did not, the plant would close and throw hundreds out of work. Tennessee officials insisted that the plant comply with more stringent standards set by the EPA. For five years, politicians and lawyers battled. Champion installed new equipment, and by 1993, the discoloration and odor from the river had been significantly reduced.[15]

But what of dioxin? Since 1989, Tennessee the river had been under a "do not consume" advisory by the Tennessee Wildlife Resource Agency for all fish taken from the Pigeon from the state line immediately downstream from Walters Dam to its junction with the French Broad in Douglas Lake. Triggering the advisory were dioxin levels in fish tissues exceeding 5 ppt parts per trillion. The warning was downgraded in 1996 to a "precautionary advisory" against eating flesh from sunfish, carp, and catfish. By 2002, the advisory had been lifted.[16] Clean-up of the river happened only because two local organizations, the Pigeon River Action Group led by Dick Mullinix and the Dead Pigeon River Council headed by Bob Seay and a handful of others, refused to be cowed by political and corporate opposition to their efforts to hold Champion and its successors to account.

Over the intervening years, the plant's owners have invested hundreds of millions in upgrading manufacturing processes with an eye to both ensuring the marketability of its products and complying with state and federal mandates. Most recently, the plant completed the change from coal-fired to gas-fired boilers, which reduced air pollution and took down its iconic smoke stack that had towered over Canton for 100 years. In many ways, the saga of Champion and its successors is the universal saga of the ongoing tension between the need to ensure the quality of air and water and the desire to sustain a small town and surrounding communities that has relied for more than a century on a single water-driven industry. Alas, in June 2023 then-owners of the mill Pactiv-Evergreen announced its closing. Though battered by this news, especially in the wake of the Pigeon River's 2021 flash flooding which killed six, as residents of Canton and the lower Pigeon watershed are now relying on their innate resilience to restore their communities' economic and environmental vitality.

RESURRECTION ALONG THE RIVER

Marilyn Ball, author of *The Rise of Asheville,* arrived in Asheville in 1977. Store fronts were sheathed with plywood and their upstairs windows, dark and vacant. Five years earlier, Asheville Mall, anchored by Dillards and Sears, had opened east of town across Beaucatcher Mountain. Interstate 240 was slicing north around the city to join I 40 and head up Swannanoa's valley toward Black Mountain, over the gap and down the Catawba into the Piedmont. An exit delivered shoppers to the mall. To revitalize downtown, the city council proposed a $40 million bond issue to raze 11 acres in the city's core occupied by 125 small businesses in 85 buildings and a couple of apartment buildings. In their place to be constructed was a fine new shopping district coupled to a convention center served by modern hotels. "In my mind, this is the best thing to happen to Asheville in a long time. If it flies, we're talking about three years

When Asheville planned to raze eleven acres of historic buildings to build a downtown mall in the early 1980s, citizens created a group—Save Downtown Asheville—and wrapped the area in bed sheets. (North Carolina History Room, Pack Memorial Library.)

of a torn-up downtown. But in the end, you'd have something super for the entire area," said Vice Mayor Ralph D. Morris Jr.

Downtown merchants were aghast. Led by Wayne Caldwell, an Asheville native and businessman then author, concerned community members came together to create Save Downtown Asheville. Said Caldwell, "For nearly two years SDA attended every meeting of city council, the housing authority, planning and zoning, and the Asheville Redevelopment Commission. They made notes, spoke at public hearings and civic clubs, asked council for money (which they never got), talked, organized, wrote letters, etc. . . . People gave two years of their lives to defeating a dragon."[17]

In a burst of brilliance, SDA member Peggy Gardner suggested wrapping the area to be bulldozed with bed sheets. Their whiteness signaled the opposite of surrender. Her scheme dramatically demonstrated all that would be lost. Capitalizing on the region's historic independence and aversion to government intrusion, SDA allied with other activists in Taxpayers Against Bonds. Together, they galvanized public support and defeated the bond issue in November 1981.[18] That opened the door for Asheville to bloom again. The community then focused attention on its beleaguered riverfront at the time, pretty much, a ruins of abandoned mills and tanneries.

A coalition of partners chaired by Jean Webb of the French Broad River Foundation and Karen Cragnolin, an attorney and communications professional hired by the Asheville Area Chamber of Commerce, developed a plan to revitalize the riverfront to retain tourists in the region for "one more day." About the same time, local businessman Bill Goacher and his wife, began buying derelict industrial buildings and renting space to artists, a movement that has grown into Asheville's well-known River Arts District. These leaders and the organizations they represented were effective in soliciting grants from TVA and a number of private sources. When coupled with the region's growing understanding that its economy future was as tied to tourism as it had been from precursors to the opening of the Buncombe Turnpike in 1827, these efforts

Residents of Asheville offer ideas for an environmental education park, a former riverside auto-crushing junkyard being transformed by RiverLink and named for its founder, Karen Cragnolin. (Photography: John E. Ross.)

led to the adoption in 1992 of a long range vision for a string of public parks, greenways, and environmentally appropriate businesses.

More than five miles of parks and hiking/biking paths have been created with more to come. Every year, outfitters serve the tens of thousands who float and frolic on the river. The nonprofit that Cragnolin helped create, RiverLink, played a leading role in attracting craft beer maker New Belgium Brewing Company to remediate and occupy in 2016 a former stockyard across the French Broad from the River Arts District. A year earlier, Sierra Nevada had opened its craft brewery in Mills River. Small craft breweries are proliferating, as is the country music scene. The city tops numerous national "Best Places to . . ." lists. As this goes to press in 2021, a half dozen new hotels are under construction in Asheville, and more are planned as is an expansion of the connection between heavily used Interstates 40 and 26.

WILMA'S QUESTION

In *The French Broad,* Wilma Dykeman asked what had the river been to those who live in the watershed.[19] Prescient as ever, she was pointing to the future. During her life in East Tennessee and Western North Carolina, she saw the unparalleled growth of the French Broad's communities. None is more dramatic than the explosion of Gatlinburg from a few houses in 1912 to the top of the bustling corridor that stretches down the Little Pigeon through Pigeon Forge and Sevierville, across the French Broad at Kodak, and on out along Tennessee Route 66 to its junction with I-40. Upwards of 16 million tourists visit the watershed annually, drawn as much by the natural splendors of Great Smoky Mountains National Park, Blue Ridge Parkway, and Pisgah National Forest as by the opportunities to visit Biltmore Estate in Asheville and other cultural attractions and to shop sales at outlet store malls. Yet traffic congestion and affordable housing are of increasing concern. Tim Ezzell, former director of the Institute for a Secure and Sustainable Environment, noting the increasing number of Asheville area residents relocating across the mountain to Erwin, wonders if he may be seeing early signs of out-migration.[20] Given the region's record of boom and bust, how can we know?

THIRTEEN

The Planners' Paradox

From the first day the first Paleo family entered the watershed, spears carried low, ready to stab a mastodon 14,000 years ago, the region's land and water have supported human habitation. Of this, evidence is ample. So too are the troughs and crests of civilization among the mountains and rivers reaching to the present. With uncertainty increasing with each coming year, each coming electoral cycle, each coming decade, each coming generation, we can be certain of little that lies ahead.

Could nomadic Paleo Indians have foretold, other than perhaps in their prayers, the Medieval Warm Period that gave rise to sustained agriculture, life in villages, and an end to their ceaseless wandering? Could the Hopewell, trekking five hundred miles south from Ohio to the mounds at Garden Creek and Biltmore 1,500 years ago, have foreseen making that journey in the same number of hours today as it took them in weeks? How might the earliest Cherokee, 800 years ago, have grasped the calamitous specters of starvation from crop failure, devastating disease carried by the first European explorers, and their invasion, which stripped them of their homeland . . . all wrought to greater or less degree by the onset of the Little Ice Age and a pair of global pandemics?

With greater certainty, poor Scots Irish and German pioneers who grubbed out farmsteads on the rich floodplains of the French Broad, its tributaries, and gently sloping hillsides might well have known that a day would come when their axes, plows, and hoes would no longer support their growing families. Surely when the Buncombe Turnpike opened in 1827, there were those who imagined that an endless future of commerce would follow its route. But who among them foresaw that the industry that would be sustaining the region three centuries hence would be waves of tourists who first salved their aches in warm springs in 1779 or gloried in the cooling breezes of Little Charleston in the Mountains?

And what of the last 100 years? Could Andy Huff, when he opened his home on Baskins Creek around 1910 to take in a few visiting timber cruisers, have envisioned that the tiny hamlet of about a dozen houses called Gatlinburg would host the lion's share of the 14 million tourists visiting the Great Smokies National Park every year? Surely many of entrepreneurial bent foresaw Asheville's spectacular growth with the coming of the railroad in 1880. But what about Asheville's all but utter collapse with the Great Depression, its abandoned industries and boarded up storefronts of the 1960s and 1970s, and its resurrection today as one of the nation's prime tourist and retirement destinations?

Of only one thing can there be great assurance. Human endeavor is accelerating the pace of change. Left alone, the planet would go through natural cycles characterized by periods of relative warmth and cold, of eruption and subsidence, and of habitation by flora and fauna evolving in synchronicity with their environments. Humans, though, are ecological wildcards, hosts of intellectual and emotional behaviors beyond prediction. And, in some humans, the ability to imagine the future runs as rampant as in others it does not.

Meteorologists are schooled in the most accurate form of predicting the weather: persistence forecasting. Simply put, absent an element of dramatic change such as pending passage of warm or cold frontal system, tomorrow's weather will be much like today's. Politicians and planners tend to think similarly, failing to connect emerging trends, as economist Robert J. Samuelson writes, bowing "to an impulse to stay with what's familiar."[1] Though state and federal highway planning attempts to look 10 and 20 years into the future, planning by local governments seems seldom effective beyond the current electoral cycle. Zoning, for instance, enacted by one county board of supervisors or commissioners can be readily changed by the next.

THE BIG FIVE FACTORS

Over the next 50 years, the future of the French Broad watershed, like that of all watersheds everywhere, will be delineated by natural and cultural evolution along five vectors: population, climate, energy, transportation, and industry. These five factors have defined the development of the watershed from its very beginning. While climate as determined by the earth's position in the solar system has, without a doubt, the greatest impact of the five on the watershed over millennia, humans are the source of greatest change from one decade to the next. Further, the behaviors of human populations hold the reins to the other four, at least in the short term. Only our collective vision and will can return the progression of climate change to what might be considered a more natural cycle.

We rely on energy, first from wild and farmed foods that nourished our sinews and skeletons. Following, within a few generations, came feed for domesticated dogs, and later, horses, mules, swine, and oxen. Wood fires warm us still, but most of the verdant hillsides and ridges we enjoy today had been stripped of trees by the early 1900s not just for building material but for fuel. Water turned millstones and cycled saws up and down as they ripped logs into lumber. Then, in the 1740s, Virginians discovered veins of the metamorphosed residue of ancient swamps, and coal found its way onto our hearths and into the fireboxes of our boilers, producing steam. Six generations later, in 1859, in Pennsylvania, Col. Edwin Drake sank the first commercial well that tapped petroleum. Our desires to move ourselves and the goods we produce from one location to another fostered the creation and renewal of transportation infrastructure and equipment that uses it. In the inescapable context of population and climate, the sum of energy—human and otherwise—and transportation, gives birth to industry-prolonged personal endeavor to produce something of value that generally sustains us but at times also threatens our existence.

Every day each of us is buffeted by the currents of these five vectors of natural and cultural evolution. Singly and collectively, they drive decisions by elected planning and zoning boards, city and county commissions, state legislatures, Congress, and the presidency. No corporation, profit or nonprofit, can long exist without concentration on long-term factors influencing their abilities to generate financial revenue and human resources. These five axes offer a host of conundrums, providing the paradoxes to which planners are called to offer a publicly acceptable resolution.

POPULATION

Over the past 14,000 years, the human presence in the watershed has evolved from the first itinerant Paleo Indians; through the Cherokee, their ancestors, and Scots-Irish-German settlers; to today's vibrant mix largely comprised of

Anglos, Hispanics, and African Americans. Regional planners forecast the number of people living in the French Broad watershed will increase by about 40 percent from about 1,018,000 in 2010 to around 1,388,000 in 2037. Racial diversity will likely see little change with about 11 percent being Hispanic and 4 percent African-American, a slight decline from current levels. In-migration will account for all of the growth. Immigration is predicted to be driven as it has been since the early 1800s by the region's scenic beauty and salubrious climate offering opportunities for healthful outdoor recreation and for employment provided by the watershed's hospitality industry. Most of the growth will occur in the more densely settled environs of Knoxville, Asheville, Hendersonville, Brevard, Gatlinburg, and Sevierville. Populations in Madison, Cocke, and Unicoi counties are projected to decline slightly while Yancey remains about the same size.

Yet the population of the region is aging. From 2000 to 2016, the number of residents 60 years of age and older grew by 55 percent. Planners expect that trend to continue. Is this a symptom of a steady reduction in the number of well-paying entry-level jobs available for young adults? Is this a result of an anticipated reduction in number of millennials choosing to make their home in the watershed? According to several directors of economic development in the watershed's counties, the region is experiencing increasing "aging-in-place." Is the region also seeing "tourism-in-place," where retirees move into the watershed for their "golden" years before returning to "home" to live their final years near family, long-time friends, and deeply familiar surroundings?

Aging-in-place fuels the expansion of continuing care retirement communities and of medical services aligned with geriatric care. Increasingly, the most prevalent causes of death in the watershed are heart, respiratory, and brain-blood circulation diseases along with Alzheimer's. Private long-term care communities are expanding and provide an alternative for the affluent. But what about residential options for increasing numbers of elderly retirees who cannot afford such facilities? Among those of pre-retirement age are the very unclear long-term implications of opioid addiction. While not related to a greying population, a growing health concern throughout the watershed is increasing obesity among children, addiction to opioids, and pandemics like Covid-19.

The Covid-19 pandemic of the early 2020s reminds us that public health is a salient concern when considering population trends. The region has weathered previous pandemics—diseases brought by Spanish explorers that killed an estimated 90 percent of native Indian populations and the great 1918–1919 influenza that felled 675,000 Americans according to the Center for Disease Control and Prevention. That we are increasingly compacted, living in towns and cities and traveling frequently among states and countries raises our vulnerability to pandemics. So too do those few among us who value their personal freedom over protecting themselves and others by following recommended safety measures based on verified medical science.

Because of increasing numbers of affluent retirees and tourists, housing for families of moderate and lower incomes presents a growing challenge. In Asheville, the core of the city is rapidly gentrifying as structures like conversion of the former BB&T tower on Pack Square to condominiums costing in the high six and even seven figures. And, as of this writing, several new hotels are either under construction or being planned for downtown. Planners and the public are wrestling with the long-term impact of such development. Will increasing congestion of automobile and pedestrian traffic limit the attractiveness of the city's core? Will future generations' exasperation with glacial traffic and scant and expensive parking lead to the conversion of downtown hotels and residences for the rich result in their degeneration into low-income housing as has happened in the centers of other cities? Will pressure to expand housing options for the affluent into the next ring beyond the core result in the conversion of former industrial sites along the French Broad into mixed-use residential properties as is being proposed for land formerly occupied by the massive Ecusta plant in Brevard? Is that a likely future for the River Arts District in Asheville?

Beyond city limits, how rapidly will housing and related services and commercial establishments consume small farms and green spaces? Is compaction of development within city limits initiating a trend toward out-migration to South Carolina's Greenville-Spartanburg area as reported by the Asheville Chamber of Commerce or to Erwin as noticed by Tim Ezzell and his colleagues at the Institute for A Secure and Sustainable Environment at the University of Tennessee Knoxville?

Further, is the compaction of residential housing in forested steep-slope developments that offer stunning mountain views providing fuel for future wildfires such as the lethal Gatlinburg fire in November 2016? That fire killed 14; injured 134; destroyed or damaged 2,000 homes, businesses, and other buildings; forced the emergency evacuation of 14,000 residents and tourists; and charred 15 square miles in the Great Smokies and adjacent private land. All one has to do is visualize each wooded deep ravine stacked with house after house built of wood as the chimney of one of those early stone blast furnaces pioneers used to smelt iron ore.

Zoning and similar land-use protections are only as durable as the current terms of elected members of the governing jurisdiction. Enforcement of ordinances and laws passed today relies solely on the collective will of those who vote. Will future generations share the visions of the current cohort of public servants? Is the political schism between rural and urban residents a force of nature like the river or will the residents of the region generate the courage to bridge or contain it?

WHITHER THE WEATHER

Ice cores from the Arctic and Antarctic show beyond any reasonable doubt that the earth's climate migrates through warming and cooling cycles. So too does evidence of up-slope migration of boreal species-spruce, fir, and related plant and animal communities from formerly much warmer floodplains to crests of the Blue Ridge. One only has to look at the formation of those same wide floodplains along the French Broad and the presence of compact car-sized boulders in knee-deep trout streams in its tributaries to understand that the region was once subject to eras of intense precipitation. Ice cores as well demonstrate the relationship between concentrations of carbon dioxide in the atmosphere and worldwide climatic temperatures.

Climatologists all but uniformly agree that the world is experiencing a period of unparalleled warming. Its negative effects are quite visible from the Blue Ridge Parkway and US 441. Standing starkly grey against the deeply green mountainside forest are the skeletons of eastern hemlocks (*Tsuga canadensis*). Known as "redwoods of the East," hemlocks are giants of the forest standing more than 125 feet tall and reaching 6 feet in diameter. They are being felled by infestations of hemlock woolly adelgid (*Adelges tsugae*). A little oval brown insect about .8 mm in length, it possesses four threads that function as parts of its mouth and suck nutrients from the underside of tender hemlock branches. At the same time, it may be injecting a toxin into the tree. As a result, the tree begins to starve, can no longer produce new growth, and ultimately dies. As little as two decades ago, colder winters froze larvae, preventing explosion of adelgid populations.

Walk almost any trout stream in the Great Smokies or Pisgah National Forest. With few exceptions, fallen trunks of large hemlocks will jumble your path. You will note as well ragged and withered clumps of once-robust rhododendron that formerly thrived in the shade of these great trees. Lack of shade from hemlocks and rhododendron opens mountain streams to heating by radiant sunlight. To feel the heat, place your hand on a black streamside boulder. This, along with increased air temperature, is warming the water to levels that brook trout cannot tolerate.

Native to the French Broad watershed since the beginning of the Pleistocene, brook trout have been long used as a species to indicate the adverse impact of climate. Their decline throughout the Blue Ridge was initially documented in the mid-1900s and linked to acid rain, snows, and mists caused by emissions from power plants and engines using hydrocarbon fuels. For the past 40 years, the University of Virginia's Shenandoah Watershed Study and Virginia Trout Stream Sensitivity Study has measured stream acidification and brook trout populations. Data from the study were instrumental in amendments to the Clean Air Act in 1990, which limited toxic emissions. As a result, brookies returned to a handful of streams from which they had been extirpated.[2] Ultimately climate warming will likely drive brookies, a living relic of the Ice Age, to extinction.

Increasing periods of extreme weather, a hallmark of climate evolution, include tropical storms with torrential downpours sometimes accompanied by hail and high winds and extended rainless periods of temperatures in the high 80s and 90s. University of Tennessee-Knoxville researchers are reporting that medical personnel and social workers are noticing increased infectious disease, temperature-related illness and death, and mental distress related to extreme weather events. Most likely to be impacted are the poor, homeless, children, and aged adults living alone.[3] The watershed is fortunate to host a number of universities actively engaged in climate research and more than 100 independent businesses providing climate resilience services and networked through a local nonprofit, The Collider. In addition, the headquarters of the National Centers for Environmental Information and the USAF's 14th Weather Squadron are located in Asheville. Personnel from these organizations are deeply involved with communities throughout the watershed providing verifiable information about climate evolution, long-term scenarios describing potential impacts, and strategies for mitigating effects.

When queried about natural issues facing watersheds in the Blue Ridge, Joe Hankins, former head of the Conservation Fund's Fresh Water Institute, said that the most significant challenge is not climate change but the availability of water for residential, commercial, and industrial use. With increasingly intense rain events occurring, this concern seems counterintuitive. Yet, heavy rainfall runs off rapidly, and the metamorphic geology of most of the watershed—with the exception of carbonate lithology in the Tennessee Valley—provides little natural storage.

For most of its water, Asheville depends on the 354-acre North Fork and the 41-acre Beetree reservoirs fed by streams draining a surrounding 17,000 acre watershed. The watershed is protected by a conservation easement. The most recent version prohibits logging. However, while extremely difficult to overturn, laws enabling easements are only as viable as the will of the courts to sustain them. In addition, the city receives water from a treatment plant on the Mills River, shared with Hendersonville. According to a regional director of economic development, Asheville has an excess water capacity of 20 million gallons a day. Gatlinburg and Sevier County rely on both the West Prong of the Little Pigeon and the French Broad for its water. In the face of rampant growth, will that be enough?

Erratic climate patterns over the watershed include extended periods without significant precipitation. Since 1968, Asheville has experienced three cycles of intense drought each lasting four years or so.[4] During long-term rainfall deficits, municipalities will be forced to draw water from the French Broad, and prolonged drought will subject existing agreements to legal challenge. Rivers also cool both coal-fired and nuclear power plants making them susceptible to shutdowns caused by low water flows. During the drought of 2007, Duke Energy was forced to reduce output from coal plants on the Catawba River. McGuire Nuclear Station on Lake Norman, which serves Charlotte and the surrounding area, was nearly forced to suspend generation.[5] Though water districts may mandate reductions in nonessential water uses such as lawn watering and car washes, climate evolution raises significant concerns about long-term viability of water supplies, and the ability of rivers and streams to carry away our sewage. Access to water and related sewage treatment is the one factor limiting population growth. For water there exists no natural or synthetic substitute.

ENERGY

Imagine the watershed in 2050. It could look much different. Many of rolling meadows where livestock once grazed 30 years earlier might now be called solar pastures. Electricity, like tobacco in the past, has become the cash crop. An acre or two of inexpensive solar collectors enable farmsteads to generate not only enough electricity to power themselves and keep electric vehicles fully charged, but also to sell to regional electric cooperatives that provide energy to small towns. Solar panels have been improved to the point where they are efficient even during periods of all but the heaviest cloud cover. Battery technology has improved as well. They are light in weight, retain a charge for long enough to outlast two weeks of thickly clouded skies, and recharge rapidly in even partial sun. To a large degree, the hard-wired power grid has been replaced by a combination of systems involving satellites, microwaves, and lasers.

Solar electricity will power geothermal residential heating and cooling units particularly in suburban and rural areas. Twin wells will be sunk 200 feet or so to tap and return water to the water table in fractured bedrock. At that depth, it averages 56°F or so. High-efficiency heat pumps will extract warmth in winter and provide chilling in summer. Deep heat sinks, layers of water-filled pipe from recycled plastic (all plastic is recycled these days) laid in beds of crushed rock, will underlie new construction. Like basements in buildings of the 1900s, subterranean heat sinks average 20°F cooler or warmer than high and low surface temperatures, thus reducing the load on heating and air-conditioning systems.

Traditional gas stations are now all but an old folks' memory. Only antique cars requiring costly and rigorously defined carbon footprint licenses are permitted to operate on public highways. Lawn mowers and other gasoline-powered yard tools, including weed whackers, garden tillers, chain saws, and snow blowers (yes, despite climate warming, the region experiences sometimes heavy snowfall), all significant but long-ignored sources of air pollution, are all battery powered. Batteries are no longer comprised of lead or lithium but of nontoxic materials. The age of biofuels will have come and gone with the death of the internal combustion engine.

Wind power, once touted as the premier alternative source of electricity, is fading into an environmental relic. Vast off-shore wind farms installed in the 2020s, have been stripped of materials that will toxify when submerged in salt water. Blades and supporting pylons have been sunk to provide artificial reefs. They are habitat for species of commercially important fish that feed thousands. Visionary activists were successful in fighting ridge-top wind turbines, thus preserving the verdant views that continue to attract tourists to the watershed. Though nuclear power plant technology has advanced far beyond that of disastrous installations at Three Mile Island, Chernobyl, and Fukushima, public sentiment continues to equate atomic power with bombs and warheads. Despite efforts to educate otherwise, the public continues its fear of radiation as a lethal flood that no one can see or feel until it is too late.

Pie-in-the-sky visioning? Perhaps. But the anticipated combination of natural climate evolution accelerated by human endeavor suggests that sustainable energy ecology will continue to expand as an extremely fertile field for research, development, manufacturing, installation, and maintenance. As science and engineering in this area thrives and economies of scale are achieved, will the watershed's increasingly aging population be willing to adapt? Will planners be successful in convincing elected officials to adopt emerging technological advances?

TRANSPORTATION

For millennia, valleys carved by the French Broad and its tributaries have provided primary transportation corridors, first afoot, then by hoof, and next by wheel on primitive roads. In 2050, wheeled vehicles will continue to dominate transportation. Residential areas have become much more densely populated. In 2014, the average American house contained 2,500 square feet. Single houses were preferred. That has changed. Dwellers within future city limits are comfortable with 1,000 square-foot abodes. Duplexes and triplexes are increasingly popular.[6] Those not using the Internet, now universally available via satellite, to commute to work will take two-, three-, or four-wheeled cycles. Either pedal-powered or solar-electric, most will be enclosed with cockpits resembling those on sail planes. Canopies will slide open so passengers can enjoy clement weather. And each will contain composting or similar ecologically appropriate sanitary equipment. Autonomous vehicles will be the norm, though still requiring drivers. Think pilots of aircraft that ride electronically beamed signals effective no matter what the weather from one destination to the next. Still, like pilots on airliners, human drivers are needed for emergencies and thus must keep their eyes on the road.

Recently developed highway pavements will collect solar energy and transmit it via microwave to vehicles' electric motors. With smart-tag technology similar to that used on the high-occupancy vehicle lanes of the past, vehicle owners will be pay per mile traveled. Old iron and steel bridges and related infrastructure will have been replaced by inexpensive high-tensile, noncorroding composites. Solar-powered highways will warm themselves as needed to melt ice and snow.

Permeable pavements will have eliminated run-off except during the most intense deluges. Rather than widening rights-of-way to accommodate more traffic, major highways will add upper decks. New suburban and rural roads are being paved with similar materials with the goal of eliminating old-fashioned asphalt and cement pavements by 2070.

Most freight and increasingly passengers traveling long distances will move by intermodal means. Diesel locomotives will have become as old-fashioned as coal-fired steam engines of yesteryear. Like highways, railroad tracks will be fitted with the latest electro-microwave technology transmitting power to sleek, high-speed locomotives. Goods will be packed in containers containing chips that define content and destination and be loaded aboard automatically. Similarly, people will drive their personal passenger vehicles onto triple decked railcars for journeys between major cities, much like the old airline hub city concept. Commercial aircraft will increasingly be solar powered and massive on the scale of military C-17 transports of the early 2000s. They will be designed to accommodate personal solar electric vehicles that, occupied with passengers, will be loaded like containerized freight; however, each will be a window seat, thanks to smart screen technology.

Is this the stuff of science fiction? Perhaps. But read the adventures of Tom Swift. Premiered in 1910 as the profile of a boy wonder traversing technologies just beyond the horizon, the most recent series, *Tom Swift Inventor's Academy*, was published by Simon and Schuster in 2019. Titles include *The Drone Pursuit*, *The Sonic Breach*, *On Top of the World*, and *Rocket Racers*. To savor his imagination, don't read Tom swiftly.

When it comes to transportation, the challenges for planners are multifaceted, but largely political. Increasingly, cities and counties must think and act regionally. Councils of governments serving the watershed—Southwest, Land of Sky, and High Country in North Carolina and First Tennessee and East Tennessee—first established by the Appalachian Regional Commission in the 1960s provide effective venues for intergovernmental collaboration.

INDUSTRY

Industry is the production of goods or services by human endeavor. Conventional usage suggests group or corporate activity engaged in manufacturing a product. But according to the *Oxford English Dictionary*, original usage also included products that were grown or cultivated. On a macro scale, tourism seems destined to remain the watershed's dominant industry. Gone are the days of most massive industrial endeavors such as Ecusta in Brevard, Enka in Asheville and Lowland, Tenn., and Beacon Manufacturing in Swannanoa, some with attendant company towns. Automation continues to reduce the number of employees required to produce and package a product and prepare it for shipment. However the strength of the region's industrial foundation will be as it always has been: individual craftsmanship, reliability, and pride in doing a job well. Aerospace and automotive parts, a mainstay of manufacturing at the opening of the 2020s, will need to evolve with developments in fuels, modes of transportation, and artificial intelligence.

Education is the key to future industrial vitality. Among major factors determining whether corporations expand current facilities and invest in new and extensive renovations is the quality and availability of educational resources, from preschool through graduate study. By the 2050s, pre-kindergarten through high school, curricula will prepare the population for learning not just mathematics and science undergirding technology, but also the humanities—language, culture, and society—which facilitate the abilities of people with diverse backgrounds to work together. Teaching will be a hybrid of in-class and on-line learning. Increasingly schools are employing curricula that emphasize problem solving. Availability of applied technological education offered by community colleges continues to ensure workforce readiness. Advanced studies available through graduate programs and faculty scholarship support industrial research and development. As well, how corporate leadership perceives the quality of a community's public school system is a factor in their ability to recruit and retain managers with families.

Unlike the 2020s, funding for pre-K–12, community colleges, and state colleges and universities no longer remains closely tied to public perceptions of quality based largely on performance on standardized tests. Funding debates often turned on input issues—teacher pay, supply budgets, and class size. Now outputs matter more, both in the context of preparation of young people for local career opportunities and for participation in interstate, national, and transglobal economies. Despite spates of regional and national isolationism, citizens of the French Broad watershed in the future will be increasingly mobile and less likely than their forebearers to reside in one county or state all of their lives.

Throughout the region, agriculture has taken on the characteristics of micro industry. One need only look at the empty tall, brown, glazed block silos standing next to weathered two-story barns with gable or gambrel roofs and adjacent cement block milking parlors to grasp once wide-spread commercial production of milk, butter, and cheese. The advent of refrigerated railroad cars facilitating the interstate transportation of dairy products sounded its death knell almost two centuries ago. Ditto with empty tobacco barns. Apple orchards, operated on almost industrial scale in Haywood and Henderson counties, continue to thrive because they are almost entirely dependent on hand labor. Will hemp and marijuana for medical and perhaps recreation become the new tobacco? In the 2020s, as hemp began to emerge as a local crop in the watershed, processing to extract increasingly popular CBD—cannabidiol—oil was extremely expensive. Will hemp growers in a region band together in co-operatives to extract, purify, and market CBD oil from small plots, much like tobacco allotments of the 1950s and 1960s?

In addition to vast acreage devoted to raising vegetables for supermarket chains and packing houses, specialty agriculture is taking root throughout the watershed. Small farms using sustainable and environmentally sound practices are growing crops and raising meats for local restaurants and tailgate markets. Will agribusiness in the region continue on small individual scale as it has been largely since the first crops planted by ancestors of the Cherokee 1,000 years ago?

RESOLVING PLANNERS' PARADOXES

For planners and the population, the future is full of paradoxes, full of choices of *this* rather than *that*. How can the public be assured that it has timely access to accurate information on which to make decisions? How can it learn to differentiate between fact and falsehood? How can it accept that accommodating differing views increases the likelihood of finding solutions that benefit the greatest number of people? Does the answer to resolving the conundrums that will continue to bedevil us lie in the watershed's underlying and hopefully enduring spirit of resilient community that led one settler to help a neighbor in times of need?[7]

Notes

INTRODUCTION

1. Robert D. Hatcher Jr. and David C. Prowell, "Modern Appalachian Topography, Product of Miocene to Recent Uplift: Not a Relic of Paleozoic Orogeny, and Not the 'World's Oldest Mountain Chain'," professional presentation (Geologic Society of America 2019 Annual Meeting, Phoenix, Arizona, Sept. 22, 2019.

2. Wm. Jack Hranicky, "Pre-Clovis in Virginia: A Matter of Antiquity," *Archaeology of Eastern North America, Eastern States Archaeological Federation* 38 (2010): 53–61.

3. Jim Wood, ed., *Great Smoky Mountains Biosphere Reserve: History of Scientific Study*, U.S. Man and the Biosphere Program U.S. MAB Report No. 5, Southern Appalachian Research/Resource Management Cooperative and Western Carolina University, Cullowhee, NC, 1982, 63.

4. Wilma Dykeman, *The French Broad* (Knoxville: University of Tennessee, 1973), 14.

ONE | THE HEADWATERS

1. Robin A. Beck, "From Joara to Chiaha: Spanish Exploration of the Appalachian Summit Area, 1540–68," *Southeastern Archaeology* 16, no. 2 (Winter 1997): 162–69

2. John Sinclair, curator of Meteorites, Pisgah Astronomical Research Institute, in discussion with author, September 2018.

3. Geologic Map of North Carolina: North Carolina Department of Natural Resources and Community Development, North Carolina Geological Survey (NCGS), 1985.

4. Bart Cattanach, North Carolina Geologic Survey, in discussion with author, September, 2018 and March, 2020.

5. John Hack, "Grandfather MTN Glacier Grooves Refuted," *Science* 184 (April 5, 1974): 88–89.

6. H. Trawick Ward and R. P. Stephen Davis Jr., *Time before History: The Archaeology of North Carolina* (Chapel Hill: University of North Carolina Press, 1999), 24.

7. Matthew T. Boulenger and Metin I. Eren, "On the Inferred Age and Origin of Lithic Bi-Points from the Eastern Seaboard and Their Relevance to the Pleistocene Peopling of North America," *American Antiquity* 80, no. 1 (January 2015): 134–45.

8. Jerry N. MacDonald, *An Outline of the pre-Clovis Archaeology of SV-2, Saltville, Virginia, with Special Attention to a Bone Tool Dated 14,510 yr BP.* Virginia Museum of Natural History, Martinsville, Va., November 30, 2000.

9. Roy S. Dickens, *Cherokee Prehistory–The Pisgah Phase in the Appalachian Summit Region* (Knoxville: University of Tennessee Press, 2002), 72.

10. Jefferson Chapman, *Tellico Archaeology: 12,000 Years of Native American History*, 3rd ed. (Knoxville: University of Tennessee Press, 2014), 39–40.

11. Chapman, *Tellico Archaeology*, 46.

12. Ibid., 43–72.

13. William E. Meyer, *Indian Trails of the Southeast, Extract from the 42nd Annual Report of the Bureau of American Ethnology 1924–25* (Davenport, IA: Gustav's Library Publishing) 771–72.

14. Lorie Hansen, *Rock Art in North Carolina* (North Carolina Rock Art Survey, USDA), 40.

15. Trawick H. Ward and R. P. Stephen Davis Jr. *Time Before History: The Archaeology of North Carolina* (Chapel Hill: University North Carolina Press, 1999), 80.

16. Chapman, *Tellico Archaeology*, 52.

17. Ibid., 56–69.

18. Ibid., 70.

19. Larry R. Kimball, Thomas R. White, and Gary D. Crites, "Biltmore Mound and Appalachian Summit Hopewell," *Early and Middle Landscapes of the Southeast*, ed. Alice P. Wright and Edward R. Henry (Miami: University of Florida Press, 2013), 122–37.

20. Chapman, *Tellico Archaeology*, 52.

TWO | CHEROKEE, THE PRINCIPAL PEOPLE

1. C. C. Royce, Map of the Former Limits of the Cherokee "Nation of" Indians (Washington, DC: Smithsonian Institution Bureau of Ethnology, 1884).

2. James Mooney, *Cherokee History, Myths, and Sacred Formulas* (Cherokee, NC, Cherokee Publications, 2006), 17, 189.

3. Ibid., 231–34.

4. Ibid., 189–90.

5. David G. Moore, professor of anthropology, Warren Wilson College, Swannanoa, N.C., personal discussions with author. January, 2017–July, 2020

6. Ibid.

7. Roy S. Dickens Jr., *Cherokee Prehistory: The Pisgah Phase in the Appalachian Summit Region* (Knoxville: University of Tennessee Press, 1976).

8. Chapman, *Tellico Archaeology*, 61–63.

9. Sam White, *The Little Ice Age and Europe's Encounter with North America—A Cold Welcome* (Cambridge: Harvard University Press), 1–8.

10. Chapman, *Tellico Archaeology*, 79.

11. Charles R. Cobb, and Brian M. Butler, "The Vacant Quarter Revisited: Late Mississippian Abandonment of the Lower Ohio Valley," *American Antiquity* 67, no. 4 (October 2002): 625–41.

12. Mooney, *Cherokee History*, 408.

THREE | CONQUISTADORS

1. Charles Hudson, *Knights of Spain, Warriors of the Sun: Hernando de Soto and the South's Ancient Chiefdoms* (Athens: University of Georgia Press, 1997), 43–44.

2. Ibid., 172–93.

3. Roderigo Rangle, "A Narrative of Desoto's Expedition," in *The Expedition of Hernando de Soto to North America in 1539–1542*, trans. J. Worth, ed. L. A. Clayton, V. J. Knight Jr., and E. C. Moore (Tuscaloosa: University of Alabama Press, 1993), 281.

4. Chester B. DePratter, Charles M. Hudson, and Marvin T. Smith, "The Route of Juan Pardo's Explorations in the Interior Southeast, 1566–1568," *The Florida Historical Quarterly* 62 (1983): 125 .

5. Alfred W. Crosby, "Virgin Soil Epidemics as a Factor in the Aboriginal Depopulation in America," *The William and Mary Quarterly* 33, no. 2 (1976): 293.

6. Hakluyt, Richard, 1552?–1616. The Discovery And Conquest of Terra Florida, by Don Ferdinando De Soto . . . (London: Printed for the Hakluyt society, 1851).

7. De la Vega, Florida of the Inca, Hernando de Soto's Trails, desototrails.com.

8. Charles A. Grymes, Ed. Http://www.virginiaplaces.org/settleland/treaties.html.

9. Washington County History before 1796, Mildred S. Kozsuch Papers—Archives of Appalachia, East Tennessee State University, Johnson City, TN.

10. Wilma A. Dunaway, "The Southern Fur Trade and the Incorporation of Southern Appalachia into the World-Economy, 1690–1763," *Review* (Fernand Braudel Center) 17, no. 2 (Spring 1994): 225.

11. William Talbot, The Discoveries of John Lederer in Three several Marches from Virginia, to the West of Carolina, and other parts of the Continent: Begun in March 1669 and ended in September 1670. (London: Samuel Heyrick, 1672): 26–27. https://quod.lib.umich.edu/e/eebo2/A49917.0001.001.

12. Dunaway, "Southern Fur Trade," 215–42.

FOUR | A LAND UNSETTLED

1. Francis Parkman, "The Jesuits in North America in the Seventeenth Century," in *France and England in North America*, Vol II (Little, Brown, and Co.,1867); http://www.gutenberg.org/files/6933/6933-h/6933-h.htm.

2. Henry Timberlake, *The Memories of Lt. Henry Timberlake: The Story of a Soldier, Adventurer, and Emissary to the Cherokees*, ed. Duane H. King (Cherokee, NC: Museum of the Cherokee Indian Press, 2007), 37.

3. William Waller Hening, ed., The Statutes at Large; Being a Collection of All the Laws of Virginia from the First Session of the Legislature in the Year 1619 (New York: R. & W. & G. Bartow, 1814), 324. Accessed July 25, 2020 https://www.encyclopedia virginia.org/Treaty_Ending_the_Third_Anglo-Powhatan_War_1646.

4. Alan S. Taylor, *American Colonies: The Settling of North America* (New York: Viking/Penguin, 2002), 323–24. http://nationalhumanitiescenter.org/pds/becoming amer/growth/text3/text3read.htm.

5. Gun Shop and Forge, North Carolina Highway Historical Marker Program P-28, North Carolina Department of Cultural Resources, 1951 accessed July 21, 2020, http://www.ncmarkers.com/Markers.aspx?MarkerId=P-28.

6. John Mack Faragher, *Daniel Boone: The Life and Legend of an American Pioneer* (New York: Henry Holt & Company, 1992), 31.

7. Ibid., 30–35.

8. Ibid., 58.

9. Mrs. R. L. McCown, letter, 21 January 1964, Mary Hardin McCown Collection, Archives of Appalachia.

10. Proclamation of 1763, Key Treaties Defining the Boundaries Separating English and Native American Territories in Virginia, http://www.virginiaplaces.org/settleland /treaties.html.

11. Paul M. Fink, "Jacob Brown of Nolichucky," *Tennessee Historical Quarterly*, Tennessee History Society, 21. No 3 (September 1962): 235.

12. Max Dixon, *Wataugans: First "free and independent community on the continent…"* (Johnson City, TN: Overmountain Press, 1989), 4–11

13. Carl S. Driver, *John Sevier, Pioneer of the Old Southwest* (Chapel Hill: University of North Carolina Press, 1932), 8.

14. Fred S. Rolater, 2017, "Treaties," *Tennessee Encyclopedia*, accessed July 20, 2020, https://tennesseeencyclopedia.net/entries/treaties.

15. Robert L. Ganyard, "Threat From the West: North Carolina and the Cherokee 1776–1778," *North Carolina Historical Review* 45, no. 1 (January 1968): 47–66.

16. F. A. Sondley, *Asheville and Buncombe County* (Asheville: The Asheville Citizen Company, 1922,) 52–53.

17. Parris, John. 1955, "Roaming the Mountains 'Eden's Land' Echoes With Sounds Like a Piper's Melody." *Asheville Citizen-Times,* July 10, 1955, 35.

18. William Bartram, *Travels and Other Writings* (New York: The Library of America, 1996), 286–88.

19. Cherokee Defeat. North Carolina Highway Historical Marker Program Q-7, North Carolina Department of Cultural Resources, 1939 , http://www.ncmarkers.com /print_marker.aspx?MarkerId=Q-7.

20. The Rutherford Expecition. Accessed July 20, 2020, https://www.ncpedia.org /anchor/rutherford-expedition.

21. Randall Jones, *The Overmountain Men and the Battle for Kings Mountain*, https://www.ncpedia.org/anchor/overmountain-men-and-battle.

22. Pat Alderman, *Overmountain Men* (Johnson City, TN: Overmountain Press, 1970), 52–96.

23. Jones, *Overmountain Men*.

24. J. G. M. Ramsey, *The Annals of Tennessee to the End of the Eighteenth Century* (J. B. Lippencott & Co, 1860), 262–64.

FIVE | EDEN OF THE MOUNTAINS

1. Stephen J. Yerka, Historic Preservation Specialist, Tribal Historic Preservation Office, Eastern Band of the Cherokee Indians, Cherokee, NC, in discussion with author, October, 2018.

2. Barbara Duncan, Education Director, Museum of the Cherokee, Cherokee, in discussions with author, November, 2018 and David Moore, Professor of Anthropology, Warren Wilson College, ongoing discussions, 2017–2019.

3. Process for Receiving a Land Grant: Bounty Land, Geneaological Services, Government and Heritage Library Blog, State Library of North Carolina, Dec. 12, 2014. Accessed 2018, https://statelibrarync.org/news/2014/12process-for-receiving-a-land-grant-bounty-land/.

4. A Short History of Fines Creek, North Carolina, Fines Creek Community Association, accessed July 20, 2020. https://finescreek.org/history/.

5. F. A. Sondley. 1913. Samuel Davidson (address, commemorative exercises when the monument was unveiled, Asheville, NC, September 25th, 1913) https://babel.hathitrust.org/cgi/pt?id=loc.ark:/13960/t1khovvo2&view=1up&seq=3.

6. Wilson Lyday, Lyday-Leeden Family, Mary Jane McCrary Family Collection, Rowell Bosse North Carolina Room, Transylvania County Library, Brevard, NC.

7. Barbara Ilie. 2016. Bison in North Carolina, University of North Carolina Library, accessed July 20, 2020, https://blogs.lib.unc.edu/ncm/index.php/2016/07/07/bison-in-north-carolina/.

8. Alex S. Caton. 2004, The Buncombe Turnpike, Western Northj Carolina Historical Association and Smith-McDowell House. Asheville, NC, accessed July 20, 2020. https://www.ncpedia.org/anchor/buncombe-turnpike.

9. Preston A. Arthur, *Western North Carolina: A History (1730 to 1913)* (Asheville, NC: Daughters of the American Revolution, 1914), 231.

10. Ora Blackmun, *Western North Carolina, Its Mountains and its People to 1880* (Boone, NC: Appalachian Consortium Press, 1977), 163.

11. Arthur, *Western North Carolina*, 233.

12. Paint Rock, North Carolina Highway Historical Marker Program P-27, North Carolina Department of Cultural Resources, 1950, accessed July 20, 2020, http://www.ncmarkers.com/Markers.aspx?MarkerId=P-27.

13. Ramsey, *Annals of Tennessee,* 178.

14. Sondley, Asheville and Buncombe County, 106.

15. Blackmun, *Western North Carolina*, 220.

16. Katherine Calhoun Cutshall, "In the Grip of Slavery: The Rise of Slave Society Surrounding the Establishment of Stock Stands along the Buncombe Turnpike, 1790 to 1855," (undergraduate thesis, University of North Carolina-Asheville, 2015), 12–13.

17. Alex S. Caton, 2004, *The Buncombe Turnpike*, accessed July 25, 2020, https://www.ncpedia.org/anchor/buncombe-turnpike.

18. Jean H. Seaman, 2006, *Gold Rush*, NCPedia, accessed July 20, 2020, https://www.ncpedia.org/gold-rush.

19. Williams, David. "Such Excitement You Never Saw": Gold Mining in Nineteenth Century Georgia, *The Georgia Historical Quarterly* Vol. 72 no. 3 (Fall 1992) 695–707.

20. Steve Inskeep, *Jacksonland* (New York: Penguin Press, 2015), 41–50.

21. Bourbon, Jeffery Normand, *"All Must Have a Say": Internal Improvements and Andrew Jackson's Political Rise in North Carolina in 1824,"* *The North Carolina Historical Review*, 91, no. 1 (January 2014) 63–92.

22. Gen. Winfield Scott, 1838. General Winfield Scott's Address to the Cherokee Nation. Accessed July 20, 2020, http://www.thomaslegion.net/generalwinfieldscotts addresstothecherokeenation.html.

SIX | WHERE THERE'S WATER

1. All-time statewide extremes: Jan. 1, 1870 to July 22, 2020. North Carolina Climate Office, accessed July 20, 2020, http://climate.ncsu.edu/nc_extremes.

2. Darin J. Waters, "Life Beneath the Veneer: The Black Community in Asheville, North Carolina from 1793 to 1900" (PhD diss., University of North Carolina, Chapel Hill, 2012), 10.

3. Sondley, 87.

4. Gail (Gaillard) Tennet, The Indian Path in Buncombe County (map), D. H. Ramsey Special Collections, UNC-Asheville.

5. Sarah McCulloh Lemmon, *Dictionary of North Carolina Biography*, ed. William S. Powell (Chapel Hill, NC: University of North Carolina Press, 1979–1996).

6. "Ice Ages," National Park Service, www.nps.gov.

7. Floods on Swannanoa River and BeeTree Creek in the Vicinity of Swannanoa, North Carolina, TVA Division of Water Control Planning, Knoxville, Tenn., 1963, 23–26.

8. Dykeman, *The French Broad*, 23.

9. F. A. Sondley, *Asheville and Buncombe County* (Asheville: The Citizen Company, 1922), 89.

10. Michael Allison et al, 2008, *Transylvania County Heritage North Carolina* (Waynesville, NC: County Heritage), 10.

11. Mills River. Accessed July 24, 2020, http://hendersonheritage.com/mills-river/.

12. Ross, John. 2019. *Flat Rock's St. John in the Wilderness.* The Laurel of Asheville, Asheville, NC, Vol. 16 No. 12. 28.

13. Horse Shoe. Accessed July 24, 2020, http://hendersonheritage.com/horse-shoe-2/.

14. Lewis, J. D. 2018. North Carolina Railroads–Hendersonville & Brevard Railroad. Accessed July 24, 2020, http://www.carolana.com/NC/Transportation/railroads/nc_rrs _hendersonville_brevard.html.

15. Ross, John, 2019, *From Turnip Seed Grew Marshall.* The Laurel of Asheville. Asheville, NC, Vol. 16 No. 11. 34.

16. Della Hazel, Moore, *Hot Springs of North Carolina* (Johnson City, TN: The Overmountain Press, 2002), 32.

17. Sondley, Asheville and Buncombe County. 117.

18. Manley Wade Wellman, *The Kingdom of Madison* (Chapel Hill, NC: University of North Carolina Press, 1973), 33.

19. Charles Lannam, "Hot Springs–100 Years ago," (The State, March 27, 1955) In *Hot Springs of North Carolina,* Della Hazel Moore (Johnson City, TN.: Overmountain Press, 2002), 33.

20. "Meet the Original Maggie," https://maggievalley.org/maggie-valley-history.

21. Plott-Duke, Cynthia. 2016. Plott Hound–The State Dog of North Carolina. Accessed July 24, 2020, https://plottfamilyclanofnorthcarolina.weebly.com/plott -hounds.html.

22. Haywood County North Carolina. Vol. 1. (Waynesville, NC: Walsworth Publishing Co., Waynesville. 1994), 1.

23. Newport, Tennessee. n.d. accessed July 23, 2020. https://www.cityofnewport-tn.com.

24. James A. Goforth, *Building the Clinchfield: A Construction History of America's Most Unusual Railroad* (Johnson City, TN: Overmountain Press, 1989), 110–14.

25. Burton, Tom, "The Hanging of Mary, a Circus Elephant," in *A Tennessee Folklore Sampler,* (Knoxville: The University of Tennessee Press, 2010), 219–27.

26. Gatlinburg, Tennessee. n.d. accessed July 23, 2020. https://www.gatlinburg.com.

SEVEN | UNCIVIL WAR IN THE MOUNTAINS

1. John Carlyle Sitterson, *"Economic Sectionalism in Ante-Bellum North Carolina,"* North Carolina Historical Review 16, no. 2 (1939): 144.

2. James C. Inscoe and Gordon B. McKinney, *The Heart of Confederate Appalachia–Western North Carolina in the Civil War* (Chapel Hill, NC: University of North Carolina Press, 2000), 12–29.

3. Ibid., 34–35.

4. *The Harper's Ferry Affair,* The Asheville News, Oct. 27, 1859. 3.

5. William G. Brownlow. n.d. accessed July 24, 2020. https://en.wikipedia.org/wiki /William_Gannaway_Brownlow.

6. E. Merton Coulter, *William G. Brownlow Fighting Parson of the Southern Highlands (Knoxville:* University of Tennessee Press, 1999), 18.

7. W. G. Brownlow, *Sketches of the Rise, Progress, and Decline of the Secession; with a Narrative of Personal Adventure s among the Rebels* (Philadelphia, PA: George Childs, 1862), 279–80.

8. Coulter, *William G. Brownlow,* 182–84.

9. William R. Trotter, *Bushwackers–The Civil War in North Carolina. Book 1–The Mountains* (Winston-Salem, NC: John F. Blair, 1988), 10–11.

10. William Cicero Allen, *Centennial of Haywood County and Its County Seat* (Waynesville, NC: Courier Printing Co., 1908), 163.

11. Milas Alexander Kirkpatrick, *Reminisces: Milas A. Kirkpatrick, 16th North Carolina Infantry Regiment, Company L*. n.d. accessed July 24, 2020. http://digital.ncdcr.gov/cdm/ref/collection/p15012coll8/id/12105.

12. George A. Mills, 1901. *History of the 16th North Carolina Regiment in the Civil War* (John C. Mills, Rutherfordton, NC). accessed July 24, 2020 https://digital.ncdcr.gov/digital/collection/p15012coll8/id/1923/ 1–2.

13. Ibid. Kirkpatrick, http://digital.ncdcr.gov/cdm/ref/collection/p15012coll8/id/12105.

14. Will A. McTeer, *Among Loyal Mountaineers: The Civil War Reminiscences of an East Tennessee Unionist, Maryville: '27/37 Publishing. 2009.* 13–20.

15. Beulah Karr, *One Moment of Glory–A Tribute to our Civil War Solders of Sevier County. (Evansville, IN:*Evansville Bindery, 2009), 225–27.

16. Confederate States of America Tax and Assessment Acts, and Amendments. The Tax Act of 24th April 1863, as Amended, n.d. accessed July 24, 2020. https://docsouth.unc.edu/imls/taxasses/taxasses.html.

17. Inscoe and McKinney, *The Heart of Confederate Appalachia, 166–207.*

18. Ibid., 70–73, 187–207.

19. Library of Congress, Map showing the distribution of the slave population in southern states. Compiled from the census of 1860, https://www.loc.gov/resource/g3861e.cw0013200/?r=0.01,0.19,0.892,0.356,0.

20. Blackmun, *Western North Carolina*, 335–36.

21. Wilma Dunaway, *Slavery in the American Mountain South*, 166; as quoted in review by Jenny B. Wahl. 2003. accessed July 24, 2020. https://eh.net/book_reviews/slavery-in-the-american-mountain-south/.

22. Karr, *One Moment of Glory–A Tribute to our Civil War Solders of Sevier County* , 7.

23. Joan Markel, "First Regiment of Colored Troops Heavy Artillery Formed in Knoxville in 1864," *Knoxville News Sentinel*, November 29, 2014, http://archive.knoxnews.com/entertainment/life/first-regiment-of-colored-troops-heavy-artillery-formed-in-knoxville-in-1864-ep-799797453-353866271.html.

24. Albert Richardson, *The Secret Service, the Field, the Dungeon, and the Escape* (Hartford, CT: American Publishing Company.1865), 444.

25. E. Stanley Godbold, Jr. and Mattie U.Russell, *Confederate Colonel and Cherokee Chief, The Life of William Holland Thomas* (Knoxville: University of Tennessee Press, 1990), 8–28.

26. Philip Gerard, Little Will's Cherokee Legion: A white man and the Indians, war and love, and the dream of freedom, *Our State*, Aug. 31, 2012, accessed July 24, 2020 https://www.ourstate.com/william-holland-thomas/.

27. Inscoe and McKinney, *Heart of Confederate Appalachia*, 117–19.

28. Ibid., 176–83.

29. Sondley quoted from William R. Trotter, *Bushwhackers–The Civil War in North Carolina.* Vol. II: *The Mountains* (Winston-Salem, NC: *John* F. Blair, 1988), 291.

30. Inscoe and McKinney, *The Heart of Confederate Appalachia*, 242–43.

31. Hardy, Michael C., *Kirk's Civil War Raids Along the Blue Ridge* (Charleston, SC: History Press, 2018), 146.

32. Trotter, *Bushwhackers*, 294.

33. Inscoe and McKinney, *The Heart of Confederate Appalachia*, 252–59.

EIGHT | THE WEED, THE DOCTOR, AND THE IRON HORSE

1. Steven E. Nash, *Reconstruction's Ragged Edge–The Politics of Postwar Life in the Southern Mountains* (Chapel Hill: The University of North Carolina Press, 2016), 108, 78.

2. Rob Neufeld, "Post-Civil War Crimes Attest to Anger of the Vanquished," *Asheville Citizen-Times*, April 24, 2016.

3. Eric Foner, *Reconstruction–America's Unfinished Revolution, 1863–1877* (New York: Harper Perennial Modern Classics), 157.

4. Nash, *Reconstruction's Ragged Edge*, 30.

5. Robbie D. Jones, "Isaac Dockery," *Tennessee Encyclopedia*, March 1, 2018, https://tennesseeencyclopedia.net/entries/isaac-dockery.

6. Nash, *Reconstruction's Ragged Edge*, 108.

7. Ramsey, *Annals of Tennessee*, 13.

8. Mark Twain and Charles Dudley Warner, *The Guilded Age–A Tale of Today*, May 25, 2018, https://www.gutenberg.org/files/3178/3178-h/3178-h.htm.

9. H. P. Gatchell and E. A. Gatchell, eds. *Western North Carolina: Its Resources, Climate, Scenery and Salubrity* (New York: A. L. Chatterton Pub. Co., 1885).

10. Mary Rothrock, *The French Broad-Holston Country: A History of Knox County, Tennessee*, East Tennessee Historical Society, 489–90, 499; https://en.wikipedia.org/wiki/Peter_Staub

11. Henderson Springs Resort, Tennessee Historical Marker Project, 2014, https://www.historicalmarkerproject.com/markers/HM1F6F_henderson-springs-resort_Pigeon-Forge-TN.html

12. Amy C. Manikowski, Historical Inns of Asheville, https://ashevillehistoricinns.wordpress.com/2013/08/27/sulphur-springs/

13. W. E. Trout, III, and Nancy R. Trout, *The French Broad River Atlas–Rediscovering River History in the Land of the Sky* (Madison Heights, VA: Virginia Canals and Navigations Society, 2016), 32–51.

14. Edwin R. Walker, III, *Cocke County Tennessee Pages from the Past* (Charleston, SC: Henry Press, 2007), 190.

15. Zoe Rhine, *Black Lives Built Western North Carolina Railroad*, Pack Library, North Carolina Room, Asheville, NC, 2018.

16. Lou Harshaw, *Trains, Trestles and Tunnels Railroads of the Southern Appalachians* (Asheville, NC: Hexagon, 1977), 12.

17. Bascom Lamar Lunsford, *Ballads, Banjo Tunes and Sacred Songs of Western North Carolina*, Smithsonian Folkways SF CD 40082, accessed July 24, 2020, http://www .traditionalmusic.co.uk/folk-song-lyrics/Swannanoa_Tunnel_2.htm.

NINE | MORNING GREETS THE WATERSHED

1. Oliver, Duane, *Hazel Creek from Then till Now,* (Maryville, TN: Stinnet Printing, 1989) 56-86

2. Richard D. Starnes, "'A Conspicuous Example of What is Termed the New South': Tourism and Urban Development in Asheville, North Carolina, 1880–1925," *The North Carolina Historical Review* 80, no. 1 (January 2003), 53.

3. Ibid., 59.

4. Haywood County Genealogical Society, *Haywood County Heritage North Carolina 1* (1994): 49.

5. N. Buckner, "The Hydro-Electric Development of the North Carolina Electrical Company," *Southern Electrician,* January 1912, 135.

6. Douglas C. Brookshire, "William Trotter Weaver: Pioneer in Electric Power Development," *Asheville Citizen-Times,* April 10, 1949, 2.

7. "Mohawk Milling Company One of Oldest Mills in Operation," *Newport Plain Talk,* March 2, 1972

8. Thomas Robinson Dawley Jr., *The Child That Toileth Not* (New York: Gracia Publishing Co. 1912), 134.

9. Ina W. Van Noppen and John J. Van Noppen, *Western North Carolina Since the Civil War* (Boone, NC: Appalachian Consortium Press, 1973), 355–56.

10. Rob Neufeld, "The Cotton Mill Saved and Slaved, by Various Accounts," Visiting Our Past, *Asheville Citizen-Times,* March 27, 2016.

11. Dykeman, *French Broad,* 171–75.

12. *Asheville Citizen,* January 23, 1890, 1; Scott Shumate, Biltmore historian, personal communication with the author, March 2019.

13. Lloyd R. Bailey, ed. *The Heritage of the Toe River Valley,* Vol. VI (Durham, NC: Lloyd Richard Bailey, 1994), 108–11.

14. Dykeman, *French Broad,* 199.

15. Ibid., 195–209.

16. Lou Harshaw, *Asheville Mountain Majesty* (Fairview, NC: Bright Mountain Books, 2007), 123.

17. Howard E. Covington Jr., *Lady on the Hill: How Biltmore Estate Became an American Icon* (Hoboken, NJ: John Wiley & Sons, 2006), 19.

18. Leonard Wilson, *Samuel Westray Battle,* accessed July 24, 2020, http://files .usgwarchives.net/nc/buncombe/bios/battle56gbs.txt

19. Harshaw, *Asheville Mountain Majesty,* 128.

20. Covington, *Lady on the Hill,* 19.

21. David McCullough, *The Greater Journey: Americans in Paris* (New York: Simon & Schuster, 2011), 190.

22. Bill Alexander, *Around Biltmore Village* (Charleston, SC: Arcadia Publishing Co., 2008), 38

23. Covington, *Lady on the Hill*, 21.

TEN | HARDWOODS, HIDES, AND OVER HERE

1. George B. Sudworth, *The Forest Flora and Conditions of Middle and East Tennessee*, paper, special meeting Nashville, TN, Sept. 22, 1897, proceedings American Forestry Association. 122.

2. Robert S. Lambert, "Logging in the Great Smokies, 1880–1930," *Tennessee Historical Quarterly* 20, no. 4 (December 1961): 350–63.

3. Carl Alvin Schenck, *Cradle of Forestry in America–The Biltmore Forest School 1898–1913* (Durham, NC: Forest History Society), 26-28.

4. Schenck, *Cradle of Forestry in America*, 37.

5. Ronald C. Sullivan, *If Rails Could Talk–Logging the North Carolina Mountains: Crestmont & Champion Fibre*, Vol. 1, 5.

6. Ibid., 10.

7. Ibid., quoting from *Polly Remembers: Reflections of Ninety-Seven years in East Tennessee* (Knoxville, TN: Tennessee Valley Publishing Co., 2002), 45–56 passim.

8. Sullivan, *If Rails Could Talk*, 20.

9. Ibid., 6.

10. Ibid., 3.

11. Ibid., 17.

12. Cory Vaillancourt, "*Sunburst's Forgotten African-Americans,*" broadcast Blue Ridge Public Radio, February 21, 2019.

13. Sullivan, *If Rails Could Talk*, 54.

14. Ibid., 122–25.

15. Virginia Daffron, "The Rise and Fall of a Giant: A.C. Lawrence, America's Largest Leather Company," *Shop Talk!*, January 2016, 16.

16. Rob Neufeld, "Visiting Our Past: Hans Rees, 1st factory in Asheville," *Citizen-Times*, Nov. 6, 2016, accessed July 24, 2020, https://www.citizen-times.com/story/news/local/2016/11/06/visiting-our-past-hans-rees-1t-factory-asheville/93299312/.

17. Riverside Park in Asheville, NC (June 29, 2017, Lost Amusement Parks Series), accessed July 24, 2020, http://www.imaginerding.com/2017/06/29/riverside-park-in-asheville-nc/.

18. National Centers for Environmental Information, Investigating the Great Flood of 1916, https://www.ncdc.noaa.gov/news/investigating-the-great-flood-of-1916.

19. Asheville Victims Claimed by Flood, The Asheville Citizen. July 17, 1916, 1.

20. Ashley McGhee, "Flood of 1916," *The Great War in the Land of the Sky*, UNC-Asheville, accessed July 24, 2020, http://unca.centuryamerica.org/flood-of-1916/.

21. M. Anna Farielio, *The People: Francis Goodrich*, 2006, Craft Revival, Shaping

Western North Carolina Past and Present, accessed July 24, 2020, https://www.wcu
.edu/library/DigitalCollections/CraftRevival/people/franceslgoodrich.html.

22. Michael Yates, "Cecil Sharp in Appalachia," https://www.mustrad.org.uk
/articles/sharp.htm.

23. Richard Winter, "Hot Springs, North Carolina–A World War 1 Internment
Camp," http://www.ncpostalhistory.com/wp-content/uploads/2016/05/Hot_Springs
.pdf; Yates, "Cecil Sharp in Appalachia."

24. Jacqueline Burgin Painter, *The German Invasion of North Carolina–A Pictorial
History* (Johnson City, TN: The Overmountain Press, 1992), 26.

25. The OTEEN, Vol. I, #1 November 9, 1918, 1.

26. The OTEEN, Vol. IV, #10, September 20, 1919, 3.

27. The OTEEN, Vol. 1, #10, 1919, 18.

28. Calder, Thomas, "Asheville Archives: The 1918 influenza changes social norms,"
The Mountain Xpress, Oct. 31, 2018, and "Asheville Archives: Death During the 1918
influenza and its lasting toll," *The Mountain Xpress*, May 24, 2020.

ELEVEN | PROMISE AND PERIL

1. Michael Kruse, "Gatsby's Asheville," *Our State*, July 2, 2014.

2. "1878–Grove's Tastless Chill Tonic Invented," accessed July 24, 2020, https://
grovearcade.com/timeline/groves-tasteless-chill-tonic/

3. Thomas Wolfe, "Boom Town," in *The Complete Short Stories of Thomas Wolfe* (New
York: Charles Scribner's, 1987), 127.

4. Charles F. Waddell, *Report to Asheville Chamber of Commerce*, July 17, 1929, Pack
Library North Carolina History Room.

5. Tetrachloroethylene (PERC), Toxic Substance Portal, Agency for Toxic Substance
and Disease Registry, accessed July 24, 2020, https://www.atsdr.cdc.gov/substances
/toxsubstance.asp?toxid=48

6. Virginia Daffron, "Beacon Site in Swannanoa Subject of Public Comment
Period," *Mountain Express*, September 15, 2017.

7. "American Enka Locates Great Plant Here," *The Asheville Sunday Citizen*,
September 23, 1928, 1.

8. A. M. Moser, ed., *Buncombe County: Economic and Social*, a laboratory study by
the Rural Social Economics Department of the University of North Carolina (June
1923), 26.

9. Bryan, Charles F. Jr, Wetherington, Mark V. Eds, *The Gentle Winds of Change–A
History of Sevier County, Tennessee, 1900–1930* (Sevierville, TN: The Smoky Mountain
Historical Society, 1989), 5–80.

10. Ed Trout, ed., *Gatlinburg–Cinderella City* (Pigeon Forge, TN: Griffin Graphics,
1984), 61.

11. C. Bren Martin, "From Golden Cornfields to Golden Arches: The Economic
and Cultural Evolution of Pigeon Forge, Tennessee," *Journal of the Appalachian Studies
Association* 6 (1994), 165.

12. Daniel Pierce, *The Great Smokies–From Natural Habitat to National Park* (Knoxville: University of Tennessee Press, 2015), 58–59.

13. Horace Kephart, *Our Southern Highlanders* (Knoxville: University of Tennessee Press, 1976), xxxviii.

14. Nan K. Chase, *Asheville, A History* (Jefferson, NC: McFarland 2007), 109–10.

15. John Boyle, "Answer Man: Was Asheville's Depression-Era Debt Repaid," *Asheville Citizen-Times*, February 5, 2015.

16. Carlos C. Campbell, *Birth of a National Park in the Great Smoky Mountains* (Knoxville: University of Tennessee Press, 2009), 12.

17. *Knoxville (TN) Journal*, August 17, 1925, as quoted in Margaret Lynn Brown, "Captains of Tourism: Selling a National Park in the Great Smoky Mountains," *Journal of the Appalachian Studies Association* 4 (1992), 43.

18. Ibid, 44.

19. John Daugherty, *John D. Rockefeller, Jr.*, Biographical Vignettes, National Park Service: The First 75 Years, accessed July 25, 2020, https://www.nps.gov/parkhistory /online_books/sontag/rockefeller.htm.

TWELVE | RIVERS OF RESILIENCE

1. Brian M. du Toit, *Ecusta and the Legacy of Harry H. Straus* (Baltimore, MD: Publish America, 2007), 38.

2. Pure Mountain Water Was Deciding Factor, *Transylvania Times*, May 5, 1938. 1.

3. Whistle at ECUSTA Blows First Blast, *Transylvania Times*, June 15, 1939. 1.

4. Du Toit, Brian M., *Ecusta and the Legacy of Harry H. Straus*, (Baltimore: Publish America, 2007) 72–98.

5. Mark Todd, "Ecusta Cleanup Nearing End," *Transylvania Times*, March 1, 2011. 1.

6. Foundry Commercial marketing brochure, https://www.foundrycommercial.com /properties/land/brevard-nc-davidson-river-village.stml.

7. Max Hunt, "Chemtronics: from Chemical Weapons to Conservation Easement," *The Mountain Express*, Asheville, N.C. March 24, 2016, accessed July 25, 2020, https:// mountainx.com/news/chemtronics-the-long-road-to-remediation/

8. Charles Johnson and Charles Jackson, *City Behind a Fence: Oak Ridge, Tennessee, 1942–1946* (Knoxville, TN: University of Tennessee Press, 1981), 6–8.

9. Tennessee Valley Authority, *The Douglas Project: A Comprehensive Report on the Planning, Design, Construction, and Initial Operations of the Douglas Project*, Technical Report No. 10 (Washington, DC: US Government Printing Office, 1949).

10. "Shuford Says He'll Ask for New Park Highway," *Asheville Citizen–Times*, August 26. 1956, 1.

11. Boyle John, "From the Archives: Impact of Frances, Ivan lingers Years Later," *Asheville Citizen-Times*, September 6, 2017.

12. James E. Hibdon, "Flood Control Benefits and the Tennessee Valley Authority," *Southern Economic Journal* 25, no. 1 (July 1958), 48–63.

13. Benjamin Schoenberg, "The Upper French Broad Defense Association, A

Moment When American Democracy Worked" (baccalaureate thesis, University of North Carolina–Asheville, April, 2017).

14. Ibid., 19.

15. Richard A. Bartlett, *Troubled Waters: Champion International and the Pigeon River Controversy* (Knoxville: University of Tennessee Press, 1995).

16. George M. Denton, Debroah H. Arnwine, *Dioxin Levels in Pigeon River Fish 1996–2002*, Tennessee Department of Water Pollution Control, October 2002.

17. Zoe Rhine, "The Fight to Save 11 Acres of Downtown," April 2016, Heard Tell: Stories from the North Carolina Roon at Pack Memorial Library, accessed July 25, 2020, https://packlibraryncroom.com/2016/04/20/the-fight-to-save-11-acres-of-downtown/

18. Marilyn Ball, *The Rise of Asheville,* (Charleston, SC: The History Press, 2015), 28.

19. Dykeman, *The French Broad*, 14.

20. Tim Ezzell, assistant research professor, Institute for a Secure and Sustainable Environment, University of Tennessee-Knoxville, in discussion with author, May 23, 2019.

THIRTEEN | THE PLANNERS' PARADOX

1. Robert J. Samuelson, "Have We Lost Our Economic Dynamism?" *Washington Post*, September 1, 2019.

2. Rick Webb, former projects coordinator Virginia Trout Stream Sensitivity Study, personal communications he author, 2016–2019.

3. Lisa Reyes Mason, Aaron R. Brown, Kathy Ellis, Jennifer Erwin, and Jon M. Hathaway, "Health Impacts of Extreme Weather Events: Exploring Protective Factors with a Capitals Framework," *Journal of Evidence Based Social Work* (July 27, 2018): 579–93.

4. J. Curtis Weaver, "The Drought of 1998–2002 North Carolina–Precipitation and Hydrologic Conditions," USGS Scientific Investigations Report, 2005–5053.

5. Sue Sturgis, South's Power Plants Stressing Drinking-Water Supplies, Facing South, Institute for Southern Studies, November 15, 2011, https://www.facingsouth.org/2011/11/souths-power-plants-stressing-drinking-water-supplies.html.

6. Hasten Willis, "Downsizing the American Dream: The New Trend Toward 'Missing Middle Housing," *Washington Post*, February 14, 2019.

Selected Bibliography

Anderson, David G. "Climate and Culture Change in Prehistoric and Early Historic North America." *Archaeology of Eastern North America* 29 (2001): 143–86.

Anderson, David G., and Kenneth E. Sassaman. *Recent Developments in Southeastern Archaeology From Colonization to Complexity*. Washington, DC: Society for American Archaeology, 2012.

Anderson, David G., Ashely M. Smallwood, and D. Shane Miller. *Pleistocene Human Settlement in the Southeastern United States: Current Evidence and Future Directions.* College Station, TX: Society for the Study of the First Americans, 2015.

Arneach, Lloyd. *Long-Ago Stories of the Eastern Cherokee.* Charleston, SC: The History Press, 2013.

Arnow, Harriet Simpson. *Seedtime on the Cumberland.* Lincoln, NB, 1965.

Arthur, John Preston. *Western North Carolina: A History.* Raleigh, NC: Daughters of the American Revolution, 1914.

Bartram, William. *Travels and Other Writings.* New York: The Library of America, 1996.

Brown, Margaret. *The Wild East: A Biography of the Great Smoky Mountains.* Gaines-ville: University of Florida Press, 2001.

Burnett, Edmund Cody. "Hog Raising and Hog Driving in the Region of the French Broad River." *Agriculture History Society* 20 (1946): 99–102.

Burton, Tom. "The Hanging of Mary, a Circus Elephant," in *A Tennessee Folklore Sampler.* Eds. Ted Olson and Anthony Cavendar. Knoxville: University of Tennessee Press, 2010.

Chapman, Jefferson. *Tellico Archaeology: 12,000 Years of Native American History.* 3rd ed. Knoxville: University of Tennessee Press, 2014.

Chase, Nan K. *Asheville: A History.* Jefferson, NC: McFarland Publishing, 2007.

Davis, Donald E. *Where There Are Mountains: An Environmental History of the Southern Appalachians.* Athens: University of Georgia Press, 2003.

Deaderick, Lucille, ed. *Heart of the Valley: A History of Knoxville, Tennessee.* Knoxville: East Tennessee Historical Society, 1976.

Dickens, Roy S., Jr. *Cherokee Prehistory: The Pisgah Phase in the Appalachian Summit Region.* Knoxville: University of Tennessee Press, 1976.

Dykeman, Wilma. *The French Broad.* New York, Rhinehart, 1955; Knoxville: University of Tennessee Press, 1973.

Eller, Ronald D. *Miners, Millhands, and Mountaineers: Industrialization of Appalachian South, 1880–1930.* Knoxville: University of Tennessee Press, 1982.

Ellison, George. *Mountain Passages: Natural and Cultural History of Western North Carolina.* South Norfolk, VA: History Press, 2005.

Faragher, John Mack. *Daniel Boone: The Life and Legend of an American Pioneer.* New York: Henry Holt & Company, 1992.

Hudson, Charles. *Knights of Spain, Warriors of the Sun: Hernando de Soto and the South's Ancient Chiefdoms.* Athens: University of Georgia Press, 1997.

Inscoe, John. *Mountain Masters, Slavery, and the Sectional Crisis in Western North Carolina.* Knoxville: University of Tennessee Press, 1989.

Inscoe, John, and Gordon McKinney. *The Heart of Confederate Appalachia: Western North Carolina in the Civil War.* Chapel Hill: University of North Carolina Press, 2000.

Keel, Bennie C. *Cherokee Archaeology: A Study of the Appalachian Summit.* Knoxville: University of Tennessee Press, 1987.

Kephart, Horace. *Our Southern Highlanders.* Knoxville: University of Tennessee Press, 1976.

King, Duane H., ed. *The Cherokee Nation: A Troubled History.* Knoxville: University of Tennessee Press, 1979.

Meeks, Scott C., and David G. Anderson. *Draught, Subsistence Stress, and Population Dynamics: Assessing the Abandonment of the Vacant Quarter, Soils, Climate, and Society. Archaeological Investigations in Ancient America.* University Press of Colorado, 2013.

Mooney, James. *Cherokee History, Myths, and Sacred Formulas.* Fairview, NC: Cherokee Publications, 2006.

Nash, Steven E. *Reconstruction's Ragged Edge: The Politics of Postwar Life in the Southern Mountains.* Chapel Hill: University of North Carolina Press, 2016.

Orr, Doug. *The North Carolina Atlas.* Chapel Hill: University of North Carolina Press, 2000.

Orr, Doug, Douglas Milton Orr, and Fiona Ritchie. *Wayfaring Strangers: The Musical Voyage from Scotland and Ulster to Appalachia.* Chapel Hill: University of North Carolina Press, 2014.

Ramsey, J. G. M. *The Annals of Tennessee to the End of the Eighteenth Century.* Philadelphia, PA, J B Lippincott & Co., 1860.

Rothrock, Mary U., ed. *The French Broad-Holston Country.* Knoxville: East Tennessee Historical Society, 1972.

Shumate, Scott. *Archaeological Investigations of the River Arts District of the Proposed Wilma Dykeman Riverway.* Asheville, NC, Blue Ridge Archaeological Consultants, 2010.

Silver, Timothy. *Mount Mitchell and the Black Mountains: An Environmental History of the Highest Peaks in Eastern America.* Chapel Hill: University of North Carolina Press, 2003.

Sondley, Foster A. *Asheville and Buncombe County.* Asheville, NC: The Citizen Company, 1922.

————. *History of Buncombe County.* Asheville, NC: Advocate Printing Co., 1930.

Ward, H. Trawick, and Steven Davis Jr. *Time before History: The Archaeology of North Carolina.* Chapel Hill: University of North Carolina Press, 1999.

Wellman, Manley Wade. *The Kingdom of Madison.* Chapel Hill: University of North Carolina Press, 1973.

Wetmore, Ruth Y. *An Archaeological Survey of Transylvania County.* Brevard, NC, Transylvania Historic Properties Commission, 1993.

PERSONAL INTERVIEWS AND CORRESPONDENCE

Baumann, Tim. Research associate professor and curator of archaeology. McClung Museum. University of Tennessee–Knoxville.

Chapman, Jefferson. Director, McClung Museum. University of Tennessee–Knoxville.

Moore, David. Professor of archaeology. Warren Wilson College.

Riggs, Brett H. Sequoyah Distinguished Professor of Cherokee Studies. Western Carolina University, Cullowhee, North Carolina.

Townsend, Russell. Tribal Historic Preservation Officer, Eastern Band of Cherokee Indians, Cherokee, North Carolina.

Index

A. C. Lawrence Leather Company, 160
Abingdon, Va. (formerly Wolf Town), 63
Abraham Lincoln: The War Years (Sandburg), 119
Adair, James, 26
Adena (Native American) culture, 20
African Americans/freedmen/slaves, 87,
   94, 102, 105, 112–13, 123–24, 202. *See also*
   enslaved peoples; race/racial diversity
aging-in-place, 202
air pollution, 195, 207
Alabama, 18, 53, 60, 68, 79–80, 104
Alcoa, Tenn. (formerly North Maryville),
   97, 188
Alcoa Corporation, 188
alcohol. *See* whisky/whiskey
Alexander, James, 75
Alexander, Rebecca, 70
Algonquian Indians, 25
Allanstand Cottage Industries, 163–164, 165
Allegheny River, 57
Allen, Lawrence, 115–16
Altapass, N.C., 8, 96, 161
alternative energy (wind/solar), 207
aluminum industry, 188
Ambler, Chase P., 177
American Enka Company, 172, 187, 210
American Forestry Association, 152
American Revolution: Battle of Kings Moun-
   tain, 8, 64, 68, 70, 88; Battle of Lexington

and Concord, 59, 61; Battle of Stony Point,
   70–71; British capture of Charleston, 63;
   Rutherford campaign, 60–63; winning the
   War of Independence, 68–69
American Tobacco Company, 126, 184
*Among Loyal Mountaineers: Reminiscences of
   an East Tennessee Unionist* (McTeer), 110
Andersonville Prison (Georgia), 111
Anglo-Powhatan War (third), 47
*Annals of Tennessee to the End of the Eighteenth
   Century, The* (Ramsey), 73
Apalachee Indians, 41
Appalachian Mountains, 2–3, 7–11, 34–35, 41,
   53–54, 77, 83
Appalachian Regional Commission, 209
Appalachian Scenic Highway. *See* Blue Ridge
   Parkway
Appalachian School (Penland), 163
Appalachian Summit region, 35
Appalachian Valley, 18, 53
Appomattox River, 47
archaeology/archaeological culture: Appala-
   chian Summit region, 35; Cherokee Indi-
   ans, 25–39; Joara village (Berry site), 41–44,
   47; Paleo Indians, 3–4, 13–15, 16, 19, 23, 183,
   199, 201; Vacant Quarter, 38; Woodland
   period, 13, 22, 23, 37
Archaic era/period/culture, xiii, 13, 16, 17–19,
   23, 37, 73

Macon County, 71
Madison County, 68, 71, 81, 92, 108–9, 112,
    115–16, 122, 163–64, 190, 202
Maggie Valley, N.C., 8, 35, 38, 88, 93–94, 190
Malvern Hills Country Club, 128
Mammoth Cave, 179–80
marijuana and hemp, 211
Marshall, John, 92
Marshall, N.C. (formerly Lapland), 9, 11, 75–
    76, 81, 91–92, 115–16, 122, 139, 141, 162, 190
Marshall Milling Company, 139, 141
Masa, George, 177
McCalla, R. C., 130
McCullough, David, 148
McDowell, Charles, 63–64
McGuire Nuclear Station, 206
McKinley, William, 177–78
McNamee, George, 147
McTeer, Will A., 110–11
Medieval Warm Period, 19, 35–38, 46, 199
Memphis, Tenn., 44
Menninger, Christopher, 119
Merrill, Ransom P., 108, 122
Methodist Church, 73–74, 106, 108
Mighty Mary (circus elephant), 96–97
Miles, George H., 109
Mills River, 56, 89–90, 154, 185, 192, 206
Mills River, N.C., 89–90, 198
Mills River Academy, 90
Mississippi River, xiv, 8, 26, 38, 44, 46–47,
    57–58, 69, 149, 152, 180
Mississippian (Native American) culture, 13,
    23, 35, 37
Mitchell County, 70
Mobile, Ala., 46
Monk, I. E., 172
Monongahela River, 57
Mooney, James, 25–276, 33
moonshine. *See* whisky/whiskey
Moore, William, 70–71
Morgan, Lucy, 163–64
Morgan, Thomas, 73
Morganton, N.C., 41, 64, 77, 102, 109, 111,
    117–18
Morris, Ralph D., Jr., 195
Morristown (renamed Asheville). *See*
    Asheville, N.C.

Mount Le Conte, 174
Mount Mitchell, 21, **22**, 95, 136, 180
Mount Pisgah, 7, 21, 67–68, 128, 136, 147, 172, 180
Mount Prospect, 94
Mountain Lily (riverboat), **129**, 130–31
Mountain Lodge, 77
Mountain Park Hotel, 92–93, 136, 137, **166**
Mountain View Hotel, 174–**175**
Mud Cut (Swannanoa railroad tunnel), 132
Mullinix, Dick, 195
Murphy, N.C., 35, 157, 185
Museum of North Carolina Minerals, 180

Nantahala Mountains, 62
Nantahala National Forest, 173
Nantahala River, 35, 185
Nasty Branch, 87
National Association for Stock Car Racing
    (NASCAR), 4
National Centers for Environmental
    Information, 205
Needham, James, 48, 54
Neilson, William, 73–74
New Belgium Brewing Company, 198
New Orleans, La., 46
New York, 18, 53, 166
New York City, Central Park, 148
New York Times, 148
New-York Tribune, 113
Newfound Gap, 9
Newport, Tenn., 2, 8, 16, 68–69, 76, 88, 91, 93,
    94–95, 97, 117, 126, 129–30, 139–140, 142–45,
    156–57, 160, 165, 190, 191, 193
Nikwasi (Indian mound), 21
Nixon, Richard, 159
Nolichucky River (aka "the 'Chucky"), **xviii**,
    2, 8, 16, 27, 35, 44, 48, 57–59, 65–**66**, 67–68,
    71, 86–87, 91, 95, 130, 144, **168**, 185, 187, 191
Norris Dam (TVA), 188
North Carolina: Cherokee removal, 68, 70,
    80, 94, 115; Civil War in, 106–19, 122–23;
    creation of Buncombe County, 71, 86;
    creation of Buncombe Turnpike Company,
    75–76, 159; discovery of gold, 77, **78**, 79;
    exhaustion of the soil, 85; highway (I 40)
    s, 189–90; leather tanning industry, 159–60;
    minerals/mining, 143–44; naming the state

U.S. Army Corps of Engineers, 130, 158–59
U.S. Centers for Disease Control (CDC), 203
U.S. Department of the Interior, 179
U.S. Environmental Protection Agency
  (EPA), 186–87
U.S. Forest Service, 149, 157, 173
U.S. Internal Revenue Service, 124
U.S. Route 19 (US 19), 33, 94
U.S. Route 23 (US 23), 61
U.S. Route 25 (US 25), 138
U.S. Route 276 (US 276), 91
U.S. Route 321 (US 321), 97
U.S. Route 441 (US 441), 9, 99, 190, 204

Vacant Quarter, 38
Van Camp Packing Company, 145
Vance, David, Jr., 75, 85, 91–92, 101
Vance, Robert B., 130
Vance, Zebulon Baird, 85, 105, 116
Vanderbilt, Cornelius, 129, 145
Vanderbilt, Eliza, 146
Vanderbilt, George Washington, III, 134,
  145–47, 153–55, 173, 177
Vanderbilt, Maria Louisa Kissam, 134, 145–47,
  179
Vanderbilt, William H., 145
Virginia Trout Stream Sensitivity Study, 205

Waddell, Charles F., 171
Walden Creek, 70
Walker, Felix, 86, 114
Walnut, N.C. (formerly Jewell Hill), 81, 92
Walnut Bottom, 156
Walters Dam, 93, 191, 193–94
War Ford, 61, 94–95
Warm Springs, Ga., 93, 137
Warm Springs Hotel, 92, 137
Warm Springs, N.C., 73, 74 ,76, 102, 118, 136.
  See also Hot Springs, N.C.
Warm Springs, Va., 73, 93, 137
Warner, Charles Dudley, 126
Warren Wilson College, xiv, 70; Archaic
  Indian sites, 16, 17, 19–20, 36, 47
Washington, George, 58
Washington, Jackson, 123
Watauga Association, 58
Watauga River, 44, 58, 65

Watauga Settlement, 71, 73
Waterville, N.C., 93, 94, 155, 190
Waterville Lake, 193
Wayah Gap/Creek, 62
Wayfaring Strangers: The Musical Voyage from
  Scotland and Ulster to Appalachia (Orr and
  Ritchie), xvi
Wayne, Anthony (Gen. "Mad Anthony"),
  70–71, 94
Waynesville, N.C., 8, 27, 30, 68, 88, 94, 117, 138,
  156, 160, 175, 190
Wear, Samuel, 70–71
Wear's Cove, 108
weather. *See* climate
Weaver, W. T., 138
Weaverville, N.C., 115, 141, 163
weaving and spinning. *See* crafts industry
Wedgewood, Josiah, 144
West Prong of the Little Pigeon River, 3,
  9, 12, 97–99, 173–74, 206. *See also* Little
  Pigeon River
Western North Carolina: Its Agricultural
  Resources, Mineral Wealth, Climate,
  Salubrity and Scenery (H. P. Gatchell,
  MD), 126–27
Western North Carolina Railroad
  (WNCR), 102, 126, 129, 131, 132, 143
whisky/whiskey, 4, 74, 75, 94, 124–25, 164,
  167
White, James, 99
White Oak Flats. *See* Gatlinburg, Tenn.
White Sulphur Springs Hotel, 138
whitewater rafting/float trips, 8, 91, 94, 191,
  194, 198
Wilkesboro, N.C., 118
Williamson, Andrew (Col.), 60–63
Wilmington, N.C., 189
Winchester, Va., 55
wind energy, 207
WNOX radio station, 176
Wolf Creek, Tenn., 125–26, 131
Wolfe, Thomas, 169, 170–71
Wolfe, William Oliver, 170
women: enslaved, 70, 112–13; life during the
  Civil War, 116, 121–22; life in Archaic
  Indian society, 17, 37; Pi Beta Phi sorority,
  97–98, 163–64, 174; role in Cherokee

women (*cont.*)
  society, 34, 62; role in mountain families,
  97, 135–36, 162–63; service during WWI,
  169; service during WWII, 184; surviving
  the Great Depression, 181
Wonderland Hotel, 176
Wood, Abraham, 47–48
Wood, W. B. (Rev. Col.) 108
Woodfin, N.C., 139
Woodland prehistoric era, 13, 22, 23, 37
Woody, Mary, 193
Work, Hubert, 178–79

Works Progress Administration (WPA),
  181
World War I, 158–59, 165–166, 169
World War II, 183, 186, 188–89
Worry, N.C., 41

Yadkin River, 56–57, 64, 185
Yancey County, 71, 122, 202
Yerka, Stephen J., 68
Yonaguska (Cherokee chief), 114

Zimmerman's Island, 16, 18, 44, 188